T0271382

SEEKING ADAM SMITH
Finding The Shadow Curriculum of Business

SEEKING ADAM SMITH

Finding The Shadow Curriculum of Business

Eli P Cox III

University of Texas at Austin, USA

NEW JERSEY · LONDON · SINGAPORE · BEIJING · SHANGHAI · HONG KONG · TAIPEI · CHENNAI · TOKYO

Published by

World Scientific Publishing Co. Pte. Ltd.

5 Toh Tuck Link, Singapore 596224

USA office: 27 Warren Street, Suite 401-402, Hackensack, NJ 07601

UK office: 57 Shelton Street, Covent Garden, London WC2H 9HE

Library of Congress Cataloging-in-Publication Data
Names: Cox, Eli Peace, author.
Title: Seeking Adam Smith : finding the shadow curriculum of business /
    Eli P. Cox, III, University of Texas at Austin, USA.
Description: New Jersey : World Scientific, [2017] | Includes bibliographical references and index.
Identifiers: LCCN 2016049469| ISBN 9789813206724 (hardback : alk. paper) |
    ISBN 9789813206731 (pbk. : alk. paper)
Subjects: LCSH: Microeconomics. | Capitalism. | Smith, Adam, 1723–1790.
Classification: LCC HB172 .C598 2017 | DDC 338.5--dc23
LC record available at https://lccn.loc.gov/2016049469

British Library Cataloguing-in-Publication Data
A catalogue record for this book is available from the British Library.

The cover image is *The Ancient of Days*, frontispiece to *Europe a Prophecy* by William Blake (1757–1827). This version is Copy D, found at the British Museum.

Desk Editor: Philly Lim

Typeset by Stallion Press
Email: enquiries@stallionpress.com

Printed in Singapore

To Ardis for her love, support, patience, and decades of proofreading.

Adam Smith's Observations on the Nature and Causes of a Nation's Wealth

In his jurisprudence lectures, Smith observes

> The wealth of a state consists in the cheapness of provisions and all other necessaries and conveniences of life ... [i]

In *An Inquiry into the Nature and Causes of the Wealth of Nations*, he declares

> In the midst of all the exactions of government, this capital has been silently and gradually accumulated by the private frugality and good conduct of individuals, by their universal, continual, and uninterrupted effort to better their own condition. It is this effort, protected by law and allowed by liberty to exert itself in the manner that is most advantageous, which has maintained the progress of England towards opulence and improvement in almost all former times, and which, it is to be hoped, will do so in all future times. [ii]

---

[i] *Lectures on Jurisprudence* (Indianapolis, IN: Liberty Fund, 1982), 82.
[ii] *An Inquiry into the Nature and Causes of the Wealth of Nations* (Indianapolis, IN: Liberty Fund, 1981), 342–3.

Foreword

I have worked in the belly of the Wall Street beast for more than 30 years. I started in institutional equity sales at Merrill Lynch in 1984, before there was such a thing as a fax machine. Talking to super smart portfolio managers and hedge fund analysts about stocks was very heady. It was especially fun in the 1990s when the markets soared to all-time highs. It was also heart stopping when the markets corrected severely in 1987 (down 23% in one day), 1994 (worst bond market in 40 years), 1998 (the devaluation of Russia's currency and overleveraged brokerage firms), 2000 (the internet bubble and burst), and 2008 (the Great Recession).

Some of my clients included Julian Robertson's Tiger Management, George Soros' Soros Fund Management, Jim Cramer's Cramer Berkowitz Capital, GE Pension, some subsidiaries of Franklin Templeton, and a host of other exceptional firms and talented money managers. I went on to be a partner at two substantial hedge funds for 5 years and later helped initiate the hedge fund relationship program as a senior managing director at Bear Stearns. Yes, that's the same Bear Stearns that went under in 2008, and I have a host of stories on that subject having stayed until the bitter end!

Investment banking has undergone many changes since my arrival. There has been considerable growth in financial innovation, particularly securitization, which offers great opportunities along with the increased risk typically involved with new untested products. I have seen electronic trading go from 0% of the New York Stock Exchange (NYSE) volume to 80%, often watching the "quants" gain an unfair advantage over those trading in the cash market. Investment banks have changed their organizational form from partnerships where the managers invest their own money to corporations where the managers invest the money of stockholders who assume much of the risk once borne by the partners. Incentive systems designed to attract the best managers have sometimes misaligned their interests and those of stockholders. Additionally, strictures imposed on Wall Street after the Great Recession have significantly reduced the banks' abilities to innovate and to take on risk.

I have seen great projects and businesses like Google and AOL financed and go on to create wonderful products. In 1996, I helped sell the first Chinese IPO (a state-owned oil company) in 70 years. We also financed Peru's wireless telephone system, which was incredibly impactful on that poor country. We financed Jack Nicklaus' company, Golden Bear, Inc., which eventually failed and the financing had to be restructured. Other companies that came to life or raised capital during my tenure at Merrill Lynch were EuroDisney, Genentech, Turner Broadcasting, and many others. The Dow Jones Index went from 1,200 in 1984 to around 19,250 today.

I have observed the great struggle between the forces for good and those for bad with the balance shifting back and forth. Although Willie Sutton was not thinking about Wall Street when he said that he robbed banks because that's where the money is, many unscrupulous individuals have gone to Wall Street with the same rationale. One of my former colleagues sold stock to the notorious insider trader Ivan Boesky in the 1980s. Boesky would trade a briefcase full of cash for inside information. Others who played outside the lines were Steve Cohen of SAC Capital, Raj Rajaratnam of The Galleon Group, Bernie Madoff at BLM Investment Securities LLC, and the list could be much longer. Greed has always coexisted with large quantities of money but greed has been glorified and its prominence was revealed by the investment banks' voracious appetite for subprime bonds.

A great country and a superpower like a stool must have four sturdy legs: a strong military, a healthy political system, a rich culture believing in the individual, and a vibrant economic system. The banking system is critical to our economy. Banking is still, however, an art and not a science. The Fed is an experiment created in 1932 to try to make financial extremes more manageable. It is very powerful, but it is not perfect. The banking system is based totally on confidence that exists when people believe it is generally fair and is run by honest people. In the words of Adam Smith, it will "crumble into atoms" when it can no longer be trusted.

In *Seeking Adam Smith: Finding the Hidden Curriculum of Business*, Eli Cox, professor at the McCombs School of Business, offers evidence that a creed of greed has been perpetuated as an ethereal shadow curriculum in business schools. The creed traces its origins to Adam Smith's *Wealth of Nations*. Smith is claimed to have promoted selfishness and greed as the driving force of free-market capitalism. It has also been claimed that competition channels the vice of greed into the virtue of economic growth when there is no government interference.

Professor Cox demonstrates that *laissez faire* government works only if most of those engaged in commerce do not use deception or force to harm others. He cites Milton Friedman in identifying a natural history of government intervention in which governments necessarily intervene to the extent that business or individuals are not trusted. Professor Cox claims that the alternative involves a shift toward anarchy.

From the boardroom to the mailroom, to the trader and to the portfolio manager, all business people need a constant reminder that ethical behavior is a critical part of their jobs. They are professionals in charge of the financial markets and they must maintain the public trust. These leaders must be taught to realize that moral decisions will result in significant profits and greater economic stability.

It is time for business schools and companies to get more serious about teaching the importance of character and ethics, not just profits. Adam Smith would have expected nothing less. We will all benefit immeasurably in the long run. Professor Cox's book is a thoughtful, manageable read on this important subject and well worth the reader's time. Let's start educating and graduating professional men and women from our business schools and executive programs who get what Adam Smith

xii   *Seeking Adam Smith: Finding The Shadow Curriculum of Business*

was really all about. It is imperative that we listen and learn from this book. The book should be required reading for every first year MBA or undergraduate business school student.

Thomas J. Ward
New York

Acknowledgments

Researching and writing this book have been more like moonlighting than the typical academic process of compiling papers, which I had presented at conferences or published in academic journals into a summary of what I had learned over the course of a career. Because of this I have sought out many individuals and organizations for advice and feedback. My records are incomplete and my memory is unreliable, so it is likely that I have omitted some who should receive my thanks. This is reflected in the nature and number of individuals and organizations that have helped me along the way. If you are among them, then I offer my sincere apology.

The first group consists of individuals who helped me with the substance of the various manuscripts I produced over the course of my efforts. None of them has seen the final work and for this reason alone none of them may be accused of aiding and abetting its shortcomings. Members of this group include Urton Anderson, Mark Alpert, Wayne Baker, Michael Brandl, Floyd Brandt, Michael Granof, John Martin, Robert Mettlen, Bob Johansen, Joe Pluta, Ramesh Rao, Joe Valle, and Tom Ward. Max Bazerman, Alexander Broadie, Anne Colby, Thomas Ehrlich, Tamar Frankel, John Highbarger, Raj Sisodia, Kapil Jain, Rakesh Khurana, Lisa Koonce, James Marroqiun, John R. McIntosh, Alexander J. Murdoch, Roth Nelson, Stephanie Nelson, and Ramesh Rao were vitally important in pointing me in the direction of important information sources. Finally,

John Bogle, William Cooper, William O'Hara, Robert Prentice, and Paul Woodruff provided inspiration and guidance by example.

I have also received very considerable editorial help in directing me through various versions of the manuscript and in catching and correcting many errors, including some that seemed to appear spontaneously. Within this important group are Anthony Cox, Jeanne Barker-Nunn, William Bishel, Rochelle Kronzek, Kathleen Davis Niendorff, Dick Mercer, Ellen Morrison, Anne Payne, Rebecca Schorin, and Lanie Tankard. I would also like to express my gratitude to the staff members at World Scientific Publishing Company for giving life to this project.

Additionally, I wish to express my thanks to many general audiences before whom I tested my ideas. Foremost are the classes I have taught since my search for the real Adam Smith began. They include alumni groups in Austin, Houston, Atlanta, and Miami as well as Sunday school classes at the Westminster Presbyterian and the Tarrytown and Northwest Hills Methodist churches. Finally, there were larger groups including the Texas Exes Alumni College, the LAMP, SAGE and QUEST programs of the Osher Life Long Learning Institute, and the McCombs Annual Alumni Business Conference.

Contents

*Adam Smith's Observations on the Nature and Causes
of a Nation's Wealth*   vii
Foreword   ix
Acknowledgments   xiii

Chapter 1	Introduction	1
Chapter 2	Preparing for the Journey	6
	Who was Adam Smith?	6
	Defining *Greed*	8
Chapter 3	Why Were Business Schools Established?	12
	Promise of Professionalism	12
	Whiz Kids and the Public Rebuke	18
	Lee Bach and the Carnegie Experiment	23
	Contrition and Rehabilitation	27
Chapter 4	How Has Economics Influenced Business?	29
	BGH and the Twin Pillars of Free Markets	30
	AGH: Economics Rules	38
	Economic Theories and the Twin Pillars	40
	Rational Choice Theory	41
	Game Theory	42
	Reputation Theory	44
	Theory of the Firm	46

Transaction Cost Theory 47
Michael Jensen and Agency Theory 50
CAUTION: Hazardous Assumptions 56
How Does Ethics Fit into Mainstream Economics? 60

Chapter 5 What is the Shadow Curriculum of Business? 65
The Formal Curricula 66
The Shadow Curriculum 68
The Epidemiology of Greed 74

Chapter 6 Is *Homo Economicus* Contagious? 87
Are We Greedy and Indifferent to Others' Welfare? 88
Does Taking Economics Make Us Like Economic
Men? 93
The Importance of Culture 98

Chapter 7 What if the Twin Pillars Prevailed? 101
Blame the Disease, Not the Patient 101
Economic Man as Shareholders' Agent 103
Economic Man as Team Player 107
Jeff Skilling: Economic Samurai 108
Pogo Economics and the Great Recession 113

Chapter 8 Why has Radical Individualism been Promoted? 121
Frederick Hayek and the Birth of Neoliberalism 122
Milton Friedman and Neoliberial Ascendance 127
Mischievous Errors of the Chicago School 141

Chapter 9 Would Smith Agree with the Twin Pillars? 152
Invisible Hand Not About Selfishness or Greed 152
The Invisible Hand of God 154
Adam Smith's Philosophy was Not Laissez–Faire 162
The Invisible Hand Needs a Hand 167

Chapter 10 What are Alternative Views in Economics? 173
The Sport of Business 173
The Natural History of Government Intervention 176
Paradox of the Invisible Hand 180
Imperfection as an Ideal 185

Chapter 11   What Lessons Can be Learned?   194
                 Resisting Groupthink   194
                 Identifying What Is Legal but Unethical   195
                 Working in a Bad Barrel   197
                 Where People Are the Bottom Line   200
                 What's Next?   201

Afterword   204

Notes   207

Bibliography   231

Index   253

Chapter 1

Introduction

This story describes my 15-year intellectual journey in search of Adam Smith's authentic views concerning economics and public policy. It began when I chose *An Inquiry into the Nature and Causes of the Wealth of Nations* for my nighttime reading. I had just read and reread Patrick O'Brian's 20-volume historical fiction about a British navy captain and his ships' surgeon during the Napoleonic Wars and was looking for something else. I had become a mature reader undertaking tasks beyond my abilities as a younger person, so I took up the copy of *Wealth of Nations* I had purchased 50 years earlier but had tried and failed to read on several occasions.

I had no idea at the time that ultimately I would identify the great intellectual forces contributing to the corruption of our nation's investment banks and to what the former Federal Reserve chair, Ben Bernanke, labeled "the worst financial crisis in global history, including the Great Depression".[1] I would also come to understand the significance of Harvard Business School Dean Nitin Nohria's declaration that "The public has lost trust in business, and some of our graduates seem to be responsible for that".[2] Whether or not it was his intention, the dean's statement was an indictment of the nation's business faculty members — with many notable exceptions, especially in the field of management. I plead guilty as charged but ask for leniency on the grounds of ignorance.

For the first four of more than five decades spent as a student and professor, I had learned about Smith's writings only secondhand. I had come to believe Smith was the father of economics and that he had identified and promoted what I term *the twin pillars of free-market capitalism.* The first pillar is that greedy and rational individuals comprise the engine of economic growth, a notion captured in the concept of *economic man.* The second pillar is that economic prosperity is maximized under conditions of *perfect competition.* Perfect competition is achieved in a single market when: (1) buyers and sellers are so numerous and small that none can influence the market, (2) all products are identical, (3) all buyers and sellers possess perfect information, (4) sellers' revenues are only adequate to recoup their costs of doing business, and (5) government interference is undesirable except in protecting property rights.[3]

In plowing through the 950 pages of *Wealth of Nations,* I uncovered evidence indicating that Smith would not have accepted the twin pillars if they had been explained to him. I resolved to find the real Adam Smith and began a reading program consisting of thousands of pages and continuing for well over a decade. I read the five other volumes of Smith's collected works, eight biographies about him, and many history, philosophy, psychology, biology, sociology, law, and business books relevant to my inquiry. I also read many economics books and articles, beginning with the 19th century.

Over the course of my journey, I discovered two conflicting views of Smith. Mainstream economists, especially those promoting a minimal role for government, hold the most prominent and historically influential view that is outlined in Chap. 4. A few economists and numerous historians and philosophers hold the second view of Smith that I have come to share and describe in Chap. 9.

Seeking Adam Smith is organized using a series of questions that directed my intellectual journey. Chaps. 3–8 begin with a brief history of the early years of business education. It continues by describing the public humiliation of business schools in 1959 when the Ford and Carnegie foundations issued reports identifying them as trade schools unworthy of their place in the university community. As business schools addressed these concerns, mainstream economics gained ascendance over other basic disciplines such as psychology and sociology in offering respectability to the business curricula. However, the science of economics served as a Trojan Horse introducing a political philosophy promoting the twin pillars of free-market capitalism: greedy and rational economic man and the self-regulating power of perfect competition. The conflation of economics and political philosophy may have served well in the discipline's traditional realm of public policy but its effects were calamitous in the arena of business education and practice. Although the consequences were surely unintentional, some business students concluded they should disregard the welfare of others in their pursuit of personal wealth because Adam Smith's invisible hand transformed the personal vice of greed into the public virtue of economic growth. The unfortunate result was seen in the dot.com and subprime bubbles and busts brought about by self-appointed economic men who had acquired positions of leadership in some of our nation's largest and most powerful corporations.

Chaps. 9–11 comprise a rebuttal of the false belief in the logic and efficacy of the twin pillars of free markets. First, Adam Smith, alleged father of the twin pillars, never stated that greed or selfishness is good but instead criticized political philosophers who had taken that position. Secondly, although he favored the elimination of poor government policies, he recommended many others — including public religious education, food subsidies, a minimum wage, and progressive taxation.

I also criticize use of the theory of perfect competition as a foundation for business curricula on a number of grounds. It portrays free-market capitalism as essentially a competitive, even Darwinian, system, while Adam Smith and libertarian Ludwig von Mises make the strong case that its success depends on a fine balance between competitive and cooperative forces. Perfect competition is neither a useful standard against which businesses can be judged nor does it offer useful insights about business strategy and practice. *Monopolistic competition* is superior to *perfect competition* as part of the theoretical foundations of business education because it is more realistic, accommodates insights from other academic disciplines, and is not encumbered by political bias.

The foundational premises of this book are that economic and political freedoms are valued as ends and as the primary means for achieving prosperity and happiness in a society. However, freedom does not give us license to harm others and members of an ideal society should be pleased to accept and abide by the social contract governing their interaction. To the extent a society is not ideal, it must have the institutions and rules of conduct to preserve freedom and justice. The calamitous dot.com and subprime bubbles and busts of the first decade of the 21st century reveal our society's failure on both counts: some of our business leaders enriched themselves at the expense of customers, stockholders, and taxpayers, and the government proved impotent in preventing fraud and in punishing those who committed it.

Much has been written about the dot.com and subprime disasters that disrupted the lives and devastated the fortunes of millions of Americans. Among the explanations for these events are: the development of innovative but poorly understood securities; failures of corporate governance; the action, inaction, or untimely action by the federal government; low interest rates; and the inevitable highs and lows of stock markets caused by greedy investors whose "irrational exuberance" inevitably turned to fear.

I consider these circumstances to be enabling factors, and assert that the underlying cause of our economic calamities has been the notable decline in the trustworthiness of many of our corporate leaders. I also believe this decline has taken place, in part, because of what continues to be taught in economics and business classrooms.

Although I am highly critical of the assumptions and implications of mainstream economics, I have great respect for the discipline and the many brilliant scholars who have contributed to it. This book reveals my lifelong interest in economics and political philosophy. It also reveals that many of the authorities I use to support my criticism of mainstream economics are found within the discipline's crosscurrents. Using the words of the British economist Stanley Jevons, my goal is to make a modest contribution to "the true basis and form of a science which touches so directly the material welfare of the human race".[4]

This book focuses on malevolent acts taken by individuals, through neglect or intention, which have resulted in significant bodily injury or property loss to others. I am especially concerned where such grievous acts go unpunished. My hope is that readers of all political persuasions will agree that such acts are always unethical, often illegal, diminish economic efficiency, and can ultimately undermine the institutions of free-market capitalism. I have intentionally avoided any mention of social or distributive justice; I make no reference to poverty and the growing disparity in wealth in the United States and Europe or of social programs that should or should not be provided by the state. I avoid, likewise, discussing corporate social responsibility and the theory of multiple stakeholders because they might divert your attention from the critical relationship between personal ethics and economic activity.

Some of my examples are drawn from personal experience but they are used only to illustrate broad generalizations. I have the utmost respect and affection for my students past and present, my colleagues, my profession, and the University of Texas where I have spent most of my career and where my father taught and received his PhD in marketing. I hope my efforts will contribute to the well-being of all parties concerned.

My perspective is informed by a lifetime spent as a business student, professor, and administrator. For much of this time, I presented my students with a hash of the two conflicting business philosophies that are the focus of this book. I told them that they should maximize shareholder wealth and that the customer is king. I hope it has taken those very bright young women and men less time to discover the incompatibility of these positions, as they have been commonly understood, than it has taken me.

I have based *Seeking Adam Smith* on extensive scholarly research. At the same time, I have tried to make the book user-friendly by avoiding formality and minimizing technical language found in scholarly journals and texts. My hope is that the issues I raise are debated within business faculties and that business faculty members in all of the functional areas instruct students to use constructively the powerful tools they have been given.

Chapter 2

Preparing for the Journey

Some background information should make more comprehensible the journey I am about to describe. I start by providing a short biography of Adam Smith and a brief description of *Wealth of Nations* and his other works. I continue by defining *greed* because the term has been used carelessly and it is central to this book.

Who was Adam Smith?

Adam Smith was born in Kirkcaldy, Scotland, on 16 June 1723, 20 years before Thomas Jefferson's birth. It is claimed the most exciting event in his life occurred when he was an infant: Adam was kidnapped by gypsies and rescued by his maternal uncle who raced on horseback to save him.[5] One biographer observed Smith turned out to be a better professor than a gypsy because he was a sickly child and absentminded as an adult.[6] Although he received a graduate degree from Oxford University, he remained single and lived with his mother and maiden cousin in Kirkcaldy and Edinburgh for most of his life.[7]

Despite his simple personal life, his intellectual life was extraordinary for he lived and traveled at the epicenter of the Enlightenment. Smith knew many of the great figures of his time including: philosophers David Hume, Voltaire, and Rousseau; politician Edmund Burke; authors Edmund Gibbon, Samuel Johnson, and James Boswell; inventors James Watt and Benjamin Franklin; and painter Joshua Reynolds.[8] After teaching at the

University of Glasgow and touring Europe with a young aristocrat, Smith spent the remainder of his life revising his books and serving as a tax collector, as his father had before him.

Smith occupied the University of Glasgow's chair in moral philosophy and taught a course consisting of four sections, each foundational for the next.[9] The first concerned *natural theology* and examined the "proofs of the being and attributes of God, and those principles of the human mind upon which religion is founded". The second dealt with *ethics*. The third pertained to *jurisprudence*, "that branch of morality which relates to justice" and is "susceptible of precise and accurate rules". The fourth was on *political economy*, or what today would be called *public policy*. The comprehensive nature of this course suggests that the modern equivalent of his academic position would be *chair of the social sciences and liberal arts* rather than *moral philosophy*.

There is no indication Smith ever planned to publish work on natural religion and the subject appears primarily in his ethics book, *The Theory of Moral Sentiments*, published first in 1759. He had worked on a jurisprudence manuscript, but didn't complete it, and he convinced the executors of his estate to destroy 16 volumes of his papers just 6 days before his death on 17 July 1790.[10] Fortunately, two sets of student lecture notes on jurisprudence have been found and published.[11] Finally, *Wealth of Nations*, written by Smith to influence London policymakers, represents political economy as the fourth part of his course.

Smith combined these four topics in a single course and saw them as related and meaningfully sequenced. Of the 3529 pages of the Glasgow edition of his works, *Wealth of Nations* accounts for 1080. To focus exclusively on *Wealth of Nations* is to ignore 69% of Smith's published work. Further indication of the integrated nature of Smith's writings is that the *invisible hand* metaphor appears in his essay "History of Astronomy", in all six editions of *Moral Sentiments* and in all five editions of *Wealth of Nations*.[12]

Smith hated the act of writing and did little of it. He dictated *Wealth of Nations* to an assistant and it reads as if he were lecturing. He makes sweeping statements, perhaps to engage sleepy students, and then goes on to support and refine them. He is didactic at times and speculative at others. The range of his knowledge was immense and his prose, which could be tedious or poetic, contains hints of many modern economic concepts. Reading *Wealth of Nations* is not unlike reading tealeaves, as interpretations still vary with the reader. The Family Tree of Economics found inside the back cover of my 1961 copy (and others since then) of *Economics: An Introductory Analysis* by Paul Samuelson (Nobel Prize 1970) indicates that all of the major economists of the 19th century, including Marx and Lenin, and all mainstream economists of the 20th century are Smith's intellectual heirs.[13]

For readers interested in learning more, *The Life of Adam Smith* by Ian Simpson Ross is most meticulously researched among the eight biographies I have read.[14] Incidentally, Ross was a graduate student at the University of Texas at Austin, and he dedicates his work to his professor and mentor, Ernest Campbell Mossner, and his wife. Mossner, a professor of English, wrote *The Life of David Hume*.[15]

Defining *Greed*

An attorney and friend deposed a salesman for a propane distributor in two separate lawsuits. The salesman had sold propane to a retailer required by law to make sure its customers' heating systems met state-mandated safety standards as a condition for filling them with the highly explosive gas. Explosions occurring about a year apart had resulted in a customer's death. In the deposition after the second death, the attorney asked the salesman if he would continue selling propane to that retailer or others who did not inspect their customers' propane systems. His response was that he would sell propane to anyone with good credit. The propane distributor settled out of court with the victims' heirs and the retailer vanished.

In the eyes of the law, propane distributors, like automobile manufacturers, are responsible for the safety of their customers' customers. So the salesman's behavior was clearly illegal, but how could he feel no remorse? He didn't know the victims and had no personal reason to harm them. What was his state of mind when he continued business as usual after the first death? Would he sell the fuel with an explosive power greater than TNT to someone he suspected of being a terrorist if that person's credit was good? Did he rationalize that he had not forced anyone to buy the gas or that someone else would have sold it to the retailer if he hadn't done so? Was he motivated by self-interest, selfishness, or greediness?

It may seem odd that a familiar word like *greed* needs special attention, but I have found it defined only once in my readings. Instead, it has been used interchangeably with *self-interest* (which Adam Smith called *prudence*) and *selfishness*. The distinctions among these terms are not subtle and should be clear to a 5-year old. If a family leaves a jack-o'-lantern full of candy bars on their front porch during Halloween, trick-or-treaters would be acting prudently by taking one, selfishly if they took a fistful, and greedily if they took the jack-o'-lantern and all the bars in it. Distinguishing these terms is vital to understanding Smith's views and the views of those who have written about him.

I restrict my use of the term *greed* to describe individuals who display a wanton disregard for the welfare of the other party engaged in a business transaction as well as for third parties who might be harmed. By this definition, the propane salesman was greedy, as were these individuals:

- Bernie Ebbers, the Sunday school teacher, former WorldCom chairman, and "angel to many desperate charitable causes" who defrauded his stockholders of $2 billion.[16]
- Chuck Cunningham, war hero and influential member of the US House of Representatives, who took bribes to pay for antiques, oriental rugs, and a graduation party for his daughter.[17]
- William McGuire, former CEO of UnitedHealth Group, who agreed to repay $618 million to the firm for backdating stock options.[18]
- Mark Ciavarella, former judge, who was convicted of sending youth offenders, including an 11-year old, to for-profit detention centers in exchange for $2.8 million in bribes.[19]
- Eighty-three-year-old Houston billionaire Oscar Wyatt, who pleaded guilty in 2007 to the charge of wire fraud. He was sentenced to jail time and forfeited $11 million.[20]

This restrictive and secular definition of greed excludes those who:

1. Suffer from alcoholism, drug addiction, gluttony, or hoarding
2. Spend all the money they can earn and borrow to buy more

3. Own numerous mansions containing rare antiques and precious art
4. Have acquired great wealth
5. Have inherited great wealth
6. Do not give money to the poor

In the first and second of these situations, the behavior is imprudent, sometimes to the point of self-destruction, but it does not indicate a wanton disregard for the welfare of others, except perhaps for their loved ones. Adam Smith describes the third as vanity but adds that it cannot harm others directly. The fourth may result from diligence and frugality and is indicative of contributions valued by society. The fifth reflects a fortunate choice of parents, and the sixth suggests miserliness, considered a sin of omission by many religions, but is excluded here because the stingy person does not necessarily engage in dishonest and harmful economic exchanges.

Greed is an act of wanting, an addiction to money or power. Because it is a motive, it can only be inferred from the behavior it prompts. Consequently, the examples of greed in this book involve individuals who appear to have been motivated by money to cause egregious harm to others.

*   *

The Washington Post published a column by George Will entitled "Greed does have its saving graces".[21] He joked that greed is cyclical, in fashion when the Republicans occupy the White House and out of fashion when the president is a Democrat. He went on to cite a study of football ticket scalpers who used the Internet site stubhub.com. The results revealed that "greedy" sellers who were asking too much had to wait and sell their tickets at significantly lower prices. Will's conclusion was that deregulated markets punish greed.

Parenthetically, scalping tickets to sporting events signifies that the organization that first sold the tickets failed to price them correctly. It is prudent, not greedy, behavior for scalpers to buy and resell something as unimportant as football tickets. It would be another matter if they were trying to corner the market for a lifesaving drug.

Adam Smith wrote eloquently about the beauty of free markets where sellers employ their time and resources as they see fit in offering products to the market, and those same individuals, when acting as buyers, employ their time and resources to obtain wanted products. The aggregate interaction of all buyers and sellers establishes the price at which products will be sold. If the market approximates perfect competition, defined earlier, then no single buyer or seller can have any impact on the operation of the price mechanism. Under these conditions, it is impossible for buyers or sellers to act greedily.

This price mechanism still operates when a differentiated product is sold. In the case of football tickets, the price varies considerably with the game and seat's location. Those asking too much for football tickets in George Will's example did not display greed as I have defined it but were overly optimistic about what others were willing to pay. Those asking too little were not altruistic but had underestimated ticket demand. As another example, if one person tries to sell a pair of Bernie Madoff undershorts on ebay.com for $1000 and another thinks they are a bargain, then both seller and buyer will consider themselves better off if the sale goes through.

Some people complain it is unfair for a young person to earn more as a waiter than as a schoolteacher, but the market has outvoted them. Still others complain that certain companies make excessive profits. But the truth is that the market may be rewarding these companies for undertaking risks when providing useful products to the public. The most successfully innovative firms like Apple are awarded the largest share of profits in a free-market system.

Opportunities for greed arise when buyers or sellers are large enough and powerful enough to interfere with the price mechanism. Moreover, informational asymmetries, where sellers possess critical knowledge unavailable to the buyer, are commonplace. They provide opportunities for greed, especially among individuals or organizations selling complex products such as financial derivatives, automobiles, or pharmaceuticals.

Chapter 3

Why Were Business Schools Established?

After the Civil War, an avalanche of new products, manufacturing technologies, modes of transportation and communication, and large manufacturers and intermediaries spilled westward across the continent. Corporations run by salaried managers working on behalf of stockholders were rapidly displacing small family-owned businesses not unlike the straight-pin maker Adam Smith famously describes in *Wealth of Nations*.[22] The demands placed on this new class of managers were unprecedented because they were responsible for designing, producing, distributing, promoting, and selling products to millions of customers with whom their firm had no direct contact.

Promise of Professionalism

There was considerable skepticism among academics and those interested in higher education about whether business management should join the ranks of the prestigious professions that had for so long occupied prominent positions within the university community. Nevertheless, the first undergraduate business program was established at the University of Pennsylvania in 1888, and in 1900, Dartmouth College offered the first graduate business degree. Other public and private universities soon followed as the popularity of business degrees grew.

A few visionaries like Joseph Wharton, who donated $100,000 to the University of Pennsylvania, believed that the emerging class of managers would benefit from a university education in the manner of medicine and law. After all, they were responsible for running the immensely complex business systems that had become so vital to national prosperity.[23]

This was a tall order and skepticism was understandable. After all, university-based medical and law programs originated in Europe during the Middle Ages and trained physicians and attorneys immigrated as the American colonies were founded.[24] The nation's first medical school was established at the University of Pennsylvania in 1765 and the first law school was launched at the College of William and Mary in 1779.[25] In contrast, the small but growing group of managers for whom a professional education was being proposed had existed only a few decades, and the notion of what it meant to be a business professional resembled those of medicine and law only in broad outline.

According to law professor Tamar Frankel, these ancient and learned professions of law and medicine have rested on two foundational premises. The first is that they possess sovereignty over well-defined bodies of technical knowledge and skill sets vital to society but beyond the capabilities of laypeople. The learned professions have been self-governing throughout their histories and exempt from laws prohibiting collusion because they have policed themselves.[26] Only trained individuals whose qualifications are recognized by a body of professionals are allowed to practice, and the license to do so can be withdrawn by that body in cases of malpractice. Today, a college diploma is necessary but not sufficient to practice medicine or law. Other requirements, usually including an examination administered by the professional body and a clear criminal record, must be met as well.

The second foundational premise is that professionals have the fiduciary duty to subordinate their personal interests to those of the general public and specifically to their patients or clients.[27] Their behavior is expected to conform to high ethical standards that are generally codified and the code is revised when deemed necessary. The modern concept of *fiduciary duty* has ancient origins and stems from the obligations of servants to masters. Such duties are spelled out in Hammurabi's Code written by a Babylonian king approximately 3700 years ago.[28] Today, fiduciary duties are embodied in professional codes of conduct, common law, and legislation.

Traditionally, the practices of physicians and attorneys were organized to avoid conflicts of interests. Physicians, for example, formed individual practices or partnerships where no superior party existed to interfere with the patient–physician relationship. Further, professionals charged standard fees for services to minimize situations where a lawyer, for example, might be tempted to extract higher fees from desperate or wealthy clients. Lawyers and physicians have done *pro bono* work for those who cannot afford their services as part of their public obligations.

The profoundly important point here is that the relationship between professionals and their clients or patients is not intended to be market based, and thus *caveat emptor*, buyer beware, should not apply. Fiduciary duties reduce transaction costs and increase economic efficiency in cases where patients and clients do not have the ability to supervise or evaluate the performance of professionals providing services. In other words, patients and clients have traditionally been willing to pay a premium above the competitive price in exchange for the trustworthiness, technical competence, and uncompromised commitment of the service provider. Few who have been charged with vehicular homicide or need bypass surgery shop for bargains.

As a final point, fiduciary duties to patients should be uncompromising, but they do not enable physicians to white wash unethical acts committed on behalf of those patients. Their fiduciary duties do not justify their implanting an organ purchased on the black market in their patient or disposing of used syringes and other medical waste improperly.[29] Likewise, corporate CEOs have fiduciary duties to stockholders but such duties do not justify their neglect or abuse of other stakeholders or to undermine the institution of free-market capitalism. No institution, including corporations, nor class of individuals, including CEOs, is above the law or exempted from the ethical restraints required by a civilized society.

Philosopher Joseph Heath asserts that attempts to address the various stakeholders directly creates an ethical morass and administrative nightmare for executives. Thus, the CEOs' ethical imperative should be that the firms they lead will undertake only those competitive acts that increase profits by bringing greater economic efficiency to the marketplace. Under the ethical CEO's leadership, the firm will avoid intentionally deceptive packaging and advertising that borders on illegality and will provide customers with the information they require for effective decision-making. The firm will avoid false economy by investing adequately in employee safety, and it will refuse to participate in lobbying efforts that perpetuate market imperfections such as banks taking on more debt than their reserves can cover.[30]

*   *

Although there were private trade schools during the first half of the 20th century, universities were uniquely suited to provide the liberal education considered essential to a professional education. It was in philosophy, history, literature, and arts courses that individuals could cultivate the sensibilities and personal and civic virtues necessary for all citizens in a democracy, but especially important for professionals with public duties. Additionally, universities had become increasingly important to society as engines of science in America and Europe, and an association with them seemed to promise that business management would become based in science.

There were early signs indicating that these scientific aspirations might be realized. Frederick Taylor and Elton Mayo exemplified the use of experimentation so that subjective judgments would be replaced with empirical findings to ground labor-relations decisions. Taylor was a mechanical engineer who had worked in the steel industry and served as a business consultant.[31] He received an honorary doctorate from the University of Pennsylvania in 1906, published *The Principles of Scientific Management* in 1911, and taught in the Tuck School of Business at Dartmouth College at the end of his career.

Taylor argued that scientific study should eliminate disputes between employers and employees concerning what and how much work should be expected when a particular job is to be performed.[32] Mechanical engineering skills, he believed, must be employed in selecting, training, supervising, and compensating workers, and "time" or "motion" experiments should be employed to design jobs that would maximize worker output.[33] He writes that: "It is only through *enforced* standardization of methods, *enforced* adoption of the best implements and working conditions, and *enforced* cooperation that this faster work can be assured. And the duty of enforcing the adoption of standards and enforcing this cooperation rests with *management* alone".[34] He recommends cooperation rather than coercion as the driving force because he believes workers will participate willingly when they share in the financial gains resulting from increased output.

It is clear Taylor's target audience did not include workers or those sympathetic to them, since he states as a general principle that "… the workman who is best suited to actually do the work is incapable of fully understanding this science …".[35] The most suitable worker for moving pigs of iron weighing 92 pounds has the intelligence and strength of an ox and requires constant supervision.[36] In discussing the broad range of application of his principles, Taylor observes "… the training of the surgeon has been almost identical in type with the teaching and training which is given to the workman under scientific management".[371]

Elton Mayo was a distinguished academic, whose formal training was in philosophy and psychology, and he is known today as the founder of the *human relations movement*. He joined the University of Pennsylvania's Wharton School in 1922 as a research associate examining labor turnover at a textile mill. He served as a professor of industrial research at the Harvard Business School from 1926 to 1947.[38] His entitled *The Human Problems of an Industrialized Civilization* appeared in 1933 and he conducted field research on human behavior, notably "clinical studies" at the Hawthorne Works of the Western Electric Company.

Mayo declared in his book that managers should recognize "the impact of applied science" in contributing to the destruction of neighborhoods and the traditional workplace.[39] His principal finding was that workers are not interchangeable parts that can be shaped according to engineering principles. Rather, workers have strong social needs that are usually fulfilled through informal organizations operating within and around the formal designs of management. In the preface to the third edition of his work, written on 1 October 1945, Mayo writes: "It is not the atomic bomb that will destroy civilization. But civilized society can destroy itself — finally, no doubt, with bombs — if it fails to understand intelligently and to control the aids and deterrents of cooperation".[40] It is useful to consider the divergent views of Taylor and Mayo concerning the design of the ideal business that are deep rooted in modern business curricula.

Business education achieved great marketplace success during the first 70 years of its history. Demand for business graduates grew continually, business schools proliferated, and the percentage of undergraduates majoring in business had to be limited on many campuses. Business schools were flooded after World War II with veterans supported by the GI Bill and administrators were preoccupied with staffing courses and acquiring military barracks for conversion into classrooms. My father's position was anomalous by today's standards because he was simultaneously a father of four, retired naval officer, doctoral student, and visiting Associate Professor of Marketing at the University of Texas at Austin during the 1950s. He was one of 129 in the nation who received a business doctorate in 1956, and one of 963 who ever had.[41]

Neither of the twin aspirations of the visionary founders of university-level business education — technical competence and public service — had been realized by the time GIs entered business programs. Just meeting the demand for classes taxed university and business school administrators to their limits. Additionally, there had been no concerted effort undertaken by business managers themselves to create a nascent profession.

In contrast, a certified public accountant's license became a legal requirement for practice in the state of New York in 1886. The New York State Society of Certified Public Accountants was organized the following year and its members were active in founding New York University's School of Commerce, Accounts, and Finance in 1900.[42]

Business school deans, apart from their discipline-based faculties, formed the American Association of Collegiate Schools of Business (AACSB) that began accrediting business programs in 1919.[43] Unfortunately, the standards for undergraduate programs remained lax and were weakly enforced, and there were no standards of any kind for graduate programs until 1958 and those established at that time were equally weak.[44]

Two other groups outside the business professoriate, the Ford and Carnegie foundations, would revolutionize business education in the 1950s after painting vivid and broad-brushed pictures of its shortcomings.

Whiz Kids and the Public Rebuke

If it were a movie, the *Whiz Kids* would tell the true story of Charles "Tex" Thornton, a college dropout from Goree, Texas. An insightful statistician with an entrepreneurial spirit, Thornton rose from obscurity in the Federal bureaucracy to form the Statistical Control Group that increased the efficiency of Air Force operations. He recruited a team of brilliant young Harvard business students who saved the Air Force billions of dollars during World War II.[45] After the war, Thornton and nine of his protégés moved on to rescue Ford Motor Company from ruin and revolutionize business education by their example.

Thornton had worked with the Harvard Business School dean to establish a program in which the top 10% of students in the Air Force Officer Training School would be taught elementary statistics. Three thousand officers went through the program and had populated the Statistical Control Group by the end of the War. The real contribution of this group was that they provided senior officers with detailed and accurate data enabling them to avoid seat-of-the pants decisions.[46] Prior to the group's creation, no one in the Air Force knew how many individuals it employed nor how many planes it possessed.[47]

After the war Thornton sent Henry Ford II a short telegram requesting a meeting, which resulted in Ford's employing Thornton as well as nine of his top staff members from Statistical Control. Ford relied on this group to transform the faltering automobile manufacturer inherited from his father. Company insiders mocked Thornton's team, branding them as "Whiz Kids", but they embraced the label as they once again proved their great worth. The intellectual leader and most famous Whiz Kid was Robert McNamara, who would later serve as Secretary of Defense during the Vietnam War.

Leaders at the Ford Foundation and other like-minded individuals outside of Ford Motor Company appreciated the astonishing value of the Whiz Kids, but worried about whether comparable Whiz Kids could be found if the Cold War with the Soviet Union became a hot one. They also recognized that our nation's economic success served as an example for nations around the world that were wavering between capitalism and communism. The foundation's leadership concluded that MBA programs across the country should produce consistently and in large numbers "management scientists" like the Whiz Kids.

In the early 1950s, the Ford Foundation leadership initiated a decade-long campaign with three objectives. The first was to expose the poor quality of business curricula, faculty, and students in most of the nation's undergraduate and graduate programs. The second was to propose sweeping changes in the vision of business education, and the third was to fund and manage educational programs that would transform such a vision into reality.

The foundation started a fellowship program in 1955 to enable business schools to recruit individuals with doctorates in the scientific and quantitative disciplines. Top MBA students entering business doctoral programs were also given financial support. In the same year, Ford committed $3.3 million (the equivalent of $28.9 million in 2015) to enhancing the doctoral programs at the Harvard Business School, Carnegie Institute of Technology's Graduate School of Industrial Administration (GSIA), Columbia University's business school and Yale University's economics department. From 1956 to 1958, Ford established centers of excellence at HBS, GSIA, and the business schools at Columbia, Chicago, and Stanford to serve as incubators for developing cutting-edge curricula and as models for other programs around the country.

As the reforms gained traction at these centers of excellence, Ford spent several million dollars between 1956 and 1959 on what they considered to be second-tier schools such as Berkeley, UCLA, and MIT. Ford then sponsored a series of workshops and seminars targeting faculty members at third-tier schools.[48]

By 1959, when the Ford Foundation's reform efforts had reached all the major business programs, they and the Carnegie Foundation released companion reports that were highly critical of the state of business education. Both covered the topic broadly, but the Ford Foundation, or Gordon-Howell, report focused primarily on graduate programs while the Carnegie, or Pierson, report concerned undergraduate programs principally.[49] There had been other critiques of business education, but they had gone largely unnoticed outside of academic circles.[50]

The Gordon–Howell report especially received widespread attention within both the academic and business presses. Presentations were made on the proposed reforms at academic conferences and papers were published in scholarly business journals. Copies of the report were distributed to hundreds of college and university presidents, business leaders, and business journalists. The senior editor of *BusinessWeek* was hired to write a digest of the report for those who did not have time to read the original's 491 pages.[51]

The Gordon–Howell and Pierson reports noted that business programs across the country did not recognize a standard curriculum, as would be expected of legitimate professions (they still do not). Pierson found that of the 22 undergraduate majors identified in the study, only three were available widely: accounting (93%), marketing (83%), and finance/banking (74%). Instead, the curricula contained courses catering to local industry needs and focusing on vocational training. Most undergraduate programs had what by today's standards are skeletons in their curricular closets. A secretarial major was offered at 47% of the schools. One program offered a course in "hotel front-office procedures" and another offered "Bread and Roll Production — Practical Shop Operations".[52]

Even Chicago had a course in railroad transportation and Harvard offered one for those preparing for a career in lumber management.[53] (The University of Texas provided several courses in cotton marketing.) Although such courses are not worthy of college credit by today's standards, they did reflect local and regional demand for business graduates. Railroad, timber, and cotton executives hiring students at that time would not have known what to do with today's BBAs or MBAs. And Gordon and Howell observed that businesses had continued to send mixed messages to students and business schools. Corporate executives praised a liberal education and the personal qualities expected to come with it, while their campus recruiters looked for individuals who could hit the ground running.[54]

The 4-year colleges and universities included in the Pierson study were equally divided between public and private institutions. In contrast to the more selective programs of architecture and engineering, students gained eligibility to business programs as part of the university admission process.[55] The author cites a 1954 study finding a positive correlation between the difficulty of the subject matter and the quality of the students studying it. Chemistry, mathematics, and physics attracted the most capable students while education, business, some social sciences, home economics, and physical education attracted those least capable.[56]

Although the first doctoral programs in business were established at Chicago and Harvard 37 years earlier, the Pierson report revealed a severe shortage of qualified faculty members.[57] Fewer than half of full-time faculty members possessed doctorates and the proportion was expected to decline as business enrollment continued to increase. Business schools lacked strong doctoral programs of their own and they were often unable to recruit faculty from the basic disciplines. The typical teaching load was four courses a semester, classes were larger than elsewhere on campus, and faculty members who conducted research were expected to do so in their spare time.

The Gordon–Howell report was especially critical of undergraduate business programs and recommended enrollment in them be curtailed nationally. However, they did recognize the value of the specialization that could be acquired over 4 years but not in a 1- or 2-year graduate program. BBA graduates with specialties might work in corporate staffs (corporate enlisted men), but MBA students entering the chain of command and advancing toward the executive office (corporate officers) would need a more general business education.

At the turn of the 20th century, the founding visionaries had expressed the lofty vision of business management as a profession. To fulfill this vision, business schools needed to meet two goals: to provide students with the necessary technical skills and to imbue them with the sense of public responsibility required of those who influenced the nation's welfare so profoundly. Gordon and Howell reaffirmed those lofty goals, declaring:

> the American businessman will play a dominant role — not only as a leader in the insistent drive for greater economic output, but as a shaper of opinion and public policies that will affect the welfare of the American people in a thousand directions, from local action to cope with

juvenile delinquency to national policy in the precarious field of international relations.[58]

The Gordon–Howell and Pierson reports declared loudly that scant progress had been made during the six decades since the Wharton School was founded. Both reports provided detailed curriculum recommendations as roadmaps for reforming both undergraduate and graduate programs.

The discredited *institutional approach* of business schools had studied business institutions and functional areas within them as medical schools continue to study anatomy and physiology. This approach was gradually replaced by the *managerial approach* that de-emphasizes the differences among businesses and industries and emphasizes the best theories and methods that can be applied across a vast range of circumstances. Other disciplines across campus have been the principal sources of these theories and methods even as doctoral programs in business raised their quality and increased their output.

Importantly, economists Gordon and Howell, at Berkeley and Stanford respectively when their report came out, wrote: "Of all the subjects which the [graduate business student] might undertake to study formally, none is more appropriate for the businessman-to-be than human behavior".[59] Elton Mayo would have been delighted with this emphasis and it would have disturbed Frederick Taylor.

Of equal importance was the new role for economics in the proposed curricula. The traditional introductory offering in economics was *microeconomics*, focusing on mathematical models of firms, consumers, and markets, and *macroeconomics,* devoted to a mathematical model of an entire economy. Both were designed to aid public policymakers by providing accurate predictions of economic outcomes.

Consistent with the new managerial approach, microeconomics was to be replaced with a *managerial economics* course offering tools useful in determining the most efficient way to produce a product, what to charge for it, what quantity should be produced, and the like.[60] A derivation of macroeconomics was also to be offered as an aid for senior managers. This so-called *aggregative economics* course was intended to cover topics such as the role of "… nonmonetary factors in economic fluctuations, economic growth, forecasting, fiscal planning …".[61] These proposed courses began to appear in MBA programs, while most undergraduate students took the conventional microeconomics-macroeconomics sequence in the economics department before they began taking business courses.

The Gordon–Howell and Pierson reports are thorough and even-handed. The value of the reports is probably more apparent to today's business school deans and professors, who may now be able to read them without being defensive. However, the Gordon–Howell report presented a conflicted vision of the ideal MBA graduates. On the one hand, they were to be trained to view corporations from the perspective of top managers and were to be provided with general management skills but would be incapable of using the sophisticated tools employed by members of corporate staffs (Elton Mayo would have approved). On the other hand, they were to be trained as the new Whiz Kids who were technically brilliant but lacked the vision, disposition, and soft skills needed to run large complex organizations (Frederick Taylor would have approved).

Thus, MBA programs were faced with the difficult task of balancing these two visions, of capturing the dual nature of the modern corporate leader. The obvious danger was that programs would be dominated by either the soft or the hard skills with only a dash of the other. The first real test of this challenge was faced at GSIA.

Lee Bach and the Carnegie Experiment

Lee Bach was the most influential advocate for the managerial approach to business education. Born in Victor, Iowa, he studied economics at Grinnell College less than 30 miles away.[62] He entered the University of Texas School of Law, but switched to the University of Chicago where he earned his PhD in economics in 1940. After serving as a research analyst with the Federal Reserve, the thirty-year-old was hired by Carnegie Tech in 1946. He served as chair of the economics department, where he established a doctoral program and recruited fifteen other economists.[63] Bach became dean of GSIA when it was established 3 years later.

Bach served as advisor to the Ford Foundation's Program in Economic Development and Administration and was close to the Foundation's vice president, who was charged with overseeing educational programs during its most active period.[64] Bach wrote the chapter of the Pierson report entitled "Managerial Decision-Making as an Organizing Concept" and is identified in the Gordon–Howell report as one of the "distinguished group of businessmen and educators" chosen to review its final draft.[65] Bach's position as GSIA dean gave him the opportunity to implement his vision and to host six of twelve Ford-sponsored seminars for business professors from around the country between 1957 and 1962. He also published academic papers and made presentations promoting managerial decision-making.

From outward appearances, Carnegie Tech was an unlikely choice as one of the four elite institutions selected by Ford to receive support for its business doctoral programs. Harvard, Columbia, and Yale were highly prestigious universities founded in 1636, 1754, and 1701, respectively. Carnegie had evolved from a group of technical schools founded in 1900. Harvard's MBA program was founded in 1908 and Columbia's in 1916. By contrast, GSIA was founded in 1949. Yale's school of management was not established until 1976, so the grant went to support its economics doctoral program.

It was Bach's leadership position at Carnegie Tech that made the school attractive to the Foundation's leadership. GSIA had a 5-million-dollar endowment and the Foundation's grant provided additional resources to fulfill the vision Bach shared with its leaders. Although he brought the economics faculty across campus with him to GSIA, the newness of the school meant Bach had what at first appeared to be a clean slate for realizing his vision.

Bach offered his strategic perspective at a seminar sponsored by the Ford Foundation at Georgia Tech in 1957, noting that the business curriculum being prepared was intended to sustain managers as they rose to positions of presidents and general managers over careers spanning three decades.[66] He rejected Harvard's case method, believing business education should be based on quantitative research concerning individual and collective behavior.[67]

His textbook *Economics: An Introduction to Analysis and Policy*, sold several million copies and his orientation was practical rather than theoretical.[68] He had complained that during an economics lecture at Grinnell:

> the professor was explaining that theoretically there couldn't be a lasting depression in a competitive, capitalist-type economy. I looked out the window at a long line of unemployed men waiting to apply for two WPA jobs the town government had managed to get. There must be a better way for either the economists or the "practical" men who ran the system, I thought.[69]

Bach hoped to acquire two groups of faculty members united by a shared vision and complementary skills who would do groundbreaking research applying rigorous theory and methods to recognized business problems. The first group was to consist of professors offering applied courses in the various disciplines. These individuals would be recruited from the top talent at other universities or from industry. The second would be comprised of researchers drawn from the core disciplines of economics and political science, as well as operations research and quantitative methods that included mathematics, computers, statistics, and accounting. However, the 15 economists already appointed to the faculty limited severely the number who could be hired from the other disciplines.[70]

Bach proclaimed that the objective of the GSIA Management Science degree was to train administrators who would be line managers in an organization's chain of command, rather than train them as specialists advising those managers. These individuals must understand administration — that is: "... the art and the science of discovering what are the most important decisions to make in the organizational environment involved, making these decisions effectively, and seeing that the decisions made are effectively carried out".[71] Bach's vision seems to represent a good balance between the visions of Taylor and Mayo.

The program's first year would consist of courses pertaining to "administrative processes and organizational behavior", "economic analysis", "quantitative method", and "functional fields of business" (particularly production, marketing, and finance). The second year would have yearlong courses in "business policy and its administration" and "business and society", plus elective courses.[72] The role of economic analysis was modest: to provide "… the businessman, as citizen and as civic leader …", with a broad understanding of the economic environment of business, and "… some tools, but only a modest part of the necessary tools, for making managerial decisions about the conduct of the firm".[73]

Bach enlisted the help of two Chicago-educated geniuses to assemble the faculty: William Cooper, a pioneer in management science who would finish his long and distinguished career at the University of Texas, and Herbert Simon, a political scientist with extensive mathematics training.[74] They assembled an extraordinary team of faculty members drawn from the Carnegie Tech economics department and outside.[75] Roots of the research that earned Eugene Fama and Robert Shiller their Nobel prizes in 2013 can be traced to those days at Carnegie.[76] Additionally, three GSIA faculty members (Merton Miller, Franco Modigliani, and Herbert Simon) would go on to receive Nobel Memorial Prizes in economics.

A group of some of the best and brightest scholars in the history of business education had been assembled to train a new generation of assistant professors. This phalanx of young individuals would then enable BBA and MBA business programs across the country to realize the ideal of the modern manager Bach had articulated so eloquently. But it was an aggregation of independent-minded individuals and not a team. An adversarial relationship developed between the economists surrounding Modigliani and faculty members who aligned themselves with Simon. Cooper, Simon's ally, was a pioneer in the field of operation research, an area of applied mathematics that arose out of World War II and became known as *management science* in its business applications.[77] Both management scientists and economists have an interest in game theory.

Simon later described Bach's challenge as defying a law of nature, engaging in the ceaseless process of mixing oil and water.[78] Three years after the Ford Foundation ceased funding Carnegie's doctoral program, the faculty disbanded. Modigliani moved to Northwestern, Simon retreated to the Carnegie psychology department, and Bach moved to Stanford where he became dean.[79]

Although GSIA was intended to represent the avant-garde of the managerial approach, it proved to be a melodramatic illustration of problems experienced at major business schools across the country for decades to come. The Gordon–Howell and Pierson reports were highly influential but the outcomes were not those intended by the foundations' leaders and others such as Bach. In the end, the inherent conflict between the ideal of a highly trained technician and that of a manager equipped with the strategic vision, personal attributes, and social skills required to lead American corporations was decided in favor of the technician at many business schools.

Contrition and Rehabilitation

Beneath business educators' public responses to the Gordon–Howell and Pierson reports lay embarrassment, self-doubt, and the recognition that every program had to respond somehow. The process appeared relatively simple for Dean Bach since he was essentially starting from scratch and had the financial resources to implement his vision. For other deans who took the call for reform seriously, their task was analogous to a farmer attempting to replace an orchard of full-grown pear trees with apple tree saplings while increasing annual production. The two foundation reports made it relatively easy in theory to replace the old curriculum and faculty members based on the *institutional approach* with new ones based on the *managerial approach.*

In practice, the process would take years, especially at the undergraduate level. First of all, an increasing number of students were majoring in business. Gordon–Howell reports 50,090 undergraduates, 5205 master's students, and 109 doctoral students receiving business degrees in 1957–1958. Combined, they accounted for 12.6% of the rapidly growing university enrollment.[80]

As the demand for business classes grew, there was an increased concern about the shortage of individuals graduating with business doctorates. One study revealed that during the 1955–1956 academic year only 0.3%, three in a thousand, of all business graduates received doctorates.[81] The average for all fields of study was 2.3%, almost eight times greater than the business percentage. For the physical sciences, mathematics, and psychology, the figure was 8.7%, or 29 times that of business. Clearly, business deans had to find individuals trained in the basic disciplines across campus to meet the demand for classes, bring the theories and methods needed to educate students in the managerial approach, and add respectability to business schools.

Those wishing to learn about the history of business education in greater detail should read *The Roots, Rituals, and Rhetorics of Change: North American Business Schools After the Second World War* by Mie Augier and James G. March[82] and the award winning *From Higher Aims to Hired Hands: The Social Transformation of American Business Schools and the Unfulfilled Promise of Management as a Profession* by Rakesh Khurana.

Chapter 4

How Has Economics Influenced Business?

This chapter reviews the role of economics in the history of business education, rather than a broader history of economics. Economics has been a part of business curricula since the beginning, but its content and the extent of its influence changed just when business schools needed help. In the era before Gordon-Howell (BGH), neoclassical or mainstream economics was dominant. While classical economists of the 19th century had focused on the supply side of free markets, neoclassical economists took greater interest in the demand side and recognized the importance of the federal government's macroeconomic policies. Its role in business school curricula continued to be questioned because economists had shown little interest in the internal workings of firms and financial markets or in providing tools for managers.

However, just as business schools needed help in the era after Gordon-Howell (AGH), economists began groundbreaking research dealing with problems of interest to business practitioners, and they brought a degree of rigor and precision to business courses that had not been seen previously. This transition from a policy orientation to a managerial orientation within economics was made easier because the pillars of free-market capitalism that were foundational to neoclassical economics during the BGH era also underpinned the managerially relevant economic theories of the AGH era.

BGH and the Twin Pillars of Free Markets

As mentioned in the introduction, my intellectual journey began with the understanding that Adam Smith, the father of economics, promoted the twin pillars of free-market capitalism: economic man and perfect competition. As I reviewed the economics literature, I came to realize that my understanding was consistent with the views expressed in a variety of media by leading economists on both the left and right.

Economics: An Introductory Analysis by Paul Samuelson, one of the best-selling college textbooks ever written, is now in its 19th edition. It had sold more than 4 million copies in 41 languages by 1997.[83] The 1961 edition sold 331,163 copies including one I purchased and still have. This success means that Samuelson began introducing many professional economists to Adam Smith shortly after World War II.

In the 1961, 1976, and 1992 editions, Samuelson quotes Smith as follows:

> "'Every individual endeavors to employ his capital so that its produce may be of greatest value. He generally neither intends to promote the public interest, nor knows how much he is promoting it. He intends only his own security, only his own gain. And he is in this led by an invisible hand to promote an end which was no part of his intention. **By pursuing his own interest he frequently promotes that of society more effectually than when he really intends to promote it.**' Adam Smith, *The Wealth of Nations* (1776)".[84]

Samuelson does not alert the reader that this "quote" is actually an 85-word adaptation of the 215-word original.[85] Additionally, there is no way for the reader to know that Samuelson has stripped the original paragraph of its context.[86]

Three paragraphs later in *Wealth of Nations,* Smith observes: "**What is prudence in the conduct of every private family, can scarce be folly in that of a great kingdom**".[87] Thus, he uses prudence, good business sense, instead of selfishness or greed to characterize investors and nations alike. Further, Samuelson's deletion of the words *generally* and *frequently* from the original leads readers to conclude falsely that Smith said that all individuals pursue their own interest all of the time.

Later, Samuelson tries to distill the essence of Smith's massive work to 39 words: "Smith proclaimed the principle of the 'Invisible Hand'; every individual **in pursuing only his own selfish good was led, as if by an invisible hand, to achieve the best good for all,** so that any interference with free competition by government was almost certain to be injurious".[88]

After reading Samuelson's two summaries of the *Wealth of Nations*, most undergraduate students may conclude falsely that they had read Smith's words as he had written them. They may also conclude that Smith believed selfish behavior benefits society because of the *invisible hand*, and that government intervention is bad.[89]

In the first edition of his textbook, published in 1948, Samuelson offers a description of Smith's views almost identical to that appearing in the 85- and 39-word summaries referenced earlier. Samuelson then makes this astonishing statement:

> This unguarded conclusion has done almost as much harm as good in the past century and a half, especially since too often it is all that some of our leading citizens remember, 30 years later, of their college course in economics. Actually much of the praise of perfect competition is off the mark.[90]

Samuelson's next paragraph begins: "A cynic might say of free competition what Bernard Shaw once said of Christianity: the only trouble with it is that it has never been tried".

Samuelson's misquote appeared in the term paper written by a student in my Adam Smith seminar. She said she found it on the web. I used the first sentence of the misquote in a Google search and got 6450 hits. I examined some of the links and found that many of them appeared in professors' slide presentations, journal articles, or finance and economics textbooks. None made any reference to Samuelson, nor did they provide a citation so the reader could confirm the accuracy of the quote by checking it out in *Wealth of Nations*.

Incidentally, "the real tragedy of the poor is the poverty of their aspirations" has been attributed to Adam Smith, and I got over 11,000 hits using the full quote in a Google search. Then I conducted an electronic search for "tragedy" in Smith's works, and found that the word does not appear in *Wealth of Nations*. It is used 35 times in his other works, but never in reference to poverty. These investigations indicate that we should be cautious when reading secondary sources that claim to quote Smith or summarize his views.

Samuelson was not alone in advancing this distorted version of Adam Smith's views. For example, we learn from a scholarly publication what Kenneth Arrow (Nobel Memorial Prize 1972) and F. H. Hahn believed to be the prevailing view of Smith among economics professors. They connected their research to "... a long and fairly imposing line of economists from Adam Smith to the present who have sought ... a decentralized economy motivated by self-interest ...". This statement is reasonable, but two sentences later they write that the "... economy is motivated by individual greed ...".[91] In another scholarly publication, Arrow refers to "those vast forces of **greed and aggressiveness that we are assured and assure our students are the mainsprings** of economic activity in a private enterprise economy; not the best but the strongest motives of humanity ...".[92]

A group of distinguished scholars gave public lectures at the University of Colorado in 1976, on the 200th publication anniversary of *Wealth of Nations,* which were published by the university's press. Among them was economist William J. Baumol, who declared that Smith believed that **free enterprise turns "... avarice against itself, transforming it into a prime instrument of public virtue"**.[93] In comparing the views of Karl Marx and Adam Smith, he stated that according to "... Marx, the capitalist, with all his crimes, is not the product of a warped morality, but a set of circumstances that gives him no choice".[94]

Baumol went on to say that according to Smith, the capitalist **"is an inherently immoral man whom the capitalist system is designed to constrain"**.[95] Thus, Baumol claimed that Smith believed the capitalist "with all his crimes" possesses a "warped morality" and as a result Smith is alleged to be more critical of the capitalist on ethical grounds than was Karl Marx. Nevertheless, these capitalist crimes are a prime instrument of public virtue, according to Baumol's interpretation of Smith. Incidentally, Smith never used the term *capitalist,* which, according to the *Oxford*

English Dictionary, first appeared in print 2 years after his death — and he never claimed that greed is good.

George Stigler (Nobel Memorial Prize 1982) gave a public lecture in 1984 at the University of Chicago entitled "Economics: The Imperial Science?" that appeared later in a scholarly journal. In explaining the difference between the fields of law and economics, he indicates that the amoral characteristic attributed to Smithian economics also applies to modern economics: "Lawyers draw fine distinctions between cases which allow the legal system to accommodate both traditional legal principles and the infinite variety of individual cases, and this is not conducive to theoretical generalization of the type which is prevalent in economics. In particular the lawyer's preoccupation with **fairness and justice is uncongenial to a science in which these concepts have no established meaning**".[96]

After declaring that "fairness and justice" have no established meaning in the science of economics, Stigler goes a step further, explaining how economic theory can be used to view civil disputes.[97] To paraphrase his story, suppose a rancher's cattle enter a neighbor's wheat field and cause $35,000 in damages. According to Stigler, it would make no difference, from the perspective of economic theory, whether the rancher or the farmer pays to build a fence between the properties and cover the cost of the lost wheat. The sole criterion used in drawing this conclusion is that economic gain or efficiency is maximized. In this case, the cost of repairs is the same whether the rancher or the farmer pays, so an economist as judge is indifferent about who should pay. The judge might observe that the farmer would probably pay since it is in his self-interest alone to do so. These outcomes, however, ignore fairness and justice because these concepts have no meaning in the context of modern economics, according to Stigler.

Audience members might have interpreted this story in one of two ways. First, the fact that fairness and justice have no place in economics might lead BBA and MBA students and others possessing an elementary understanding of economics to construct an alternative story making the same point. Suppose a young man sees an old woman hide $100 behind a brick in her fireplace. The young man promises to double her money if she invests in his business. The young man buys goods with the $100 and sells them for $200. He claims a salary of $210 and then tells the old woman that the firm lost $10 and would be unable to return any of her investment.

Applying Stigler's line of reasoning, it is better from an economic perspective for the young man to take the money. If it remains behind the brick, the "value to society" would be $100 (old woman: $100 + young man: $0). However, the "value to society" would be $200 (old woman: $0 + young man: $200) if the young man takes her money and doubles it in business.

Putting it another way, it would cost society $100 if the young man was honest and did not take the money. In this utilitarian view, personal vice has indeed become a public virtue if the only basis for judging right and wrong is society's total wealth. This line of reasoning could provide a dangerous lesson for ambitious economics and business students listening to Stigler's lecture.

In another public lecture given at Harvard University in 1980 and later published with a collection of his essays, Stigler states that economists rarely address ethical questions because they focus on social policies and institutions rather than individual behavior.[98] According to him, economists have been able to focus exclusively on economic efficiency because societal goals had been uncontroversial for over 200 years.[99] The problem is that business students might not see Stigler's story through the lens of public policy. Instead, they may be evaluating its relevance to their careers and seeing opportunities for themselves in the story of the young man who made $200 by increasing the efficient use of the nation's resources.

Consider a second interpretation of Stigler's story. His speech is given lightheartedly, suitable for a general audience rather than a faculty seminar. However, it is quite likely that some of his fellow economists, including Ronald Coase (Nobel Memorial Prize 1991), and economics graduate students were in attendance. Stigler might have shared a smile with Coase displaying his characteristic wit. The original story was Coase's and it was offered as a thought experiment addressing the question: How would the farmer and rancher resolve their dispute if neither owned the land they occupied? The answer: They could not go to court to have an issue of property rights resolved but instead would have to reach some sort of financial arrangement.[100] Audience members who were unaware of Coase's work would likely have assumed the rancher and farmer owned their land and had given the story an entirely different and unfortunate meaning.

Gary S. Becker (Nobel Memorial Prize 1992) wrote a scholarly article proposing an econometric model of the legal justice system using an utilitarian view that balances the costs of crime to society against the costs of catching, convicting, and punishing criminals. He indicated his approach "... follows **the economists' usual analysis of choice and assumes that a person commits an offense if the expected utility to him exceeds the utility he could get by using his time and other resources in other activities**".[101] Thus, Becker provides a more expansive definition of *economic man* that has allegedly descended from Adam Smith. Rather than simply being greedy, economic man will engage in criminal activities when crime pays.

The trait of rationality is incorporated into the definition of *economic man* contained in *A Dictionary of Economics*, published by Oxford University Press: "A person who is **entirely selfish and entirely rational**. While such a person in pure form is a caricature met only in economic models, there is a sufficient element of this in enough people to make economic models relevant to real life".[102]

In a book on globalization targeting a general audience Joseph E. Stiglitz (Nobel Memorial Prize 2001) states that, "In **Smithian economics, morality plays no role ... Individuals did not have to think about what was right or wrong**, only about what was in their own self-interest; the miracle of the market economy was that, in doing so, they promoted the general welfare". [103] Stiglitz went on to observe that some economists (such as Milton Friedman who won the Nobel Memorial Prize in 1976) built on this logic to conclude that if morality enters the minds of corporate executives at all, it obligates them to focus on the stockholders' sole concern with maximizing their investment returns.

In a public lecture reprinted in two books, economist John Kenneth Galbraith wrote that according to Smith, "**Self-interest or selfishness guides man,** as though by the influence of 'an invisible hand' ... **Private vice becomes a public virtue ...**".[104] Thus, Galbraith says, Smith viewed self-interest as vicious rather than virtuous, but that free markets transform this viciousness into a public virtue.

Milton Friedman gave an essentially correct but exaggerated and potentially misleading defense of capitalism on the Phil Donahue television show in 1979 and tapes of the interview have been seen on YouTube by millions of viewers since then.[105] Concerning economic man, the first pillar of free-market capitalism, Friedman responds to a question from Donahue by asking the rhetorical question: "Is there some society that doesn't run on greed?" He is also dismissive of the value of integrity, asking: "Do you think … American presidents reward virtue? Do they select their political appointees on the basis of their virtue or their political clout?"

Concerning the second pillar, Friedman declares that governments have produced none of humankind's great achievements. He equates pursuing self-interest with greediness, suggesting greed inspired the achievements of Albert Einstein and Henry Ford. While many economists have stated greed is a prominent feature of capitalism, Friedman's words can be interpreted to mean it is a desirable one.

It is possible that impressionable young men and women who saw the original Donahue interview or its tape could take away an unfortunate personal message: If I adopt the role of economic man and accept a creed of greed, I can join the ranks of Americans who have enriched themselves without worrying about the harm they have caused to others. This idea was surely not Friedman's intention, but he could have offered a more nuanced and less misleading defense of free-market capitalism.

Economist James Buchanan (Nobel Memorial Prize 1986) writes that individuals should not cooperate with others even when it could be self-serving. Consider this retelling of his story. Aurora is an unincorporated subdivision where all 1000 residents agree it would be beneficial to add an extra lane to the road connecting it to the highway. Estimated benefits are $100 per person for a total of $100,000, and the construction costs will be $50,000 or $50 per person. Net benefits to the community if the lane were built would also be $50,000, or $50 per person.

A committee is formed to collect contributions. Ken Hanks, an Aurora resident, recognizes he and everyone else will benefit if the lane is added and considers whether or not to contribute. Ken notes that if his neighbors contribute sufficiently, he will have use of the improved road without contributing a penny himself. If his neighbors' contributions are inadequate then it doesn't matter whether or not he contributes. Buchanan argues that in such situations, individuals *"must always* rationally choose the free-rider alternative. Since all individuals will tend to act similarly, the facility will not be constructed from proceeds of wholly voluntary contributions of potential beneficiaries".[106]

But is this tactic rational on Ken's part? Suppose he estimates that 10% of the residents would be unwilling or unable to contribute, and concludes that if each of the rest of the residents contributes an average of $55.56, the net benefit for each will be reduced from $50 ($100 – $50) to $44.44 ($100 – $55.56). He might reason that his $44.44 net gain justifies his contribution. Following this line of reasoning, Ken should reject Buchanan's advice, concluding that it would be irrational not to donate $56 when he would get all of his money back if the total raised were insufficient. If Ken were a real person and Aurora actually existed we might discover that the local church relies solely on voluntary contributions. It could also be that one of the committee members owns a print shop and was making signs for contributors to place in their front yards.

*   *

The statements beginning with Samuelson's and ending with Buchanan's indicate how I and other economics students could have learned that Adam Smith promoted greed and the self-regulation of markets as the twin pillars of free-market capitalism. One might argue that the influence of the ten economists just quoted has declined and that mainstream economics has changed. After all, three of them were born before World War I began in 1914, and another four before the stock market crash of 1929.

The counterargument is that although mainstream economics has changed since these men were making their most significant contributions, their intellectual legacy remains intact. A friend who received his PhD from the University of Chicago told me that a professor there told him that if a customer overpaid for a job the only ethical question would be whether the person taking the money would tell his partner. Additionally, the twin pillars of free-market capitalism they supported in part, or in whole, have remained foundational to more recent research relevant to business practice, as the reader will see.[107]

The following section describes how economics in business curricula emerged from being a member of the supporting cast to taking the leading role. The section thereafter will introduce major economic theories and methods appearing in business schools in the aftermath of the Gordon-Howell report.

AGH: Economics Rules

Where were business deans to turn in search of faculty members who could bring to business schools the rigorous theories and methods declared to be so lacking by the Gordon-Howell report? It would not be to the anthropology or sociology departments, where doctoral students were applying "weak theories" and "soft methods" to the study of mating habits in Samoa or America's slums.[108] Those trained in experimental psychology or communications might have a small role, but they offered no grand theories and their research findings were piecemeal and tentative. Besides, these social scientists were brought up in an academic tradition where business was dismissed as vocational training and business problems were not considered interesting or worthy.

The choice was obvious. Economics is arguably the oldest social science, tracing the mathematical modeling for which it is famous to the early 19th century. The Frenchman Augustin Cournot published *Research into the Principles of the Mathematics of the Theory of Wealth* in 1838.[109] Further, a discipline characterized by the law of diminishing marginal product, the law of diminishing marginal utility, the law of scarcity, the law of supply and demand, and others appears to place economics in a class with physics. Economists make definitive statements about universal principles with a degree of precision and certainty found nowhere else in the social sciences. Certainly no other social science has as its foundation the irrefutable rules of mathematics.

Parenthetically, the institutional approach was rejected in economics as it was in business. The American Economic Association was founded in 1885 by institutionalists who opposed neoclassical economics but were deposed by "neoclassical-Keynesian" synthesis with its focus on mathematics and statistics. Those interested in this attempted revolution should read Yuval Yonay's *The Struggle over the Soul of Economics: Institutional and Neoclassical Economists in America Between the Wars*.

And then of course, there's the Nobel Memorial Prize. Economics joined the ranks of physics, chemistry, medicine-physiology, literature, and peace in 1967. Thereafter, economic theories, methods, and the individuals credited with their development achieved a level of status inaccessible in virtually all other disciplines. A Columbia Business School brochure brags that "thirteen winners of the Nobel Prize in Economics have taught or studied at Columbia, including University Professor Joseph Stiglitz, who often teaches at the Business School".[110] There is double counting because Nobel Prize winners have not studied and taught at a single university, but no claim of excellence is more effective in identifying an elite business school.

Another major factor, mentioned previously, was that economists had turned their attention to business.[111] During Harry Markowitz's defense of his thesis on stock portfolio theory in 1952, Milton Friedman declared it did not justify a PhD in economics, stating: "It's not math, it's not economics, it's not even business administration".[112] Friedman's complaint was Markowitz's work lacked a solid theoretical foundation. That general criticism of research dealing with financial markets was soon to be addressed by groundbreaking theoretical work in Chicago's economics department and business school and MIT's economics department. The premise of the Chicago economists was that markets are perfect, while those at MIT argued they were imperfect, but the Chicago view grew to dominate the emerging field of financial economics which would revolutionize the way investing has been taught in business schools and practiced on Wall Street.

No longer were the inner workings of financial markets, large business organizations, and distribution channels ignored. Beginning in the 1990s, a string of Nobel Memorial Prizes was awarded to economists working in the field of financial economics that concerns the pricing of capital assets and the financial decisions made by individuals and firms.[113] The work in this area completely transformed financial theory and practice and served as a major entry point of neoclassical economics into the business school.[114] Additionally, economists began exploring why and how business organizations were formed when traditional economic theory indicated they were unnecessary because self-employed individuals could do the same work. This research work has been met with resistance within the management discipline but its impact on management practice has been considerable.

Economic Theories and the Twin Pillars

The twin pillars underpin theories and methods that have influenced both theory and practice, particularly in finance and management during the AGH era.

Of particular importance in finance is *rational expectations theory,* which claims the actual price of a product is an accurate (unbiased) estimate of its true value. Such high-quality information exists because market prices reflect the collective wisdom and knowledge of buyers and sellers. Thus, the aggregate interaction of all a product's rational buyers and sellers sets prices based on near-perfect information. *Efficient market theory* involves the application of rational expectations theory to the stock market, positing that current prices represent the best predictions of every stock's long-term value.[115] Because of their greater relevance to this story, theories and methods that have influenced management practice are the focus of this chapter.

Rational choice theory is a formal presentation of the concept of economic man and is used to describe the behavior of both individuals and firms. It underpins the theories of rational expectations and efficient markets, those just described and those that follow.

Game theory is a mathematical model used to examine how parties interact as rational choice theory predicts. *Reputation theory* predicts how firms weigh the costs and benefits of maintaining a good reputation. *Transaction costs theory* and *agency theory* are applications of the *theory of the firm,* with the former looking at the broad issue of how industries and the firms within them are organized, while the latter has been concerned principally with aligning the incentives of stockholders and CEOs. Game theory is employed in the theories of reputation, transaction costs, and agency.

Rational Choice Theory

Rational choice theory attempts to explain human behavior resulting from the choice from among alternatives the course of action that maximizes the benefits we receive and minimizes the costs we incur.[116] Parents weigh the benefits and costs in deciding whether or not to have their children vaccinated and choose the course of action appearing to offer the greatest health benefits. The utilitarian principle — the greatest good for the greatest number — is invoked when benefit-cost analysis is applied to groups. Thus, some parents may be required to have their children vaccinated in order to prevent harm that might result if measles or another communicable disease were introduced into a school system.

Francis Hutcheson, Adam Smith's moral philosophy professor at the University of Glasgow, had the intuition of utilitarianism when he wrote in 1726: "that action is best, which procures the greatest happiness for the greatest numbers".[117] Economist John Stewart Mill helped formalize the concept when he published *Utilitarianism* in 1863. Some individuals reacted to the work with hostility, and introduced the term *economic man* to ridicule the cold calculating character Mill portrayed.[118]

Economists have since responded that critics used economic man as a "straw man", but the descriptions of economic man presented earlier indicate that the notion of a cold calculating character is embraced widely today among economists.[119] Despite the consistent use of *selfishness* or *greediness* in modern descriptions of economic man, this has not always been the case. Alfred Marshall, one of the first great neoclassical economists, wrote in 1890: "When the older economists spoke of the 'economic man' as governed by selfish, or by self-regarding motives, they did not express their meaning exactly".[120] Instead, Marshall declares that *deliberateness* rather than selfishness is the principal characteristic of modern man.[121]

Although originated when classical economics acquired utilitarian foundations during Smith's time, the theory has spread throughout the social sciences. Economists have used money to denominate benefits and costs, but nonmonetary benefits and costs have been employed all over the social sciences. For example, calculating Christians are assumed by some researchers to weigh the benefits of getting into heaven against the cost of following the Ten Commandments.[122] Alternatively, low election turnout is attributed to the fact that most adults do not believe voting is worth the trouble.[123]

Rational choice theory can also be used as a self-help tool. Primatologist Frans de Waal tells of a researcher who had used computer spreadsheets to keep track of the gives and takes in five successive marriages.[124]

Game Theory

Game theory is a highly technical method of analyzing the strategies of opposing agents (individuals, firms, nations, etc.) who are joined in multiple rounds of decisions. Perhaps, the simplest way of explaining the technique is with a single-round formulation of a game referred to as the Prisoner's Dilemma.

Bonnie and Clyde have been arrested for armed robbery and placed in separate prison cells. Bonnie has no criminal record, but Clyde has been sent up twice for serious crimes. They live in a state with a "three strikes and you're out" law. The prosecutor is politically ambitious and wants to make a very public example of Clyde. She has no interest in sending Bonnie to jail but wants her help in getting Clyde.

There is no direct evidence to convict them so the prosecutor has come up with plea-bargain proposals he explains fully to each of them. First, if both Bonnie and Clyde rat on the other, then she receives a 2-day sentence and he will spend 20 years in prison. Second, if Bonnie rats and Clyde clams up, she receives probation and he gets a life sentence. Third, if Bonnie clams up and Clyde rats on her, she gets 3 days and he gets 10 years. Finally, if both of them clam up, Bonnie will serve 1 day and Clyde gets 30 years.

This game is represented with the matrix shown in Table 1, where the rows represent Bonnie's decisions and the columns represent Clyde's. The cells of the matrix illustrate the four outcomes. The pairs of numbers in each cell represent the sentences, with the first number (in **bold**) indicating Bonnie's and the second (in *italics*) indicating Clyde's.

The prosecutor set up an office pool allowing staff members and jail residents to bet on the plea-bargain decisions before she presented the offers to Bonnie and Clyde. The idealistic bettors argued that "love conquered all" and bet that both would clam up. The realists claimed that

Table 1:   Bonnie and Clyde's Dilemma.

		Clyde	
		Rats	**Clams up**
Bonnie	Rats	**2 days**, *20 years*	**Probation**, *Life*
	Clams up	**3 days**, *10 years*	**1 day**, *30 years*

although Clyde loved Bonnie dearly he could not risk a life sentence and would have to rat on her. The sexists argued "women cannot be trusted" and thought Bonnie would rat on Clyde.

Those free to move around gathered in the main office to learn who had won the pool. The prosecutor announced to the surprised audience that both prisoners had ratted on the other, so Bonnie was sentenced to 2 days and Clyde to 20 years. The audience was also surprised to learn that the sole winner was a trustee who was serving a lengthy term for fraud. They asked him how he knew and he responded that he had learned about rational choice theory in an online criminology course.

While this example is frivolous, its point is not: Game theory assumes that both agents (individuals, firms, nations, etc.) are economic men intent on maximizing their own gains without regard for the welfare of the other. It also assumes that players will select their best alternative even if it is superior to the other by a trivial amount. Whether I had expressed Bonnie's options in seconds, days, or years — or if Clyde faced the death penalty instead of a life sentence — Bonnie's decision would have been the same, according to game theory.

Incidentally, James Buchanan's view of the right decision for Ken and his fellow Aurora residents concerning whether to build the road that is presented in this chapter could be formulated in game theory as the Prisoner's Dilemma.

The *Stanford Encyclopedia of Philosophy* warns of game theory's "false, misleading or badly simplistic assumptions". It notes that the robot-like nature of insects makes them especially suitable for study using game theory, but human beings are highly complex. Our ability to reason, and the way we have been socialized, mediates our genetically determined instincts. Thus, modeling human beings with a "single comprehensive utility function, is a drastic idealization".[125] The same can be applied to the modeling of firms. This is not to say that game theory should not be used as a research tool but, rather, that it should be used with great care.

Reputation Theory

A corporation's most valuable asset is often, and ideally, its name. Apple's brand was valued at $118.9 billion in 2013 while its factories and equipment were worth $16.6 billion, or about one-seventh as much.[126] Successful firms must manage how customers, employees, suppliers, competitors, creditors, and regulators view them in order to enhance and maintain this precious but vulnerable asset. Research on corporate reputations is found in several academic disciplines.

Game theory has been employed by economists to evaluate a firm's management of its reputation in the opinion of various parties.[127] These studies must assume, of course, that the firm and the other parties possess the characteristics of economic man, weighing the economic gains from having a desirable reputation against the costs of maintaining it. Researchers tend to assume that perfect information does not exist and that the competitors or customers of a firm must instead rely upon information signals that are imperfect. For example, economist Carl Shapiro utilized a repeated game in which the players interacted repeatedly — in contrast to Bonnie and Clyde's one-time interaction. He developed a model representing a market in which buyers cannot evaluate a product's quality before it is purchased.[128] The first player in the game represents firms that have reputations for quality and can charge a premium price for their products, while the second represents firms making money by selling an inferior, low-cost product.

Shapiro identifies the optimal differential between the prices charged by the two groups of firms. He proves that the lack of an established reputation does not prevent a new quality provider from entering the market. Finally, he finds that most customers will benefit if the quality of products is evaluated and made available, and they will also benefit if a minimum quality standard is imposed through a licensing agreement, for example.

It has been claimed that the primary benefit of reputation theory is in demonstrating that the benefits of creating and maintaining a strong reputation outweigh the costs in highly competitive markets where good information is available. For example, the fact that the market value of Apple's stock is more than double that of Exxon at the time this is written, the second largest firm by this measure, is an accurate reflection of Apple's stellar job in building a strong reputation for selling quality products.[129]

It is dangerous, however, when this simplistic version of reputation theory is assumed to represent reality. Judge Frank Easterbrook rejected a charge filed by prosecutors in a federal lawsuit (before the demise of Enron's auditors, Arthur Andersen) that an accounting firm had aided and abetted the fraudulent acts of its client. The judge's rationale was that it would have been irrational for the accounting firm to do so. "The complaint does not allege that [the accounting firm] had anything to gain from any fraud by [its client]. An accountant's greatest asset is its reputation for honesty, followed closely by its reputation for careful work. Fees for two years' audits could not approach the losses [the auditor] would suffer from a perception that it would muffle a client's fraud .... *It would have been irrational for any of them to have joined cause with the client*".[130]

There are several problems with this simplistic view of reputation theory as the source of market discipline imposed on firms. First, what contributes to a firm's good reputation with one stakeholder may harm it with another. Hard-nosed investors may not be interested in a retailer that refers to its sales clerks as "associates" and pays premium wages. Second, conflicts may exist between a firm's desire for a good reputation and its employees' desires for better-paying jobs with other companies. For example, employees of a federal regulator working on-site at a major investment bank may be tempted to go native. Third, a firm's reputation doesn't matter if there is little or no competition. A cable company does not need a good reputation; it only needs to hold its customers' dissatisfaction level below the boiling point because of limited alternatives and the difficulty of switching to another provider.

There is also the danger that reputation theory itself can be misused. Take as an example, the modeling of a monopolist's engagement in predatory practices to prevent new competitors from entering its market that was undertaken by business professors Paul Milgrom and John Roberts.[131]

The conventional view is that such behavior does not occur because it isn't cost effective for the monopolist to engage in such practices. The study demonstrates to would-be monopolists that predatory pricing, for example, drives out recent entrants into the market and discourages others from trying to enter that market. It is also true that prosecutors of antitrust cases can use these research findings to undermine defendants' claims that they had not engaged in such practices because it had been irrational to do so. It would be a pity if students interpreted their professor's silence concerning the uses and abuses of reputation theory as an indication of indifference. That assumption might lead them to believe that a high volume of advertising by Internet providers, as we are seeing in the Austin area today, could compensate for shoddy service.

Theory of the Firm

Ronald Coase was a rare economist: a British expatriate, former socialist, and author of two landmark articles in which the only numbers are for identifying the pages. He entered the London School of Economics as an undergraduate business student in 1929, just 14 years after the Russian Revolution. He took an eye-opening economics class, which claimed that central planning was impossibly inefficient and that the price mechanism allocated resources nicely. The neoclassical economic theory Coase was being taught predicted that all individuals would be self-employed, when in reality many in Britain had permanent jobs paying wages. How, he wondered, could we explain the existence of large firms whose internal operations were governed by central planning?[132]

Coase found his answer to this insightful question and the seminal ideas leading to the *theory of the firm* when he studied business organization in the United States during the third year of his academic program. Economists assumed that buyers and sellers engaged in transactions (finding workers and keeping them or finding a job and keeping it) effortlessly and without cost. To the contrary, he realized these transaction costs were considerable and could be reduced substantially if workers and those who hired them made long-term commitments. Coase's ideas appeared in the economics journal published by the London School of Economics in 1937.[133]

He emigrated to the United States in 1951, and in 1960 published his second great article, the one about the rancher and farmer discussed earlier in this chapter. He joined the University of Chicago law faculty shortly thereafter, remaining there for almost 50 years.[134] It took a long time for the significance of his revolutionary ideas to be fully appreciated. He received the Nobel Memorial Prize at the age of 80, 54 years after the first paper was published and 31 years after the second. By contrast, Kenneth Arrow received his award when he was 51.

Transaction Cost Theory

One strand of Coca Cola's supply chain begins with mining bauxite for aluminum cans and ends, along with its other strands, in a store when customers place a six-pack of Diet Coke in their shopping carts. *Transaction cost theory* attempts to explain why firms comprising the supply chains are organized and operated differently for various end products — bread, soft drinks, smart phones, airplanes, and the like. The existing structure of an individual supply chain, and of the firms comprising it, is assumed in this theory to minimize the costs of coordinating and motivating all the individuals involved in providing the product.[135]

The theory has three important components. First, two firms must often commit significant resources before a relationship between them begins. As an example, a national fast-food franchisor provides turnkey operations and training, and an individual franchisee spends considerable funds to purchase the franchise and build the individual restaurant before a single taco can be sold.

Second, neither the franchisor nor the franchisee can foresee the future so it is impossible for the franchise agreement to anticipate all feasible events. For instance, the franchisor must come up with new menu items and eliminate old ones to meet changes in demand, and external pressures arise when a new competitor enters the market or customers' tastes change.

Third, the theory offers its own version of economic man, someone who is strategically "opportunistic". The opportunist tries to game the system by lying, making false promises and threats, malingering, and stealing.[136] Oliver Williamson, the economist who won the Nobel Memorial Prize in 2009 for his contributions to this theory, observes that this conception of economic man "is akin to the prevailing behavioral assumptions employed throughout microeconomics".[137]

Small firms have their own transaction costs to deal with even though they are not likely to have much influence over the supply chain. Thus, the theory is usually presented from the perspective of a single large firm.[138] In the present example, the focus is on the franchisor that has trouble policing opportunistic franchisees. These franchisees may, for example, underreport revenues, fail to maintain their facilities, offer their own menu items, or operate outside their assigned territories.

The franchisor could solve these problems by buying out a franchisee and operating the outlet itself. However, its newly acquired employees could act opportunistically as well. They might steal food, falsify time sheets, neglect the restrooms, or fake injuries. For this reason, the franchisor needs to impose a system of authority on employees through which orders are given, work is supervised, and compensation is properly dispensed. The franchisor will decide, according to this theory, whether or not to keep a particular franchise operation based upon which alternative minimizes transaction costs.

Transaction cost theory views a supply chain as a large nexus (network) of contracting parties that is comprised of smaller nexuses representing individual firms. It also assumes that information is imperfect and that the number of suppliers available to a customer may be insufficient to create strong competition among them. Under these circumstances, order and efficiency are increased over what the market would have provided when the manufacturer acquires a supplier or performs its operations internally.

The concept of economic man is more nuanced in transaction cost theory than in other theories. It recognizes that some individuals may be devoted to the organization. Others may only be motivated by compensation but are willing to play by the rules, and still others are opportunistic no matter how well they are treated.[139] Some researchers also acknowledge that the characteristics of economic man may be culturally determined.[140]

The assumption that suppliers and manufacturers behaved like economic man may have been reasonable before the Japanese forced US manufacturers to think otherwise. A company like GM once maintained adversarial relationships with its suppliers. It utilized more than one supplier for the same product, so they could be played against each other. GM concealed the maximum it would pay for a product (say $24) and suppliers would conceal the lowest price they would accept ($18), and then they battled to increase their share of the difference between these two reservation prices ($6). It was unheard of during this era for a manufacturer's and a supplier's engineers to collaborate, a common practice today.

The Japanese were a highly credible source of information for US manufacturers because they could produce products of disturbingly high quality at frighteningly low costs. One of their major innovations was the operating assumption that a manufacturer and its supplier could improve product quality and share the financial gains from doing so if they established a cooperative and trusting relationship. This revolutionary idea is the foundation of the modern concepts of *supply chain* and *supply chain management*.[141] The supply chain incorporates the channels of distribution of most of the parts and materials that wind up in the can of Coca Cola being produced. Supply chain management involves the coordination of efforts of its participants, including the suppliers of other suppliers, so they could operate as smoothly as if they were parts of a large, vertically integrated firm.

One of the best examples of supply chain management has been Proctor & Gamble (P&G), which organized itself so that one management team and its supporting staff members are now responsible for its suppliers upstream and another is focused on its distributors downstream.[142] Walmart is P&G's largest distributor and P&G has a team working at Walmart's Bentonville, Arkansas headquarters. To sell Pampers, for example, P&G's computers are linked to Walmart's so that when cash register sales data indicate that inventory is running low at any of its more than 5100 outlets, the message is sent up through the supply chain at close to the speed of light. Supply chains could not function effectively if individual firms acted as "opportunistic man".[143]

Michael Jensen and Agency Theory

The purchase of services is often far more complex and difficult than that of goods. We can't test drive a surgical procedure for removing a cancerous tumor and it will be years before we can breathe with the relief that it got everything. The assessment of a last will and testament never comes in time for its author to evaluate it, so we must trust that executors and probate judges will see to our wishes. We have faith that the electronic or paper reports of our retirement savings are not illusory and that our investment manager is not a would-be Bernie Madoff. We rely upon the integrity and technical competence of such service providers, but we must employ them before we are able to determine with certainty whether they possess either of these qualities. We would never engage such service providers if their sole objective was to maximize their wealth because we are too vulnerable and weak, and the future is too uncertain, for us to protect ourselves.

The institutions of the learned professions and the concept of fiduciary duties discussed in Chap. 3 were created to enable service recipients to place trust in the integrity and technical competence of special classes of service providers. Among these classes are physicians, attorneys, judges, elected officials who receive oaths of office, licensed financial advisors, corporate board members and officers, notaries public, executors of wills, and various kinds of trustees.

Standards can be quite high for individuals bound by such duties. Consider the actual case of a surgeon who interrupted an operation, went to his financial advisor's office to conduct some business, and returned to complete the operation successfully.[144] He lost his license to practice for violating fiduciary law. Although the patient was not harmed, the decision was based on the notion that it is bad public policy for physicians to place so recklessly their financial interests above the health and safety of their patients.

If the relationship between the surgeon and patient had been simply commercial, as when a technician takes off to go fishing in the midst of repairing a customer's air conditioner, there would be no grounds for a suit: "no harm, no foul". The waivers that patients sign before undergoing surgery appear to represent an attempt to protect surgeons from lawsuits by converting their relationships with them from fiduciary ones toward commercial (or contractual) ones.

As a financial example, consider the fictitious case of a trustee of the estate established for the care of a disabled person who outlived his parents. A sales representative for an insurance company approaches the trustee offering her an honorarium of $1000 for transferring the trust funds from a competitor's annuity to one his firm offers with better returns. It would be a violation of the trustee's fiduciary duties to accept the money, and she would be obliged to add it to the trust funds unless the trust agreement specified otherwise.

The important lesson here is that anyone providing financial services or purchasing them should realize that diversified financial service firms are likely to offer some services where fiduciary duties apply and others where they do not. If a stockbroker with no fiduciary duties recommends a particular stock, the deal may be better for him than for the customer.

Economic efficiency is increased when fiduciary duties are performed faithfully. If surgeons were untrustworthy, it might be worthwhile for a heart patient to hire a second physician to ensure that a stent is really necessary and that it is implanted properly. Likewise, it could be a fiduciary duty of mutual fund trustees to conduct their own audits if they believe public accounting firms are failing to meet their own fiduciary duties to the public by concealing a corporate client's cooked books.

The fiduciary duties of several professions have weakened considerably in recent decades.[145] However, the record of corporate executives is among the worst.[146] Adam Smith wrote extensively in *Wealth of Nations* about the East India Company, complaining of the "negligence, profusion [extravagance], and malversation [corrupt administration] of the servants of the company".[147] Because owners and managers were living in different hemispheres, and correspondence took 18 months to be sent from London to India and back again, unsupervised managers could enrich themselves with impunity by misappropriating corporate funds.[148]

State governments go to the trouble and expense of granting corporate charters because it is assumed each newly constituted firm will benefit the public. Corporations have grown in number and scale because they have contributed significantly to the increase in global prosperity despite their shortcomings. During the 1980s, however, there was widespread doubt about whether American corporations were meeting the challenge of their Japanese competitors. CEOs appeared more concerned with building their own empires by acquiring businesses they would manage like parts of an investment portfolio.

These expanded corporate domains enabled executives to command larger salaries and bonuses and to treat themselves with palatial offices, large staffs, personal jets, and staff retreats at exotic resorts. By diverting resources for their own purposes, the executives were denying stockholders their property rights and limiting corporate profitability. Corporate boards of directors who were supposed to represent stockholder interests were weak and ineffectual.

Markets for corporate stocks and as well for CEOs failed to correct these problems. CEOs kept their jobs and maintained their compensation levels even when the corporations they managed performed poorly. An intervention was needed to reduce the acute conflict of interest between managers and stockholders afflicting US corporations. Michael Jensen, a Harvard Business School professor, was the most prominent advocate of *agency theory* that was developed to solve these problems.

Jensen, now retired, is one of the finest examples of the modern business faculty member envisioned by the authors of the Carnegie and Ford Foundation reports of 1959. He was born in Rochester, Minnesota, and studied economics at McAlister College in St. Paul, about 80 miles away. He earned an MBA in finance and a PhD in economics, finance, and accounting at the University of Chicago, and he spent his teaching career at the University of Rochester and Harvard Business School. Jensen launched his career by working with some of the world's top economists: Merton Miller (Nobel Memorial Prize 1990), who served as his dissertation advisor, and Eugene Fama (Nobel Memorial Prize 2013) and Myron Scholes (Nobel Memorial Prize 1997), who were coauthors on some of his earliest publications.

The most influential of Jensen's publications has been "Theory of the Firm: Managerial Behavior, Agency Costs and Ownership", which he published in 1976 with William Meckling, who also did graduate work in economics at Chicago.[149] The Social Science Research Network ranks this paper as 19th out of the top 10,000 downloaded from its database within the past 12 months. Additionally, it has been downloaded 104,904 times and referenced by 4407 other papers since it first appeared.[150] Jensen is ranked first among the top 8000 economics authors based on the number of downloads of all his publications over the last 12 months (62,131), even though he spent his career teaching in business schools.

The 56-page article on agency theory concerns "the study of the inevitable conflicts of interest that occur when individuals engage in the cooperative behavior" occurring in corporations.[151] Jensen employed game theory to examine conditions where a CEO will divert corporate resources to his own personal use by decorating his office lavishly, paying a premium for an attractive secretarial staff, contributing to favorite charities, buying the adoration and respect of employees, or diverting business to friends.[152] Stockholders can stop such wasteful spending if they monitor the CEO's behavior sufficiently and link his compensation to the corporation's financial performance, according to the theory. Equilibrium in the model is found when the combined costs of the CEO's waste and of the incentive and monitoring systems to rein him in are minimized.

Although no data were offered to support Jensen's claims, the mathematics presented in the article are extensive and highly complex. The paper offers a *theorem* (a general proposition not self-evident but one that can be demonstrated) and a mathematical *proof* providing the necessary demonstration. Jensen's theorem is that investors will reduce what they are willing to pay for a stock to the extent that the CEO is diverting corporate funds for his or her own use. The assumption upon which this proof rests is the validity of efficient market theory: Potential investors have sufficient information to discount a stock's price properly if the CEO diverted funds for his or her own use.[153]

Quod erat demonstrandum (QED) is printed at the end of the proof to indicate that its results are consistent with the theorem. The unequivocal nature of this proof and the impressive mathematics throughout the paper imbue Jensen and Meckling's conclusions with a level of certainty and degree of exactitude associated with physics, in contrast to the tentativeness and imprecision of conclusions drawn from other social science research.[154]

In addition to the assumption of investors' perfect information, there are others that are relevant to this book. Second, corporations "are simply legal fictions which serve as a nexus for a set of contracting relationships among individuals".[155] Third, money denominates all relationships within a corporation, including the CEO's "personal relations ('love,' 'respect,' etc.) with employees".[156] Fourth, all individuals are focusing on maximizing their own wealth and are indifferent to the welfare of everyone else. Fifth, stockholders are capable of imposing the incentive and monitoring system on untrustworthy CEOs and understand that by doing so will maximize their own wealth. Sixth, a CEO's effectiveness can be captured in a single measure — the stock price. Finally, the purpose of the firm is to maximize shareholder wealth. This last assumption is especially important and it will be discussed in Chaps. 5 and 7.

The managerial implications drawn from Jensen's paper on agency theory are as plausible as the analysis appears conclusive. The first is that CEOs' incentive systems should employ stock options because their value goes up when the corporation is doing well and down when it is doing poorly. Second, corporations should focus on what they do best, their core competencies, and sell off unrelated businesses. A steel company has no business trying to sell cosmetics. Third, corporations should finance new ventures by borrowing money rather than by issuing more stock. The rationale is that the CEO will be more judicious in taking on new ventures and more aggressive in paying off the debt of those undertaken.

Finally, corporate boards should be reformed, enabling them to monitor and reward or punish CEOs based on their success in increasing stockholder wealth. One component of this recommendation is that CEOs should not serve as board chairs because that would be like assigning a fox to guard the hen house. Additionally, the proportion of outside board members (those who are not corporate employees) should be increased to dilute the influence of insiders.[157]

Agency theory has been the centerpiece of the Coordination, Control, and the Management of Organizations (CCMO) course formulated by Jensen and Meckling at the University of Rochester in 1973. It grew to become one of the most popular elective courses in Harvard's MBA program, attracting between 500 and 600 of the 850 second-year students, according to a 1997 history of the course.[158] The history is fascinating reading, at least to an academic, because it suggests the vast resources, both human and financial, devoted to this course and the interdisciplinary research supporting it. Also remarkable are the extensive course-related publications and Internet-based resources available to other business schools and interested parties. Few if any other business schools in the country could provide such support for a single elective course.

Jensen and Meckling also prepared a manuscript for the course in the early 1970s, later published as "The Nature of Man". In it they declared that human nature is "fundamental to understanding how organizations function, whether they be profit-making firms in the private sector, non-profit enterprises, or intended to serve the 'public interest.'"[159] They present five models of human behavior drawn from the social sciences and two of them are relevant to this discussion.[160] The Resourceful, Evaluative, Maximizing Model (REMM) acknowledges that human beings care for a long list of things including wealth, honor, approval, group norms, culture, and rules of conduct.[161] No one can have all of everything, so REMMs make the tradeoffs and substitutions necessary to achieve the most desirable outcome. In contrast, Jensen and Meckling reject the Economic Model that presents man as "a short-run money maximizer who does not care for others or for art, morality, love, respect, or honesty".[162]

Although they reject the Economic Model in their "Nature of Man" paper, they are forced to employ it in their "Theory of the Firm" paper because it utilizes game theory. Their rationale is that money is valued by almost everyone because it can be used for so many purposes and the amount it is rewarded is easily varied with job performance.[163] Additionally, Jensen and Meckling note that the Economic Model is used by economists because it is easier to represent mathematically.[164] In other words, they preferred the REMM to the Economic Man Model, but could not incorporate it into a mathematical model because of its vast complexity.

This discussion about alternative assumptions concerning the nature of man is not merely hairsplitting. Managers who are treated with respect are probably more likely to act respectably, and those treated as thieves may defy the restraints their boards try to impose upon them and act without compunction to maximize their own wealth at the expense of stockholders.

In the history of the CCMO course, four authors who had taught the course expressed surprise that it had been described as "ideological".[165] However, the twin pillars of free markets are apparent in the course materials. Concerning the first pillar, economic man personifies the players of game theory. Acceptance of economic man as greedy and rational is an ideological position (as will be shown in Chap. 6) without empirical evidence to support it.

The second pillar, perfect competition used for describing much of economic phenomena, is also an ideological one. "The Nature of Man" states that the stock market possesses an attribute of perfect competition: perfect information. Additionally, Jensen and Meckling write: "it is reasonable to argue that all markets are always in equilibrium, and all forces must always be in balance at all times".[166] No government intervention is required under such ideal conditions.

CAUTION: Hazardous Assumptions

When people say, "I assume you brought the airline tickets", they are making a statement — in this case a hopeful one — about what they believe to be true. In contrast, economists use the term *assumption* to refer to the appropriateness of a theory or model for use in a particular situation.[167] If a researcher incorrectly assumes that there is a correspondence (isomorphism) between the variables and their interrelationships built into a model and the corresponding forces at work in that particular situation, then biased forecasts will likely result. So if the model for monopolies is used to forecast changes in wheat production in response to a demand increase, for example, then the forecasted quantity produced will likely be too low.

Efforts to forecast wheat production or labor productivity on an assembly line should not by themselves alter the true values of the variables being forecast. However, government officials and business managers employ economic theories and models with the intention of increasing wheat production or labor productivity. Special care must be used to select an economic tool with valid assumptions because failure to do so may result in outcomes that are the opposite of those intended.

Management professors Sumantra Ghoshal and Peter Moran have argued that transaction cost theory should not be taught in business schools because of its destructive assumptions, and sociologists Frank Dobbin and Jiwook Jung published the provocatively titled article "The Misapplication of Mr. Michael Jensen: How Agency Theory Brought

Down the Economy and Why It Might Again".[168] The problems these researchers identify concerning transaction cost theory and agency theory may also afflict the other theories and methods that rest on some of the same assumptions. Thus, managers must be fully aware of the assumptions associated with an economic tool and the significance of those assumptions before they base important policy decisions on its use. The critical question is whether managers are sufficiently well informed to avoid disaster.

There is a provocative parallel between economic tools and prescription drugs in this regard. Prescription drugs must undergo clinical testing before they can be safely released for public use. In contrast, economic tools and theories may not have undergone empirical validation before authors of business textbooks introduce them to students as if they are ready for widespread application by managers or consultants.

After any drug has passed clinical trials, the Food and Drug Administration (FDA) requires pharmaceutical companies to provide physicians, pharmacists, and patients with adequate information about a drug's proper use, misuse, and the negative side effects that might result. Likewise, George Stigler argues that a new economic theory should survive a 10- or 15-year period of challenges and repeated empirical testing, the "trial by fire that is the heart of the scientific process", before it can be implemented with confidence.[169] However, it seems that similar information is generally lacking when economic tools such as game theory are presented to business students.

The purpose of this comparison is not to suggest that a business or economic equivalent of the FDA should be established. Rather, textbook authors should ensure that classroom teachers and their students are properly informed about the demonstrated efficacy of an economic tool and about the manner in which it can be used safely and effectively. Accordingly, I suggest that when potentially powerful tools are presented to business students, they should be accompanied by statements concerning: the empirical support of the developers' claims, the kinds of problems a tool is intended to address (Indications), the conditions under which the tool should be used with caution or not used at all (Contraindications), and any side effects that may result (Warnings and Precautions).

To illustrate this point, I have prepared the equivalent of a package insert for agency theory:

> **Indications:** Agency theory is a management tool used to reduce "the inevitable conflicts of interest that occur when individuals engage in cooperative behavior".[170] Its principal application is to ensure that a corporate CEO is fully devoted to maximizing shareholder wealth.
>
> **Contraindications:** Situations where agency theory should be used with caution or not at all have not been identified. Its developers claim it may be used where organizations are essentially nexuses of contracts among selfish and rational individuals and these include: firms; nonprofit institutions such as universities, hospitals, and foundations; mutual organizations such as mutual savings banks and insurance companies and cooperatives; some private clubs; and even governmental bodies such as cities, states, and the federal government; government enterprises such as the Tennessee Valley Authority (TVA), the post office, transit systems, and so forth.[171]
>
> **Warnings and Precautions:** Agency theory has not undergone empirical testing and no side effects have been indicated.

Two alternative versions of the "insert" are presented — one for use with CEOs or presidents and the other for use with employees:

> **Indications (CEOs or presidents):** Agency theory is a management tool used to prevent a selfish and rational CEO or president from diverting an organization's resources for his or her own personal use.
>
> **Contraindications:** Agency theory should be used cautiously in corporations or other organizations where the CEO or president appears conscientious in fulfilling his or her fiduciary duties. What appears to be a CEO's or president's diversion of the organization's resources may actually serve the organization's long-term interests.
>
> Agency theory should not be used when the CEO or president of an organization and its board of directors are engaged in an embrace rather than an arm's-length relationship. Nor should it be used when the corporate board does not have the independent staff or resources to supervise or reward the CEO appropriately, or where the CEO is

able to maintain the public illusion that the current price of its stock is appropriate and is an accurate indication of its future earnings. Note: It was discovered after the fall of Lehman Brothers that it had invested $44 for every dollar of its own assets and that many of the investments were in subprime mortgages.[172]

Warnings and Precautions: Indications of instances where selfish and rational CEOs are taking significant risks with stockholders' and creditors' money may be found when there are: indications of managed earnings, innovative accounting practices, accusations by senior executives that financial analysts or business writers do not recognize genius, and employment contracts rewarding executives with large bonuses whether the corporation is making money or losing. Note: Top bond ratings and impressive financial statements may be false indicators.

Indications (Employees): Agency theory is a management tool that reduces "the inevitable conflicts of interest that occur when" individual employees put their personal interests above those of the organization.[173]

Contraindications: Agency theory should be used with caution or not used at all in organizations where: worker performance is multi-faceted and difficult to measure, the desire to maximize wealth is not the sole motivator or even the principal one, teamwork and trust among workers are vital, and a strong sense of purpose is held and a sense of pride is shared by most members of the organization. Note: The apparent failure of certain individuals to cooperate may reflect personnel issues rather than problems with organizational design.

Warnings and Precautions: Absenteeism, tardiness, resignations, work slowdowns, vandalism, and theft.

Agency theory has not undergone clinical testing. Careful organizational analysis and, where possible, empirical trials should be performed to validate its assumptions before it is applied organization wide. Large organizations may be able to use multiple units to conduct a field experiment for evaluating its suitability.[174] Additionally, coworkers could be asked to play the ultimatum game [described later] face-to-face with $500 to determine their willingness to treat each other fairly.

Although the use of the package insert model may not be the most effective way of presenting the material, it should be offered in some manner. I have examined six contemporary managerial economics textbooks, each of which covers several of the economic tools discussed here.[175] They are impressive works, but none of them provides the proposed material comprehensively or explains why the validity of assumptions may really matter. Further, the lengthy examples and cases included in some of the texts would provide excellent vehicles for illustrating problems that may arise when such powerful tools are used.

How Does Ethics Fit into Mainstream Economics?

After a lecture at Cornell University in 1978, a student asked Milton Friedman if he thought it was wrong that Ford Motor Company sold Pintos with defective gas tanks after their analysis revealed it would be less expensive to deal with the injured parties than to reinforce the tanks.[176] The student claimed that over a thousand lives had been lost during the 7 years the automobile had been sold.

Friedman countered, saying that the student's question was an economic one and not a matter of principle. He asked what Ford's decision would have been if it had valued the cost of a life lost at $1 billion instead of $200,000, or if the estimated number of lives lost had been one instead of 200. He went on to say that the real question of principle is whether Ford should have informed customers about repair costs and the additional risk of death that could result if repairs had not been made. Finally, Friedman stated that the courts exist to punish firms for fraud when they fail to provide adequate warnings.

It would have been very instructive if someone in the audience had asked Friedman about the efficacy of treating cases of personal injury and death as matters of fraud. Let's use our example from Chap. 2, under "Defining Greed". Suppose a distributor's salesperson sold propane to a rogue retailer who resold it to an elderly man for $35 and the man's propane system was in violation of state safety codes when a resulting explosion caused his death. Suppose, finally, that the salesperson continued to sell the propane to the same retailer and a second deadly explosion occurred.

What laws would comprise Friedman's ideal legal system? Would good public policy allow the distributor to claim it did not defraud the two propane customers because it had not sold them anything? Should the policy allow the retailer to claim that the estates of the two deceased customers could only recover the cost of the propane if fraud were proven? Should the distributor or retailer be able to require nondisclosure agreements as part of settlement agreements with the victim's heirs? What if the heirs did not have the resources to file a lawsuit against the distributor and retailer?

William Cooper (the quantitative methods professor at Carnegie Mellon mentioned earlier, who retired at the University of Texas) claimed in a personal conversation that Friedman "may not have been the greatest economist but he was the greatest arguer". The Cornell student was certainly out of his league. Some audience members voiced outrage with Friedman's positions while others applauded. In my opinion, Friedman did a disservice to the Cornell audience and those who have seen a recording of his comments since then. He argued that businesses should make their decisions based on economic and legal considerations, but he provided no place for legitimate ethical ones.

Friedman condoned the disregard for unethical actions that were legal, but two attorneys went further by recommending illegal acts if increased corporate profits would result. Frank Easterbrook, then a University of Chicago law professor, and David Fischel, then a law professor at Northwestern University, wrote in a *Michigan Law Review* article: **"Managers do not have an ethical duty to obey economic regulatory laws just because the laws exist", rather they are duty bound to "violate the rules when it is profitable to do so".**[177] If corporations are treated as individuals in the law, then why don't the rest of us individuals have a duty to ourselves to break the law when the benefits exceed the costs?

Easterbrook would later be appointed to the position of federal judge and Fischel would join the Chicago law faculty and go on to defend the acts of the felonious CEOs Charles Keating, Michael Milken, Jeffrey Skilling, and Joseph Nacchio.[178] "Easterbrook and Fischel", according to Joseph Heath, "are among the most influential theorists of corporate law of the twentieth century, and their position has become something close to Chicago school orthodoxy".[179]

Automobile executives exposed to the views espoused by Easterbrook and Fischer might conclude that they must risk the lives of the drivers and passengers involved in accidents where their vehicles were to blame so long as the litigation costs do not exceed the costs of replacing a defective part.

Did this pernicious message get to any of the 15 General Motors (GM) employees who were fired in 2015 for concealing the faulty ignition switch in their automobiles that resulted in 54 crashes and 13 deaths.[180] And what about the GM attorneys who handled the lawsuits and the senior executives who were aware of the mounting costs? Would their fiduciary duty apply if some of their shareholders or their loved ones were among the casualties? Or were the stockholders alerted to avoid the flawed vehicles?

*   *

The failure of the leading economists referenced in this book to discuss personal ethics or to dismiss its importance has been striking. This omission is profoundly important because students and others may conclude that personal qualms about harming others may be, or even should be, parked at the corporate front door. This omission is appropriate in the realm of positive economics because illegal activities are part of all economies and should be included in the analysis. However, this exclusion should not seem to suggest that the markets for crack cocaine or child prostitutes are desirable, even though they may increase economic efficiency. Unfortunately, this neglect of ethical considerations also extends to discussions of economic policy, with a few notable exceptions.

In the *Ethics of Competition*, Frank Knight, Friedman's former professor at Chicago, recognizes that human values are beyond the boundaries of science and he criticizes scientific dogmatism that "naturally denies the existence of everything which will not pass its tests as a fact".[181] He writes that "the scientific view of life is a limited and partial view; life is at bottom an exploration in the field of values, an attempt to discover values ...".[182] He observes that economics takes values unquestioningly and attempts to explain their most efficient fulfillment, whatever they are, through the production of goods and services.

Knight dismisses the brand of economics that reduces human virtue to self-interest as "glorified economics", saying:[183]

the rational, economic, criticism [or dismissal] of values gives results repugnant to all common sense. In this view the ideal man would be the economic man, the man who knows what he wants and 'goes after it' with singleness of purpose. The fact is, of course, the reverse. The economic man is the selfish, ruthless object of moral condemnation. Moreover, we do not bestow praise and affection on the basis of conduct alone or mainly, but quite irrationally on the motives themselves, the feelings to which we impute the conduct.[184]

Knight cautions that arguing from simplified premises overlooks abstract factors necessary for drawing sound conclusions and formulating meaningful policies.[185] In my words, he seems to be suggesting that it could be as disastrous for economists to design public policy based exclusively on overly simplified models as it would be for physicists to design bridges this way.

If the purpose of economic organization is to apply a society's scarce resources to maximize the satisfaction of its members' wants,[186] then humility is required because, according to Knight:

There is a fairly established consensus that happiness depends more on spiritual resourcefulness, and a joyous appreciation of the costless things of life, especially affection for one's fellow creatures, than it does on material satisfaction.[187]

Ronald Coase concludes his paper, "The Problem of Social Cost", with the statement that: "In devising and choosing between social arrangements we should have regard for the total effect", and acknowledges, in agreement with Knight, that such "problems of welfare economics must ultimately dissolve into the study of aesthetics and morals".[188]

Economist and federal judge Richard Posner has been careful to point out in his textbook, *Economic Analysis of Law*, that efficiency "has limitations as an ethical criterion of social decisionmaking [*sic*]". "The common law attaches costs to the violation of moral principles that enhance the efficiency of a market economy".[189]

Unfortunately, Knight, Coase, and Posner fail to elaborate on these points sufficiently to illustrate where and how aesthetics and morals should constrain the actions of a firm in its pursuit of shareholder wealth.

Chapter 5

What is the Shadow Curriculum
of Business?

The concept of the *hidden curriculum*, referring to the role schools play in preparing children for the transition from family to society, is traced to the work of French sociologist Émile Durkheim.[190] The narrower but related concept of the *shadow curriculum* focuses on values and beliefs both good and bad embedded in particular educational settings. For example, a student may note the contrast between the high sanitation standards promoted in medical school and the careless behavior of a hospital staff.[191]

This chapter contrasts the formal and shadow curricula, emphasizing how the latter has promoted the creed of greed. It also discusses concepts and theories from philosophy, social psychology, and sociology that explain how the creed of greed has developed and spread. The chapter after the next presents empirical evidence supporting the claims that selfishness is not the predominant trait of individuals engaged in economic exchanges.

Like a cartoon character receiving advice from an angel perched on one shoulder and a devil on the other, a business student relies on both formal and shadow curricula to prepare for a successful career. The formal curriculum provides vital knowledge, skills, and a sense of professionalism while the shadow curriculum offers the street smarts necessary to enter, gain acceptance, and thrive in a highly demanding work environment. The distinctive quality of a formal curriculum is its idealistic, formal, coherent, and explicated nature. Student immersion usually begins with matriculation and ends with graduation. The shadow curriculum is practical, diffuse, informal, disjointed, and often difficult to reconcile with the formal one. Its influence begins early in life as young boys and girls begin to learn about the business world chiefly from conversations overheard. The shadow curriculum's influence intensifies when students begin preparing actively for a professional career, and when they are immersed in a career once they take a job.

Pioneers of business education and subsequent thought leaders intended for graduates to acquire technical skills and assume the roles of public servants, just as students in law and medicine have for centuries.[192] Those entering the three professions, however, have to reconcile the idealistic worldview implicit in the formal curricula with the harsh realities of professional practice. Medical students may not appreciate fully the extent insurance companies, government, hospitals, employers, malpractice attorneys, and time pressures interfere with their patients' care and their own independence and professional judgment. Law students may be highly trained in research methods and legal reasoning, but not possess the knowledge and skills required for courtroom success. Business graduates with excellent technical skills may have difficulty navigating a firm where major outcomes are determined by the power and ambitions of their most senior leaders rather than by methods taught in textbooks.

The Formal Curricula

Business schools provide students with state-of-the-art technical skills and imbue them with a sense of public responsibility. The Gordon–Howell report proclaimed that American business leaders are responsible for more than increasing the nation's economic output. They also shape public opinion and maintain policies that "affect the welfare of the American people in a thousand directions, from local action to cope with juvenile delinquency to national policy in the precarious field of international relations".[193]

Carnegie's dean, Lee Bach, articulated his vision of a business curriculum for equipping managers as they rose to become presidents or general managers after careers spanning three decades. The Management

Science degree he created at Carnegie was intended to train students for positions as managers in the corporate chain of command rather than as staff specialists advising those managers. The organizations Bach and most everyone else had in mind were the major industrial giants that continued to dominate the US economy, such as AT&T, DuPont, GE, GM, IBM, Standard Oil, and US Steel.

Bach proposed that business schools across the country redesign their curricula to replace the discredited institutional approach with the new managerial approach. According to Bach, the first year of a 2-year program should be comprised of technical courses dealing with business organization and management, economic and quantitative analysis, and courses in production, marketing, and finance. The second year was to offer courses in corporate policy, business and society, and electives.[194]

Undertaking major curriculum revisions such as those Bach proposed for business schools across the country involved an arduous process. Typically, every curriculum is codified in a university catalog in which faculty members are listed, degree programs are identified along with their detailed requirements, courses are described briefly, and administrative policies and procedures are included. Although outside advice may be sought, revising a curriculum is a legislative process during which drafts of proposed catalog changes must be voted upon favorably by departmental and college faculties and then approved by the dean before going through an approval process at higher levels of university administration. Changes are ultimately incorporated into the published catalog that is essentially a contract between the university and students seeking degrees there. The Association to Advance Collegiate Schools of Business (AACSB) reviews business curricula periodically and awards accreditation to programs that are properly designed and executed.

Few people other than faculty and staff members and administrators ever see catalogs or know of their existence, but their imprint is everywhere — in the design of physical facilities; organization of the university into colleges, schools, and departments; number and training of faculty and staff members; syllabi required for every course offered; course schedules; and materials describing and promoting the university and its various programs.

It took decades for the managerial approach to replace the institutional approach in business education. Business schools had continued to revise their curricula by building in a greater international focus and incorporating the realities of the computer revolution, for example, yet the managerial approach remained largely unquestioned until after the dot. com and subprime bubbles and busts. The abrupt interruption of business as usual in business schools occurred because it became obvious that many corporate executives were deficient in leadership and ethical behavior, as well as devoid of any sense of duty except to themselves.

There has been much public criticism of business education by outsiders and even more soul searching from within. Srikant Datar, David Gavin, and Patrick Cullen, in their book *Rethinking the MBA: Business Education at a Crossroads*, describe changes that have taken place at some of the top MBA programs in response to this and other challenges.[195] The principal response at the University of Texas in the College of Business Administration was to create the Department of Business, Government, and Society — the first change in the number of departments since the college was first organized in 1947.[196]

Today a business school may require students to take an ethics course or offer trips where students give advice to businesses in exotic locations. However, professors specializing in business ethics account for 0.5%, and those teaching courses in business law or the legal environment of business account for 2.7% of the 30,144 business faculty members included in a recent AASCB report.[197] A more serious matter is that students may view these courses and activities as being off-message when ethical or legal considerations are not raised in their career-relevant courses, and a Darwinian view of the world where nice guys finish last is a prominent subtext.

The Shadow Curriculum

If the formal curriculum is found in descriptions of degree programs, course syllabi, reading assignments, and prepared lectures, then the shadow curriculum is an amalgam of knowledge, attitudes, and beliefs accumulated from diverse sources over a lifetime. Shadow curricula for various career options are vague and embryonic for adolescents but become more fully developed as students prepare themselves for adulthood. Information comes from: observation, conversations overheard and participated in, books read, movies and television programs seen, and, increasingly, the Internet.

Many high school students arrive on college campuses intending to major in premed until they encounter organic chemistry and get a hint of the vast range of other majors and career options available. Or students are interested in a business major because it purportedly offers the surest path to employment. They sample courses, attend public lectures, check out student organizations, and visit with career counselors and upperclassmen in search of the right fit.

College students, left to their own devices, are at risk of putting together an uninformed and unfortunate mix of ideas and values in their general education courses. In philosophy, they may learn from Nietzsche that sin does not exist by definition because there is no God to sin against and that they should make up their own rules. They may learn in anthropology that there are no universal standards for right and wrong because values vary from one society to another. They may discover in biology that their ancestors were sea slugs and, driven by their genes, they are destined to act like "Chicago gangsters".[198] In psychology, Freud informs them that they risk becoming neurotics if they deny their *id* (appetites).

Students will find little to justify ethical behavior in the classrooms of research-oriented universities.[199] When the political scientist John Mearsheimer addressed entering freshmen at the University of Chicago in the fall of 1997, he explained that the University of Chicago made little effort to provide them with moral guidance and that they would have few opportunities to discuss ethics or morality, primarily because courses for such purposes did not exist.[200] He declared that Chicago, like other elite universities around the country, was essentially an amoral institution except for its concern about academic dishonesty. There was special irony in his remarks as he and the mostly 18-year-olds were gathered in Rockefeller Chapel — named after the university's founder, John D. Rockefeller, who declared that religion should be the "central and dominant feature" of the university.

Could there be a greater authority in the shadow curriculum of business than "Ivan the Terrible" Boesky? He had published *Merger Mania: Arbitrage, Wall Street's Best Kept Money-Making Secret,* revealing how he had amassed a $200 million fortune.[201] The book's dust jacket indicates that he was serving as Adjunct Professor at Columbia and New York University's graduate schools of business when he wrote the book. It is perhaps ironic that I had to purchase a copy of it because the two copies listed in our library's catalog were missing.

Boesky proclaimed in a commencement address to Berkeley MBA students that the secret of his success was the realization that "greed is good".[202] Not long afterward he was sentenced to 3 years in prison for filing false stock trading reports and fined $100 million.[203] But that did not prevent his statement from gaining global attention and becoming a mantra of the creed of greed. The fictional character Gordon Gekko, modeled after Boesky, declared that "greed is good" at a stockholders' meeting in the popular movie *Wall Street*. Bankers and traders celebrating the creed offered Michael Douglas, the actor who portrayed Gekko, high-fives, and handshakes when he walked down the streets of Manhattan.[204]

Perhaps students may read Ayn Rand's *Atlas Shrugged* or *The Fountainhead,* as a former Federal Reserve chair did in his youth. The gospel according to Rand is that "each person's primary moral obligation is to achieve his own well-being and he should not sacrifice his well-being for the well-being of others".[205] A few students are repelled by the competitiveness of business school and the careers it promises and seek other majors. A few others are eager to accept that creed of greed and get into the game. Most students are unfazed by such messages but may have difficulty in articulating a sound argument to counter the creed of greed.

Students taking economics may have been exposed to Nobel Prize-winning economists like Friedman, Samuelson, Stigler, Becker, and Arrow — or to the former students of these great thinkers who are now in the classroom. The students discover with a mathematical certainty that greed is the social equivalent of gravity. As they begin to take business classes, students' attitudes and beliefs about realities of the business world are shaped by war stories and offhand remarks from their economics and business professors.

The contribution of neoclassical economics to the shadow curriculum has been pervasive and insidious. The political ideology of radical individualism and unregulated markets has been given legitimacy by those Nobel Prize-winning economists who have been leaders in what has been falsely claimed to be the value-free science of economics. While most information sources constituting the shadow curriculum remain external to the formal curriculum, this political ideology has operated at its very heart — in the core and tool courses essential to the career success of business students.

In addition to influencing student views concerning the proper role of government, neoclassical economics has validated the creed of greed so evident on Wall Street and in Corporate America during the first decade of the 21st century. Whatever the intentions of those who promulgated these views, this neoclassical economics has served as a Trojan Horse introducing and giving credibility to a political ideology undermining the high aims of those promoting business as a profession in which business-people play a profoundly important and positive role in determining our nation's welfare.

Students select the right major, usually finance, and take the right courses, typically corporate finance or investments, and begin actively to prepare for careers. They attend training sessions put on by their school's career services office, recruiting events, career fairs, lectures by visiting professionals, and join professionally oriented student organizations.

The most successful students go through recruiting season during their junior year and obtain an internship with a firm they might like to work for after graduation — a trial marriage of sorts. The process begins with an interview during which the intern candidate is expected to display: a professional appearance and engaging personality, detailed knowledge of the industry, firm, entry-level job, skills required, relevant technical vocabulary, and types of questions typically asked in the interview. There is often a follow-up dinner at a posh restaurant, where the finalists are assessed concerning how well they might interact with the firm's clients. Students who either did not get an internship or whose internship did not result in an acceptable job offer must go through the recruiting process for seniors.

The process is similar for MBA students, but is compressed into 2 years with the all-important internship occurring at the end of the first year. The typical MBA student is 5 or 6 years older than the BBA student, has professional work experience, and is positioned for a more demanding job with considerably higher salary after graduation. For MBA students who have not studied business or had a job with a business, immersion in the shadow curriculum must be particularly intense.

Learning from the shadow curriculum is vital to career success. I have known students with straight A's who were unsuccessful in finding a job because they did not have a clue what to do during recruiting season. However, there is a downside when malevolent portions of the shadow curriculum undermine the effect of the formal curriculum in promoting leadership, ethics, corporate social responsibility, and even legal behavior. This situation is especially problematic when students see a close association between the shadow curriculum and technical courses in management, marketing, finance, and other fields considered essential for career success.

The formal and shadow curricula are both vital but each is inadequate by itself. If students learn too little from the shadow curriculum, they may not be equipped to deal with practical realities of the workplace. If they accept too much from the shadow curriculum, they may acquire a cynical and self-serving view of business practices. Yet students hear conflicting messages:

- The customer is king. The ultimate criterion for evaluating every marketing decision is financial.
- Corporate social responsibility is vital. Corporate social responsibility is tantamount to socialism.
- Corporate executives have a fiduciary duty to their stockholders. Corporate executives who place the interests of stockholders and other stakeholders above their own are irrational.
- In business as in sport, there must be rules and referees to enforce them. Markets are self-regulating and cleanse themselves after excesses occur.
- Success is about what you know. Success is about who has your back.

Joseph Heath laments that business students are likely to be reading Sun-Tzu's *The Art of War* because it "is far too often seen as an alternative to the study of business ethics, one that offers more 'realistic' advice for dealing with the challenges that will arise in the corporate world".[206] Or the more Machiavellian students may find that business ethics also has its uses.

In *Giving Voice to Values: How to Speak Your Mind When You Know What's Right*, business ethicist Mary Gentile tells the story of how the formal curriculum may be subordinated to the shadow curriculum. A corporate CEO was interviewing an MBA graduate for a job. The MBA mentioned he had taken a business ethics course and the CEO asked what he had learned. The MBA responded that he had learned all of the models of ethical reasoning and that knowledge enabled him to resolve ethical conflicts by picking the model that supported his decision.[207]

*　　　*

I was getting my shoes shined in Manhattan midmorning, biding my time before meeting with a former student who worked for an investment bank. An impressive young Wall Street warrior took the seat beside me. He wore an expensive-looking dark suit, a starched white shirt, and an elegant silk tie. His black cap toe oxfords were hardly in need of the attention they were getting. His hair was drawn back and combed closely to his head like Gordon Gekko's or an English aristocrat's. What made him memorable and somewhat amusing is that the black pen in his suit pocket possessed the stylized white six-point star of the Montblanc brand. I suspected that if it had been a Bic, he would have placed it in his shirt pocket.

He was in his mid to late twenties and I speculated he had a BBA, MBA, or both. I also suspected he was waiting for the all-important interview. We did not speak or make eye contact, but if he had asked me how he looked, I would have said he looked great but that he should display his pen by taking notes during the interview. I have since wondered how his interview went and where he is today. I hope he has done well on Wall Street, as have so many of my wonderful former students.

His exposure to the shadow curriculum probably began when he decided to study economics or business. As he began to narrow his focus to finance and then investment banking, he likely began to acquire the appearance, vocabulary, and worldview of an investment banker. He had probably made it through the on-campus interviews and dinners where his social skills and table manners were scrutinized, and he had now traveled to New York for his final interviews. If things went well, he doubtless became an analyst in one of the top investment banks on Wall Street, where he could observe the real superstars — if not interact with them directly. I hope he did not go on to regret some of the decisions he would make, as some of our graduates did after they became energy traders for Enron.

The Epidemiology of Greed

The mathematical models of microeconomics are designed to be consistent with the notion that buyers and sellers maximize their resources. While buyers and sellers are typically organizations and often very large ones, they are labeled *economic man* or *Homo economicus* and acquire the human traits of rationality, greediness, and others referenced in Chap. 4. There is nothing wrong with that, as long as this fictitious creature is confined to economics journals and texts, but it should be a cause for alarm if it becomes the intellectual equivalent of "Typhoid Mary" spreading the pathogen of the creed of greed.

Several concepts and a theory from philosophy, social psychology, and sociology suggest the epidemiology metaphor is a reasonable one. The concepts of *reification*, the *naturalistic fallacy*, and the *self-serving bias* help explain how this opportunistic (infecting those with weak immune systems) pathogen is contracted. The disease's transmission is illuminated with the concepts of *socialization* and the *self-fulfilling prophecy*. And *diffusion of innovation* theory helps us see the dot.com and subprime bubbles and busts as being similar to the outbreak of diseases.

Reification, naturalistic fallacy, self-serving bias

Why does it matter what Adam Smith wrote so long ago or what a bunch of professors have written and said about him since then? Who cares about the typically unstated assumptions used for a mathematical model predicting the level of unemployment or the price of gasoline? The answer is that the assumption of *economic man* as rational, selfish, and amoral has flowed out of dusty old books and arcane academic journals, through textbooks and lectures, and into the minds of university students and business professionals. A look at three common errors in reasoning — *reification, naturalistic fallacy,* and *self-fulfilling prophecy* — helps us understand how *economic man*, found in textbooks and lectures, has influenced the thought and behavior of individuals.

Reification

Reification is the logical fallacy where an abstract concept such as free-market capitalism is treated as something concrete in the real world.[208] Although concepts do not exist in the real world, they do have real-world consequences when enough of us act as if they did. Evolutionary biologist Stephen J. Gould argues in *The Mismeasure of Man* that mental ability has been reified to produce IQ scores measured with a pencil-and-paper test.[209] (Would someone get extra points by folding the test into an origami figure resembling a cuckoo clock or a dragon?) Gould claims that although the original test was intended for simple diagnostic purposes, its apparent value has expanded to the point where some believe that human beings could be placed with precision and accuracy along its single numerical scale. What questions would appear on the test if Socrates, Goethe, Newton, Beethoven, and Helen Keller were all to score toward the top of the genius range? And what would be the repercussions if a society acted as if such a scale really existed?

In a book published by the Carnegie Foundation, the organization that brought us the Pierson Report, scholars Anne Colby, Thomas Ehrlich, William M. Sullivan, and Jonathan R. Dolle and colleagues charge that reification is encouraged in business schools and carried on in business practice because of overreliance on simplistic mathematical models. The problem is made worse when "individuals remain embedded in a single conceptual framework over an extended period of time (as the dominance of the efficient market model in business almost ensures) coming to treat the model as real even if they are aware on some level that it is not".[210]

These authors also state that when analytical thinking "is emphasized to the exclusion of other modes of thought, concepts and models may become all too real for students".[211] These students will likely have professors who are deeply immersed in the same mode of analytical thinking and who also engage in reification. I would add that this tendency is enhanced in disciplines where journal editors and reviewers for the top journals in those fields, who may be intolerant of alternative modes of thinking and analysis, are gatekeepers for those on the path to tenure.

Or consider an executive who forgets that the Excel model for the corporation's budget is not the corporation itself while preparing for a meeting of the board of directors. The firm competes with all of the highflyers listed on the New York Stock Exchange, as well as with the other mine operators selling the same commodity, and the executive's stock options comprise a large portion of his or her compensation package. Environmental Protection Agency (EPA) policies have been reducing coal demand and mine safety inspectors are forcing increased operating costs. Just days before the scheduled meeting, the numbers in the spreadsheet still don't work. The executive trims the number in cell AA254 just a bit and the all-important net income figure turns from red to black. No thought is given to the 31 grimy coalminers who are 290 miles away and a 1000 feet down and whose lives depend on having proper safety equipment.

Naturalistic fallacy

The *naturalistic fallacy*, or *is-ought fallacy*, describes the mistake of concluding something is good and proper because it exists naturally. David Hume, Adam Smith's best friend, employed the concept to challenge the common belief that the world and everything in it is good because it was designed by God.[212] Opponents of homosexuality arguing that it ought not be accepted because it is unnatural, as well as proponents claiming it is natural and should be accepted, make this mistake. The pertinent question is: What harm, if any, does either natural or unnatural behavior cause?

Psychologist Daniel Kahneman (Nobel Memorial Prize 2002) observes that economics students may come to believe that the business world is "like a boxing ring or a poker game ... in which many of the rules that govern other human interactions are suspended" and they learn to accept and even value what had previously been unacceptable behavior.[213] An undergraduate student told me she had found her brother cheating for the first time after he had transferred to the business school. His defense was: "When in business, do what businesspeople do".

Self-serving bias

Criminologists Neal Shover and Andy Hochstetler note that when white-collar criminals are "ensnared by the law" they "doggedly resist" defining their actions as criminal or seeing themselves as criminals. These individuals, often from privileged circumstances and currently in positions of trust and respect, are confident that "their conduct and the reasons for it can be grasped adequately only through sophisticated and arcane interpretation beyond the capability of lay persons and prosecutors".[214] It is ironic that such flawed reasoning conforms to what logicians call a *syllogism*.

A syllogism consists of a primary premise (assumption) such as "mammals are warm blooded", a secondary premise (assumption) such as "I am warm blooded", and an inference (conclusion) such as "therefore, I am a mammal". This form of argument is inviolable but only when its premises are true. White-collar criminals may unknowingly employ the syllogism in the following manner. "Good and generous people do not commit crimes [primary premise]. I am a good and generous person [secondary premise], and therefore what you accuse me of doing is not criminal [inference]".

Rational choice theory cannot account for the self-delusion of an "honest" embezzler because it is based on the false premise that crimes are always committed after rational individuals have determined that the benefits of the illegal act outweigh the costs. Such instances of irrational behavior have interested psychologists for many years and have increasingly attracted the attention of economists working in the field of behavioral economics. Psychologist Mahzarin Banaji, Management Professor Max H. Bazerman, and doctoral student Dolly Chugh discuss four processes that can enable individuals and groups to make unethical decisions in a *Harvard Business Review* article, and Legal Environment of Business

Professor Robert Prentice reviews 12 in a *Financial Analysts Journal* article.[215] Additionally, Max Bazerman and Ann Tenburnsel summarize research results in the emerging field of behavioral ethics in *Blind Spots: Why We Fail to Do What's Right and What to Do About It.*[216]

The misuse of the syllogism by white-collar criminals is explained by the concept of *self-serving bias* that proposes we selectively receive, process, and store information in order to maintain an idealized self-concept that may enable us to justify actions seen as wrong by others. The word *bias* is appropriate because it indicates that it is a pattern of thought that enables us to ignore the ethical dimensions of our decisions.

All but one of the students who were taking an exam directed their attention to the one whose textbook had fallen to floor. When we met in my office afterward she looked me in the eyes, told me with great sincerity that she had thought the exam was open-book, and I still believe she really believed it. However, she could not explain to me why other students were not using their books and why she had hers in her lap rather than on top of the desk where she could use it more easily.

While we may be aware that we use rationalization to justify courses of action we know down deep we should not take, the self-serving bias enables us to suppress those deep-down feelings. The self-serving bias serves a mechanism for denying its own existence, enabling individuals to withstand training in ethical decision-making. The process may involve linguistic tricks such as labeling cheating as an effort to gain an advantage over other students or deciding that the reimbursement request for travel expenses was consistent with the spirit of company policy, if not its letter.

The self-serving bias can go hand in hand with the naturalistic fallacy. It is the way we justify the unjustifiable by not thinking about it very much. Science writer Robert Wright observes "… that the human brain is, in large part, a machine for winning arguments, a machine for convincing others that its owner is in the right — and thus a machine for convincing its owner of the same thing".[217] A person may rationalize that "greedy and rational economic men are just the individuals needed to make the hard decisions that will advance economic growth" (and make one's self wealthy). Or "This is what I am compelled to do because everyone else does it". Or "My investors demand it".

Socialization and self-fulfilling prophecy

Socialization, and the *self-fulfilling prophecy* illustrate how the *Homo economicus* pathogen can flourish in a suitable social environment.

Socialization

I could almost hear William Jefferson's voice as I read the story he told to a reporter visiting him in prison. A student in my freshman business ethics seminar had written vividly in a historical fiction about Jefferson's mental journey from being a respected congressman to becoming a despised convict. At the end of each semester, students discuss whether the "rogues" they had written about were psychopaths who were finally caught, or ordinary men and women who had started with small mistakes but were destroyed by an avalanche of increasingly larger ones. Almost all of my students identified their rogues as being quite ordinary. How did basically decent people wind up in prison?

Our personal identities are shaped in large measure by our group membership. *Socialization* describes the process by which we acquire a group's worldview, attitudes, beliefs, and behaviors and is the concept most closely associated with the shadow curriculum. Conformity is a condition of membership and significant deviation from group norms may result in expulsion. Groups also support us when we are threatened — that's why prisoners join gangs.

In the *Lucifer Effect: Understanding How Good People Turn Evil*,[218] psychologist Philip Zimbardo observes that our society, and our criminal justice system especially, tends to treat offenders as bad apples when the problem is often a bad barrel. This observation suggests that virtually all of us possess characteristics of both Dr. Jekyll and Mr. Hyde, and that Mr. Hyde will likely be released if we find ourselves in a toxic social situation.

A more accurate subtitle for Zimbardo's book might be *Understanding Why Good People Do Evil Things* because the extraordinary conclusion of this extraordinary book is that evildoers in toxic situations are generally quite ordinary in nontoxic ones. He illustrates the point by describing a prison simulation he set up using college-aged male students who volunteered to participate for minimal compensation. The participants underwent psychological tests to ensure their sound mental health before being randomly assigned to the role of prisoner or guard. The young men assigned to the guard's role quickly became aggressive, abusive, and brutal, while those assigned to the prisoner's role became submissive and withdrawn in humiliating conditions. The behaviors of both groups became so extreme Zimbardo terminated the simulation prematurely. Soon after the participants were released, they abandoned their toxic behavior and returned to normal life. It is noteworthy that the incentives for participating were nominal and the same for prisoners and guards.

Zimbardo observes that toxic situations explain how cigarette manufacturers and their scientists developed and promoted highly addictive instruments of death and how companies like Enron defrauded the public.[219] He would not likely be surprised at the despicable behavior of the mostly college-aged males portrayed in *The Wolf of Wall Street* book and movie.[220]

*   *

The remarkable thing about Zimbardo's study is how clearly the participants identify their roles as guards and prisoners without first-hand experience or instruction and how quickly they embrace them without encouragement. Similar findings have been obtained from controlled experiments relevant to business. Marketing professor J. Scott Armstrong, for example, conducted a role playing experiment involving undergraduate and graduate management students as well as managers from 10 countries attending an executive education program.[221]

All of Armstrong's subjects were told they were participating in an exercise in which they were to assume the roles of members of the Upjohn Company's board of directors who were to decide the fate of a controversial but highly profitable antibiotic called Panalba. There were several competitive products that were equally effective and were priced about the same. However, the use of Panalba resulted in the death of between 14 and 22 users yearly according to the estimates of scientists, and the company was experiencing increasing pressure to remove it from the market.

Subjects were divided into groups representing the board and then assigned to one of three experimental conditions. Those in the first condition were informed that the board had declared several years previously that "society's needs would best be served if the board acted in such a way as to maximize returns to the stockholders". Those in the second condition were told that they were stockholders and that the board had declared previously that "the board's duty was to recognize the interests of each and every one of its 'interest groups' or "stakeholders", while some individual board members assigned to the third condition were told they represented employees, customers, suppliers, and the local community.

Seventy-six percent of the groups in the stockholder condition decided that Upjohn should continue promoting Panalba aggressively and use all means within its power to fight efforts to ban its sale (as did the real Upjohn board concerning the real Panalba). In contrast, only 22% of the groups in the two stakeholder conditions took the same position. Of course, none of the stockholder groups decided that the production of the drug should be stopped and remaining supplies destroyed, but 21% of the stakeholder groups made that decision. The majority of the stakeholder groups took an intermediate position such as the cessation of production but leaving the remaining supplies on the market.

In a second study conducted by social psychologists Varda Liberman, Steven Samuels, and Lee Ross, pairs of male undergraduates at Stanford University engaged in an exchange in the form of a prisoner's dilemma. The game was played for seven rounds and each participant would earn the maximum of $2.80 if they and their partner always cooperated, and they would earn nothing if they never cooperated. The students were assigned to two groups. The exercise for the first group was conspicuously labeled the Wall Street Game and the exercise for the second group was identified as the Community Game. Otherwise the groups were treated identically. A total of 31.5% of the students in the Wall Street condition cooperated as opposed to 66.1%, or twice as many, in the Community Game condition.[222]

Self-fulfilling prophecy

A number of researchers[223] have used the self-fulfilling prophecy to explain the relationship between the language of economics and opportunistic behavior. Sociologist Robert Merton coined the term *self-fulfilling prophecy*, stating it "is, in the beginning, a false definition of the situation evoking new behavior which makes the originally false conception come true".[224] He offers the story of the Last National Bank that was destroyed during the Great Depression despite its financial soundness as customers withdrew their savings because they feared it was unsound. Likewise, a group of young analysts joins an investment bank, acting on the false assumption that others will undermine their chances for success and consequently act ruthlessly. In these instances, the bank's depositors and the analysts harm themselves.

Merton also gives examples in which one group may draw false conclusions about another group and brings about the negative behavior it was trying to avoid. For example, two nations suspicious of one another and wishing to avoid a war find they must counter the other's "offensive" moves with their own "defensive" ones until ultimately war does occur.

A concept related to the self-fulfilling prophecy is *reactance*, a motive induced when a person's freedom is threatened or lost; its intensity increases with the importance of the freedom.[225] Reactance seems to be a special case of the self-fulfilling prophecy, although I have not read anything about their possible connection. In Merton's bank example, the customers' false beliefs caused an unfortunate change in their behavior. In a case of reactance, the false understanding of one group causes an unfortunate change in a second group, as the following example illustrates.[226]

When David Packer, cofounder of Hewlett-Packard, was a young General Electric employee, management started locking up tools and parts because they thought there was a theft problem.[227] In fact, employees had been borrowing things so they could work at home. The employees acted defiantly to the new policy by taking even more tools and parts home. Based on this experience, Packard established a policy of open storerooms at H-P.

Imagine, a candidate offered the position of CEO for a large corporation. During contract negotiations, she discovers that her compensation will be tied directly to the corporation's stock price and that she must provide stockholders with a quarterly report detailing the complete cost of her air travel, retreats, office furnishings, remodeling expenditures, additions to staff, and so forth. She wants the job badly but is insulted that she is being treated like an unworthy hired hand rather than a committed professional.

She smiles, remembering the true story told to me by a professor David Ford at the University of Bath in England. A corporation used special machinery to produce a unique component sold to manufacturers for use in their product. The company hired a new CEO with a moderate salary and the promise of a very generous bonus based on the firm's stock price. The CEO started selling the specialty machinery as well as the components to delighted customers. Profits, the stock price, and the CEO's bonus went through the roof, while his celebrity allowed him to move on to a better job before the manufacturer with nothing to sell closed its doors.

Diffusion of innovation

In 1962, communications professor Everett Rogers published a highly influential and readable book entitled *Diffusion of Innovations* in which the spread of diseases is a metaphor for the spread of ideas. Categories of adopters and the approximate percentage of the population they comprised are: Innovators (2.5%), Early Adopters (13.5%), Early Majority (34%), Late Majority (34%), and Laggards (16%). Innovations may be new ideas, practices, or physical objects.[228]

The example of personal computers illustrates this process. The one Innovator I knew was an MBA student who had assembled a PC from parts he had received by mail from an electronics supply house before they were available for sale in Austin. I was probably an Early Adopter because I purchased a first-generation IBM PC with 64K of RAM and one floppy disk drive in April 1983 for $3,109, or what would be $7,327 today. Often early adopters are opinion leaders who provide information and reassurance to members of the Early Majority who purchased their PCs when every respectable professional finally had to have one. Members of the Late Majority acquired PCs when the computers were so prevalent they could be purchased from Walmart or a department store. Laggards are still waiting for a really good deal.

Many examples of diffusion theory begin when an innovation, the PC in the previous example, arrives on the scene and is ready for adoption. A two-stage diffusion process may be more appropriate for an economic theory or method when it is first diffused within academia, and secondly when it is introduced into and diffused in business practice. The spread of agency theory can be used to illustrate this scenario. The first phase began when Jensen and Meckling published "Theory of the Firm: ..." in 1976. A search via Google Scholar reveals that the paper was cited in 167 publications between 1976 and 1980, and 16,300 between 2011 and 2015, with the number doubling during each successive 5-year interval. The second phase was two pronged. In the first phase, it began when the paper was assigned as reading for MBA students, as it was at Harvard, and agency theory was incorporated into textbooks.

Management professor Rakesh Khurana writes that through the efforts of Jensen, Fama, and other promoters of efficient markets:

> Agency theory quickly created a unified approach to organizations and corporate governance in American business schools, catalyzing academic revolutions in the study of corporate finance, organizational behavior, accounting, corporate governance, and the market for corporate control.[229]

In the second phase, the theory was disseminated to the business audience. For example, Jensen published "Eclipse of the Public Corporation" in *Harvard Business Review* in 1989.[230] It received the McKinsey Award as one of the top three articles appearing in the periodical during that year. Sociologists Frank Dobbin and Jiwook Jung argue that agency theory took on a life of its own when it was adopted and promoted by institutional fund managers, securities analysts, and corporate CEOs.[231] Then, finance-trained executives promoted agency theory within their firms.

The dissemination of an economic theory does not fit neatly within Roger's conventional framework because the diffusion cycle begins without mention of the innovation's creator. Rather it begins with the innovators and early adopters with some of the latter group being opinion leaders. In the case of economic theories, the creator may also be the principal opinion leader. George Stigler comments that the creator of new economic theories is "an evangelist seeking to convert his learned brethren to the new enlightenment he is preaching" and that repetition of his original message is "perhaps the most powerful of the arguments".[232] Jensen's role in promoting agency theory seems to conform to Stigler's description of creators who are most likely to be successful if they are also opinion leaders.

A measure of the rise of agency theory and its premise that the purpose of the firm is to maximize shareholder wealth can be seen in the written statements of the Business Roundtable,[233] an organization of CEOs that in 2012 represented corporations accounting for over $6 trillion in sales and employing more than 12 million individuals.[234] In 1990 the organization declared:

> 1990: **Corporations are chartered to serve both their shareholders and society as a whole** ... The trust of history and the law strongly supports the broader view of directors' responsibility to carefully weigh the interests of all stakeholders as part of their responsibility to the corporation or to the long-term interests of its shareholders.[235]

When agency theory reached the height of its popularity, the new statement proclaimed:

> 1997: In the Business Roundtable's view, **the paramount duty** of management and of boards of directors **is to the corporation's stockholders; the interests of other stakeholders** are relevant as a **derivative** of the duty to the stockholders. **The notion that the board must somehow balance the interests of other stakeholders fundamentally misconstrues the role of directors.**[236]

The 2012 statement issued after the subprime bubble and bust suggests a retreat to the views expressed in the 1990 statement:

> 2012: [It] is the responsibility of the corporation to engage with long-term shareholders in a meaningful way on issues and concerns that are of widespread interest to long-term shareholders, with appropriate

involvement from the board of directors and management ... **it is [also] the responsibility of the corporation to deal with its employees, customers, suppliers and other constituencies in a fair and equitable manner and to exemplify the highest standards of corporate citizenship.**[237]

The corporate excesses contributing to the dot.com and subprime bubbles and busts occurring between 1997 and 2012 indicates how profoundly it became apparent that wayward CEOs have not been reined in as intended. Rather, the CEOs of corporations that crashed and burned during the subprime bubble profited from the lessons of Jeff Skilling, Bernie Ebbers, and Dennis Kozlowski and avoided prison.

*   *

Formal and shadow curricula coexist symbiotically in business programs because each compensates for the shortcomings of the other. Both depict and shape the reality in which they operate, for better or for worse. Particular attention has been paid in this chapter to that portion of the shadow curriculum of business that promotes radical individualism. It is inimical to efforts associated with the formal curriculum designed to advance business management as a profession or even a respectable vocation. Several concepts and a theory have been offered to indicate how a creed of greed might be formulated and spread throughout business education. So far, the connection between the content of the shadow curriculum and management practices is theoretical and anecdotal. The following chapter examines research findings taken from a variety of settings and gathered with a variety of methods that lend credibility to the discussion so far.

Chapter 6

Is *Homo Economicus* Contagious?

Two conditions must be met for the metaphor of epidemiology to be useful in explaining the *Homo economicus* pathogen. First, it must not be a preexisting trait for the vast majority of human beings. Second, there must be some evidence that individuals exposed to the pathogen are more likely to possess the trait than those with little or no exposure.

Many studies are needed to examine these two conditions because there are no critical experiments in the social sciences. Archimedes is said to have shown the Spartan king that his crown was made of adulterated gold. Archimedes took a container of water filled to the brim. Into it, he placed a quantity of pure gold equal in weight to the crown. Water was displaced and spilled to the floor. He then placed the crown into the container and even more water spilled out. Archimedes explained that the additional spillage occurred because the volume of base metal was greater than that of gold relative to its weight.

Because such experiments cannot be conducted in the social sciences, a good understanding of the relationship between taking economics courses and the possession of attitudes favorable toward greed can only be achieved as a patchwork of modest studies is assembled and findings are confirmed and refined. The following sections are intended to provide samples of two such patchworks.

Are We Greedy and Indifferent to Others' Welfare?

The short answer appears to be "no". First, there is anecdotal evidence. It seems to be common sense that the success of a family, neighborhood, school, work environment, and even a nation is dependent upon the extent to which individuals populating them care for the welfare of others. This trait helps explain our nation's founding. We might be part of the British Commonwealth today if our founding fathers had not risked everything in their fight to protect their inalienable rights and those of fellow colonists. Fifty-six colonists committed treason against King George III when they signed the Declaration of Independence.[238] The closing words of this effectual death warrant were "we mutually pledge to each other our Lives, our Fortunes and our sacred Honor". George Washington agreed to become our republic's first leader, a choice not made by Napoléon Bonaparte, another revolutionary leader who became the emperor of France less than two decades later.

President Kennedy established the Peace Corps and challenged Americans to "ask not what your country can do for you, ask what you can do for your country". Almost 220,000 have served as volunteers since 1961 and 6818 are currently serving in 64 countries.[239]

Generosity is a national trait. A recent report on charitable giving ranks the United States as ninth out of 135 countries in the percentage of its citizenry who donated money (68%), and second in total giving.[240] The Business Roundtable, an organization representing major US corporations, reported in 2012 that charitable contributions of its members totaled more than $7 billion of almost $12 billion given by US corporations annually.[241]

There is also much empirical evidence supporting this common sense view. Of particular interest are experiments involving behavioral game theory where human subjects, rather than a mathematical model, are used to make decisions when they are presented with choices in the form of the Prisoner's Dilemma *à la* Bonnie and Clyde. For example, Drew Fudenberg, David G. Rand, and Anna Dreber conducted an experiment in which 384 subjects were assigned to pairs who played several rounds of a game.[242]

Each participant was paid $10 for participating in the 90 minute experiment and received between four and $26 in winnings.

The researchers assigned the pairs to four experimental conditions, differing in the size of the gains they could obtain from cooperation. Each player sat at a computer screen displaying the four outcomes of the game and was asked to choose between cooperative and selfish alternatives. The games consisted of a number of rounds and were terminated without warning.

When players found their fellow players did not cooperate, they employed various strategies to encourage them to do so in successive rounds. The researchers selected at random one in eight rounds for each player and altered their decision in order to introduce ambiguity into the feedback the players were giving each other and reducing their confidence in selecting a strategy. The players were told when they made these "errors", but their opponents were not informed of them.

The researchers found that 71% of all players cooperated on first round and on 50% of all successive rounds. In other words, the vast majority of participants began their play with an offer to cooperate and half played cooperatively throughout the rounds. The authors found, not surprisingly, that the level of cooperation increased when the incentives for doing so were large. They also found that players were slower to punish and quicker to forgive uncooperative behaviors than those in games reported for other studies where no "errors" were introduced by the researchers. In other words, when the motive for actions of the other player was uncertain, they were given the benefit of the doubt.

The "ultimatum game" has been used for decades to examine experimentally the sense of fair play.[243] Two books by economist Robert H. Frank provide nontechnical reviews of research employing this game that assigns subjects to the roles of Proposer and Responder.[244] The Proposer is given a sum of money, often $10, and asked to indicate how he or she would divide it with the Responder. The Responder can accept the offer and the money is then divided between them as proposed, or all the money is returned to the experimenter if the proposal is rejected. If Proposers conform to the model of economic man, then they should keep as much money as possible for themselves. If they assume Responders also conform to the economic man model, they should expect Responders to accept a small share of the money because something is better than nothing. Accordingly, one would expect offers of $1 out of $10 to be made and accepted typically.

This experimental method has been employed many times in many countries, and extreme outcomes, such as giving only a dollar, rarely occur. In one study, an offer of $5 was made and accepted in more than 80% of the cases. Responders rejected offers of $1 because they considered them to be unfair. Knowing this, the Proposer as economic man should have made offers of at least $3 or $4. However, more than 80% of them offered 5$, suggesting the Proposers were attempting to act fairly. After one such experiment, Responders were asked to indicate the minimum acceptable offer and the average response was $2.59. Our ability to recognize when we are being treated unfairly is also possessed by monkeys and apes, suggesting that it is "not just the result of social conditioning or our culture".[245]

Economists Ernst Fehr and Simon Gachter have offered "the economics of reciprocity" as an alternative to the "economics of selfishness" based on research employing the ultimatum game.[246] They found that in many places around the world (including Indonesia, Russia, the United States, Israel, and Europe), Responders punish Proposers who give them unfair offers. This phenomenon occurs even when significant amounts of money are involved. For example, in a study in Moscow, the games involved what amounted to an average of 10 weeks of salary.

Researchers have also employed the simpler "dictator game" where the Proposer starts off with $10 and is allowed to give the Responder any portion of the money and the Responder must accept the offer. This non-game becomes interesting when played multiple times, with the roles of Proposer and Responder reversing. Researchers have found that if a Responder received zero from Proposer A and $5 from Proposer B, then when it is the Responder's turn to act as Proposer, she or he will likely give nothing to A and $5 to B — Tit-For-Tat responses.

Analysis of the ultimatum and dictator game results reveals that play moves toward fair solutions over repeated trials if the players have historical knowledge of their competitors, either through experience or reputation. Further, individuals will punish those who have treated them unfairly, even if they will no longer be dealing with the uncooperative person in the future and have no expectation of benefiting personally from correcting the other's behavior.

In addition to experimental game theory and the dictator and ultimatum games, there are also games evaluating individual's contributions to *public goods* — products or services provided by the government because the private sector cannot provide them effectively. The personal dilemma of whether to contribute to a public good, or be a free rider who utilizes the good without helping pay for it, was illustrated in Chap. 4 where the residents of Aurora were trying to fund the construction of a new road with voluntary contributions.

In a typical study, groups of four undergraduate students are seated around a table and each is given $5. They are told they may invest none, some, or all of their money in a group project without the knowledge of the other group members' actions. The contributions are collected and totaled, and twice that amount is divided equally among all group members whether they contributed or not. If all four contributed $5, they each would get back $10. If three contribute five and one contributes nothing, then each contributor receives $7.50 and the free rider who does not contribute gets $7.50 to add to the five that he or she had withheld.

Sociologists Gerald Marwell and Ruth E. Ames stimulated controversy and considerable research in 1981 when they published the results of 12 studies "expressly designed to maximize the probability of individualized, self-interested behavior".[247] High school and college students participating in these studies allocated tokens they had been given between a personal investment (the money they keep) and a group investment (the public good). Students received returns of about $5 in 10 studies and $10 in the other two. The highest contribution rate to the public good among the experimental groups was 84%, the lowest was 20%, and the average was 47%. Thus, slightly over half of the student subjects conformed to economists' expectations that they would be free riders. A second noteworthy result is the fourfold difference in contributions among the experimental groups. Subsequent research has confirmed the original finding that economic man may be a good characterization of individuals who have participated in public goods studies, but the results are highly sensitive to the design of the individual studies.[248]

Robert Frank also offers evidence of a sense of economic fairness in non-experimental settings. For example, workers do not evaluate their pay on the basis of what they can buy with it but rather upon how well they are paid, that is how much they are appreciated, relative to their coworkers. Thus, the optimal distribution of pay within a group is to give the lowest-rated workers more compensation than they deserve on the grounds that it will keep them from leaving the firm. Their continued presence provides a more favorable frame of reference for highly rated workers receiving the greatest compensation. Thus, the distribution of pay in most private firms is more egalitarian than economic theory would indicate.

*   *

The most compelling and fascinating evidence concerning the cooperative nature of human beings comes from the fields of psychology, brain physiology, and evolutionary biology. Psychologist Martin Hoffman's *Empathy and Moral Development: Implications for Caring* discusses how socialization, human development, and biology enable humans to abide by society's rules without regard to external sanctions.[249]

There is evidence that this sense of fair play appears at a very early age. Consider the story related by psychologist Paul Bloom about the 1-year-old boy who saw a live show in which one puppet gave a ball to a second puppet who returned it.[250] When the first puppet gave the ball to a third puppet, it ran away with it. Piles of treats were then placed in front of the second and third puppets and the boy was asked to remove one of the piles. The boy took away the "bad" puppet's treats and hit it on the head for good measure.

In *The Ethical Brain: The Science of Our Moral Dilemmas* by Michael Gazzaniga discusses research linking ethical decision-making and brain physiology in an emergent field called bioethics.[251]

Frans de Waal argues that psychologists and bioethicists explain their findings in the context of evolution theory. If that is so, then it is reasonable to view the brains of lesser-developed animals as earlier versions of the hardware enabling us to prosper in large complex societies.[252] One of de Waal's many books is *The Age of Empathy: Nature's Lessons for a Kinder Society* that focuses on his extensive work with primates, particularly chimpanzees.[253] These animals show behaviors suggestive of their more advanced forms found among human beings: respect for possessions, reciprocity when there is a significant time lapse between giving and receiving, and expectations concerning how individuals should be treated as well as how resources should be divided.[254]

Hoffman, Gazzaniga, and de Waal, all mention the consistency between the research findings in their fields and Adam Smith's *Theory of Moral Sentiments* that will be outlined in Chap. 8.

*   *

Economists Samuel Bowles and Herbert Gintis offer a growing body of theory and empirical research indicating that *Homo reciprocans* is a better description of human beings than *Homo economicus*.[255] We pursue our own interests but with a sense of fair play, reciprocating with in-kind responses to friendly and unfriendly acts even when it is not to our advantage to do so. Evidence suggests that "altruistic punishment", punishing an individual for not cooperating, led to the evolutionary success of foraging bands of human beings approximately 100,000 years ago.[256]

In *Moral Minds: How Nature Designed Our Universal Sense of Right and Wrong*, Mark Hauser claims human beings alone are capable of engaging in large-scale cooperative systems consisting of unrelated individuals. These individuals establish stable relationships characterized by reciprocity.[257] Reciprocity requires several elements: a concern for ongoing relationships; mutual expectations among the parties; emotional responses to behaviors meeting or violating those expectations; and the ability to develop, follow, and enforce rules. The grandest example of these systems, according to Hauser, is international trade that has flourished for several thousands of years.

Does Taking Economics Make Us Like Economic Men?

The article by Marwell and Ames referenced several pages previously is entitled "Economists Free Ride, Does Anyone Else?" It was one of the early studies testing the assumption that economic man is a good representation of human beings. It also started a controversy about whether economics students are more likely to be greedy than other students.

The authors consulted five economists and one sociologist prominent in this area of research while designing their studies.[258] The experts agreed that the study design offered a good test of the hypothesis that human beings are uncooperative and thus few public goods would be supported by voluntary contributions. Four predicted that none of the study participants would contribute tokens to the public good, one predicted that less than 5% would do so, and the sixth predicted that 30% would — bringing the average estimate to around 6%. The authors summarize the experts' opinions saying that even those with somewhat higher predictions "envision behavior that is primarily free riding, with only small amounts of investment resulting from 'irrationality'".[259]

The subjects in the researchers' twelfth and final study were first semester graduate economics students at Wisconsin. Their contribution to the public good was 20%, the lowest reported in the paper and hence its title. The next lowest for all other groups was 28% and their average was 48%.

All subjects were asked whether they had been concerned about the fairness of their decisions. The proportion of economics students who expressed concern was about half of what it was for the other students and some indicated the concept of fairness seemed "somewhat alien" to them in this context. More than one-third either refused to comment about fairness or gave complex answers difficult to interpret. The researchers reported that only two of the thirty-two students could name the theory upon which the study was based and stated provocatively that: "As first-year students they had yet to reap the full benefits of the remarkable education assuredly to be theirs".[260]

Economist Daniel Kahneman (Nobel Memorial Prize, 2002), Jack L. Knetsch, and Richard H. Thaler (Nobel Memorial Prize, 2013) published experimental results comparing economics and psychology students using the ultimatum game in which Proposers offer a portion of $10 to Responders.[261] As before, if the Responder accepts the offer then the money is divided as proposed. If the Responder rejects the offer, then all of the money is returned to the experimenter. The money had to be allocated in 50-cent increments. The psychology students were assigned to two groups, where those in the first were told they would be playing with other psychology students and those in the second were told they would be playing with business students.

Of the psychology students, 81% offered an equal split to other psychology students, while 79% offered an equal split to business students and 63% of business students offered one to psychology students. The minimum acceptable offers averaged $2.59, $2.24, and $2.00 for the three groups, respectively. Thus, psychology students displayed a greater sense of fairness and demanded to be treated more fairly than economics students.

Robert Frank and fellow economists Thomas Gilovich and Dennis T. Regan mailed a questionnaire to six classifications of college professors asking them to report in dollars the amounts they had given to various charities.[262] The lowest proportion of "free riders" who did not give was among professional school respondents at 1.1%. The highest was among economists at 9.3%, with the proportions for the other four classifications ranging between 2.9% and 4.2%. The average size of the economists' donations was also among the least generous.

These researchers employed experimental game theory in a second study. They found the cooperation rate was 39.6% for economics majors compared to 61.2% for students with other majors. They also found that males were 24% more likely to free ride than females, regardless of major and that economics majors were 17% more likely to free ride than students with other majors. Thus, the highest rate of free riding was among male economics majors and the lowest among females of other majors.

Economists Anthony M. Yezer, Robert S. Goldfarb, and Paul J. Poppen criticized the research by Frank and his colleagues, countering that what students say and how they play games may not indicate how they behave.[263] To support this point, they employed a "lost-letter experiment" in which envelopes containing cash were placed in classrooms where classes in economics and other subjects were scheduled to meet. Ten $1 bills and a handwritten note were placed in a stamped envelope with an address but no return address. The note indicated that the money was to repay a loan. Letters were left in 32 classrooms before intermediate economics classes began and another 32 were placed in classrooms before classes in psychology, political science, history, or other disciplines began. Eighteen (56%) of the letters left in economics classrooms were returned, while 10 (31%) left in noneconomics rooms were returned. Frank and colleagues then countered with a critique of the lost-letter experiment and offered additional evidence supporting their claim.[264]

Business professor Donald McCabe and colleagues Kenneth Butterfield and Linda Trevino have conducted extensive research on cheating at the college level. The results of two studies are combined in Table 1.[265] The undergraduate statistics are drawn for a survey of 1946 students representing sixteen "highly selective institutions". The results for graduates were based on 5,331 survey responses from students at 32 US and Canadian universities. These percentages indicate that business students at both levels are more likely to cheat than their counterparts across campus.

In other research, McCabe and fellow researchers Janet M. Dukerich and Jane E. Dutton administered a survey to entering business and law students at two universities. Respondents were asked to assume the role of individuals described in five brief stories and to indicate whether they would avoid: (1) overbilling, (2) coercing a government official to make a favorable decision, (3) taking responsibility for improperly disposing of hazardous waste, (4) engaging in insider trading, and (5) studying a stolen copy of the CPA exam.[266] MBAs chose the ethical option 67% of the time across the five scenarios, while 78% of the law students did so. Differences between the groups were small for the first three scenarios, but 49% of the business students indicated they would not engage in insider trading, compared to 69% of law students. As well, only 46% indicated they would not use the stolen CPA exam, compared to 78% of law students who would not do so. Thus law students were 41% (0.69/0.49) more likely than business students to indicate they would not

Table 1: Percentage of students who admit to cheating.

	Business (%)	Other (%)
Undergraduate	84	66
Graduate	56	47

engage in insider trading and 70% (0.78/46) more likely to report they would not use the stolen exam.

Business professors Robert J. Williams, J. Douglas Barrett, and Mary Brabston used government records to determine the number of Occupational Safety and Health Administration (OSHA) and Environmental Protection Agency (EPA) citations that had been given to 184 *Fortune 500* companies.[267] Their analysis revealed that the number of citations was greater for the firms with a high percentage of MBAs among the senior executives.

Results drawn from a variety of studies employing differing methods, measures, and subject populations indicate, with the one exception I reported, that the attitudes and behaviors of those who have taken economics courses or business courses with economic content conform more closely to the concept of economic man than those who have not. There are three possible explanations for these results and each is likely to be partially true.

The first explanation is that taking these courses causes individuals to become more like economic man. In "Business education and erosion of character", business professor Juan Elegido uses the term *indoctrination* to describe the underlying process.[268] This term indicates a degree of intention and organization that does not seem to characterize most of the shadow curricula of business and economics. If anything, attempts to introduce ethics into the formal curricula, which I applaud, can better be described as indoctrination.

The second explanation is that students select majors that offer views compatible with their own, and that students resembling economic man are more likely to study business or economics than education or nursing. (A confounding factor is that more males have tended to study the first two subjects and more females have tended to study the second two.) The research seems to indicate that this self-selection process may be more important than socialization in explaining the difference between economics and business students and those studying other subjects.

It may also be the case that the third explanation is more important than either of the first two: Individuals with greedy or selfish tendencies are more susceptible to the undesirable and unintended influences of the shadow curricula of business or economics. In other words, individuals with greedy or selfish tendencies may be more likely to embrace and absorb a self-serving view of neoclassical economics than other students. (Experimental researchers refer to this phenomenon as an interaction.) By analogy, these individuals have weaker immune systems and are more susceptible to the *Homo economicus* pathogen. This view would suggest that the creed of greed is similar to a staph (*Staphylococcus aureus*) infection that is passed along invisibly to the most vulnerable hospital patients each year.[269]

The Importance of Culture

Chapter 5 and this one so far illustrate the importance of subcultures in determining the beliefs, attitudes, and behaviors of their members. A very ingenious natural experiment sheds light on how the same point may be made about larger cultures. Researchers examined the number of parking tickets received by United Nations diplomats in New York City.[270] Parking violations meet Transparency International's definition of *corruption*, "the abuse of entrusted power for private gain".[271] They examined the behavior of diplomats who represented countries with varying degrees of corruption but who were exposed to the same opportunity to engage in corrupt behavior — getting a parking ticket and not paying for it.

Diplomatic immunity during the time of the study meant that parking tickets placed on automobiles with the letter *D* on their plates did not have to be paid. Diplomats from 146 countries received over 150,000 tickets for fines averaging more than a 1000 per country and totaling more than $18 million (averaging over $123,000) between November 1997 and the end of 2002.

The researchers found a high positive correlation between the number of violations by particular diplomats and the corruption score assigned by Transparency International to the country they represented. The 10 countries whose representatives had the greatest number of violations (along with their nations' per capita incomes) were: Kuwait ($18,620), Egypt ($1286), Chad ($222), Sudan ($407), Bulgaria ($2077), Mozambique ($218), Albania ($780), Angola ($840), Senegal ($513), and Pakistan ($483). Diplomats from Scandinavian countries and Japan had no violations and low corruption scores.[272] Those representing countries with very small diplomatic missions, such as Burkina Paso, also had no violations. Some countries, such as Bahrain ($13,149), had many violations but paid their fines.

If we assume the Kuwaiti case, is the upper limit with 246.2 violations per diplomat, then none of the other countries comes close to abusing the privilege as consistently. Egypt, second in the rankings, had 139.2 violations, and Pakistan, ranking 10th, had only 69.4. The median number of tickets was 7.7 for all 146 countries, and 30 countries had less than one ticket per diplomat on average.

Why was there such variation? A partial answer is that corruption even among the privileged members of a country is negatively correlated with a nation's wealth. This finding may suggest a vicious cycle between impoverishment and corruption. Another interesting question concerns why representatives of two of the wealthiest countries in the top 10 (Kuwait and Egypt) have the most tickets? The most intriguing question of all is why Kuwait was at the top of the list of 146 countries and Bahrain was at the bottom, when both are Arabic-speaking, oil-producing monarchies located on the Persian Gulf?

Thinking back, I may have glimpsed the answer to these questions when I took a bus during a visit to London in the early '70s. I found a stop where the bus I wanted and several others were listed on the same sign. I was puzzled because several dozen individuals formed a single line when there should have been a separate one for each bus. My bus was the first to arrive and perhaps a dozen individuals who had been interspersed along the line stepped out of it without comment, formed a new one, and entered to take a seat. I realized I had seen why a small island nation had, for better or for worse, been able to build and maintain an earth-spanning empire.

The lesson was increasingly clear when I tried to register for classes at the American University of Beirut in the mid '60s. There was no line for me to join because everyone else seemed to be trying to register first. The connection between forming lines and ruling an empire may not be immediately obvious but I believe, it is a strong one.

Consider the concept of *civic virtues*, which are the "personal qualities associated with the effective functioning of the civil and political order, or the preservation of its values and principles".[273] Examples of civic virtues include being punctual, meeting commitments, obeying laws, paying taxes, serving in the military, voting, supporting nonprofit organizations, and helping strangers.

Think also about the civil, civilized, or *civic society*, which is "that aspect of society concerned with and operating for the collective good, independent of state control or commercial influence; all social groups, networks, etc., above the level of the family, which engage in voluntary collective action".[274] It is comprised of formal organizations in the non-profit sector, such as hospitals, universities, religious institutions, and charities, as well as informal ones organized around neighborhoods and communities. Government, business, and civic society represent the three forms of social organization. The richness of a civic society flourishes when the proportion of individuals embracing civic virtues is high and prosperity and happiness are widespread.

*   *

Research presented in this chapter indicates that *Homo reciprocans* (reciprocal man) provides a better description of human beings engaging in economic activities than *Homo economicus* (economic man). Additionally, it appears that some of the college students studying business and economics resemble economic man more closely than those studying other subjects. These students are more likely to rationalize the belief that greed is good and find it supported by the shadow curriculum of business schools. The same processes of self-selection and socialization operate after students graduate and join a firm where wanton disregard for the welfare of others may be encouraged and rewarded.

Chapter 7

What if the Twin Pillars Prevailed?

The twin pillars of free-market capitalism, economic man and perfect competition, are foundational for the neoclassical economic theories and methods that have transformed business education and practice. These theories and methods were developed originally to predict economic outcomes useful for legislators and public policymakers, but their scope has been expanded to include problems relevant to business executives. Unfortunately, application of transaction cost theory, agency theory, and the related theories and methods discussed in Chap. 4 have contributed to outcomes that were the opposite of their creators' good intentions.[275] Rather than strengthening business operations, they undermined them greatly and sparked the dot.com and subprime conflagrations. I have found no evidence that reputation theory contributed directly to these disasters. However, reputation theory employs game theory and typical neoclassical assumptions, and is thus useful in helping to explain why institutions that were supposed to maintain the integrity of financial markets failed to do so.[276]

Blame the Disease, Not the Patient

I am virtually certain a friend of mine, who is very critical of publically held corporations, owns stocks or shares in stock funds. He most certainly knows, or at least takes for granted, that he could lose his money if a corporation he has invested in goes out of business but he will never be responsible for its unpaid debts. This investor protection enables corporations to raise vast sums of money allowing them to operate with greater efficiency. Corporations, unlike family businesses, are also able to maintain a succession of competent Chief Executive Officers (CEOs); for example, Walmart has done quite well since Sam Walton's departure.

Corporate investors own shares of the firm's residual cash flows (the money left over after all its debts are paid) that are traded on stock exchanges. In theory, corporations have charters that are similar to national constitutions. They are organized as representative democracies where individual shareholders have a vote for each share they own. Shareholders elect representatives who constitute a board responsible for overseeing the firm. This board of directors determines the firm's mission, approves budgets and strategic decisions, and directs the managers who are expected to act as faithful and competent agents (or else) for the principals — the stockholders.

A board subcommittee is usually responsible for hiring and supervising the public accounting firm conducting the corporation's audits, filing its taxes, and signing off on annual reports. A second subcommittee evaluates corporate success and determines the appropriate methods and levels of compensation for the top executives. If board members become unhappy with these executives, they can reduce their pay or fire them. If the stockholders become unhappy with individual board members, they can be voted out of office. In addition, state and federal regulations are designed to protect the property rights of stockholders, at least in theory.

Although corporations have contributed significantly to global prosperity (and to my friend's), it is apparent that reality has been far from the ideal. Agency theory was formulated and applied when the deficiencies of US corporations were particularly apparent. Specific recommendations were made with the intention of increasing stockholders' control of corporate CEOs. Stockholders, through their boards, were to link CEO compensation to the stock price and to monitor their CEOs' behavior to ensure corporate resources were not squandered.

These recommendations still make a lot of sense and the efforts of business and economics professors to see that they became reality should be applauded. Unfortunately, the assumptions underlying agency theory and the reality of corporate operations collided with catastrophic results.

One significant assumption is that both shareholders and CEOs are economic men focusing on maximizing their shares of the same pot of money. A second is that stockholders are able to determine the CEOs' compensation and supervise their behavior. In reality, CEOs often run the boards, frequently serving as their chairs. Thus, many CEOs pay and supervise themselves and can undermine corporate reform efforts that are not in their interests.

Economic Man as Shareholders' Agent

> The grand sailing vessel breaks the wave with its huge hull. This ship carries a crew of fearless adventurers, ready to conquer new territory on their mission to map uncharted waters... During their journey, the watch keeps his trained eyes focused on the ocean, looking for sharp rock that could sink the boat... This crew actually works at Enron, but the 50-story Houston office towers and field offices around the world are equally full of adventure. The captain of Enron is CEO Ken Lay, and the accountants are the watch who help guide the company.
>
> *Today's CPA*, Texas Society of CPAs,
> November–December 2001[277]

> We spoke recently with the top management including the CEO, CFO, chief accounting officer, and the head of wholesale services... We view Enron as one of the best companies in the economy, let alone among the companies in our energy convergence space. We are confident in the company's ability to grow earnings more than 20% annually for the next 5 years, despite its already large base.
>
> Goldman Sachs, Buy Recommendation,
> October 8, 2001[278]

On December 2, 2001, just weeks after the appearance of the publications just quoted, what had been the seventh largest company in the United States declared what was at that time its largest bankruptcy. Its market capitalization (the price of a single share of stock multiplied by the number of shares held by investors) of $65.5 billion vanished almost entirely. Enron, declared "America's most innovative company" for six successive years by *Fortune* magazine was an illusion, a hoax that came to represent the widespread corporate excess and fraud rampant during the dot.com bubble and bust of the early 2000s.

In response to Enron and the other abusers of American capitalism, the Sarbanes-Oxley Act was passed to "… set up a system of checks and balances in terms of corporate governance, auditing supervision, and responsible accounting which to the maximum extent will help to avoid similar occurrences in the future", according to Senator Paul Sarbanes. The ceremonial end of the era occurred when Enron's Ken Lay and Jeff Skilling were found guilty of fraud in May of 2006. Michael Oxley, US representative, declared:

> "Justice has been served today…. The entire debacle reminds [us] of the need for the Sarbanes-Oxley Act to help reinforce the duties of company directors and officers…. I remember those who have suffered great economic loss. Today's news should encourage them as they continue to rebuild their financial security".[279]

If Sarbanes-Oxley forced a housecleaning in corporate America, how could we have found ourselves in an even worse mess just a few years later? The answer: structural problems apparent in American capitalism were not dealt with adequately. In *The Battle for the Soul of Capitalism* (2005), John Bogle, founder and former CEO of the Vanguard Mutual Fund group, describes a "pathological mutation" of capitalism revealed by the dot.com bubble and bust.[280] This mutation continues today despite the good intentions and high hopes of Sarbanes and Oxley and subsequent legislation.

Bogle provides an analysis of the dot.com bubble and bust and the conditions leading to it. He claims that during this period, massive wealth was transferred from "public investors to corporate insiders, entrepreneurs, and financial intermediaries". The amounts he estimates are shocking: executive stock options exercised: $200 billion; profits for dot.com entrepreneurs with initial public offerings: $800 billion; fees for investment bankers and brokerage firms: $1 trillion; and payments to mutual fund managers: $275 billion.[281] These amounts total $2.275 trillion, or 4.86 times the size of the federal deficit for 2014 which is estimated to be

$468 billion.[282] Investors who entered the stock market before 1997 and held their positions survived, but those entering the market just in time to cash in on the New Economy were the primary source of these massive transfers of wealth.

Booms and busts are nothing new to capitalistic economies, but according to Bogle, the dot.com bubble and bust was different because it represented mutation from "investors' capitalism" to "managers' capitalism". In investors' capitalism, the investors possessed the capital and took risks by buying stock in firms promising marketplace success and the profits going with it. In investors' capitalism, the corporation should be organized and run approximately in the manner described in the previous section.

In managers' capitalism, investors own the capital and take the risks, but the likelihood that the firms experience marketplace success, as well as the likelihood that investors fully enjoy the profits of success, are greatly reduced. Instead, the corporation becomes a vehicle for enriching the managers at the expense of its owners, even when the firm is a marketplace failure and the owners lose capital. In managers' capitalism, it is the managers who run the board of directors and select its outside members for their own purposes.

Consider the post-Sarbanes-Oxley example of board members of the Stanford Financial Group who were responsible ostensibly for looking after investors' interests. One was James Stanford, the 81-year-old resident of Mexia, Texas, and father of the group's founder, R. Allen Stanford.[283] Another was O. Y. Goswick, an 85-year old with a 40-acre ranch outside Mexia. Goswick had a stroke in 2001 and had been unable to communicate with anyone until his death in 2009.[284] R. Allen Stanford was convicted in 2012 and sentenced to 110 years in prison for defrauding his investors of $7 billion despite the close scrutiny of his father and Mr. Goswick.[285]

In Bogle's words the bubble and bust represented "... a mutation from [a] virtuous to vicious cycle — a failure of character, a triumph of hubris, and greed over honesty and integrity in corporate America. It is facile to ascribe the wrongdoing of the era to just a few bad apples, and it's true that only a tiny minority of our business and financial leaders have been implicated in criminal behavior. But, I believe that the barrel itself — the very structure that holds all those apples — is bad".[286]

In *Pay without Performance: The Unfulfilled Promise of Executive Compensation* (2004), law professors Lucian Bebchuk and Jesse Fried report extensive empirical research documenting their claim that board members do not operate "at arms length" with corporate managers on behalf of the stockholders they are expected to represent. Rather, they serve their own interests and those of fellow managers. Corporate law does not allow stockholders to propose or vote on rules related to managers' compensation that are binding on the board.[287]

In summarizing a report on corporate bonuses on Wall Street, Anthony Cuomo, attorney general of the State of New York, wrote: "… when the banks did well, their employees were paid well. When the banks did poorly, their employees were paid well. And when the banks did very poorly, they were bailed out by the taxpayers and their employees were still paid well". Cuomo's analysis reveals that the level of bonuses paid during the bull market of 2003–2006 continued during the subprime crisis; there were numerous instances when individuals in money-losing divisions received large bonuses. Citigroup and Merrill Lynch lost a combined $54 billion in 2008, paid out $9 billion in bonuses, and received $55 billion in federal bailout money. Goldman Sachs, Morgan Stanley, and J. P. Morgan Chase together earned $9.6 billion in 2008, paid bonuses of just under $18 billion, and received a $45 billion bailout.[288]

Bebchuk and Fried observe that once a corporate governance structure favorable to managers is in place, it is very difficult to change. The authors note that stockholders could reduce the board's ability to ignore its own individual interests by removing the board's power to veto proposed changes in the way it conducts business. Unfortunately, board conduct is specified by the rules of the state in which the company is incorporated or in the corporate charter. Thus, "Under long-standing corporate law, only the board — not a group of shareholders, however large — can initiate and bring to a shareholder vote a proposal to change the state of incorporation or to amend the corporate charter".[289]

The big lesson for managers from the dot.com bubble and bust was that managers can legally obtain from their compliant boards what they once obtained foolishly by illegal means. In the $1.2 million remodeling of his office at Merrill Lynch, John Thain added a $35,000 commode on legs. In contrast, Dennis Kozlowski went to jail in part because he used Tyco money to purchase a $17,100 traveling toilet box for his apartment.[290]

Economic Man as Team Player

Until the middle of the 19th century, the typical business in the United States was small, limited in scope and market size, and run by owner-managers. This form of organization was for the most part replaced by World War I with what business historian Alfred Chandler called the *modern business enterprise* in *The Visible Hand: The Managerial Revolution in American Business* published in 1977.[291] This modern organization is essentially an amalgam of the earlier business form, but the owner-manager has become a salaried mid-level manager. These small business units comprising the modern organization would previously have competed against each other (two small shoe manufacturers) or have engaged each other as buyer or seller (a shoe manufacturer and a supplier of laces).

The visible hand of cooperation in a larger, more efficient organization replaced the invisible hand of market-based relations among small rivals. Why did this profound change in business organization take place? A summary of Chandler's analysis may be reduced to the simple statement that it happened because the effectiveness and efficiency of the new organizations were vastly superior to those of the old ones. Ronald Coase described the gains as being the result of reduced transaction costs among parties.[292]

So, why would middle managers within a large organization agree to cooperate when traditional economic theory predicted they would compete? Chandler's answer is that these managers could expect lifelong opportunities for promotions and pay raises. He described the bygone era when career managers "preferred policies that favored long-term stability and growth of their enterprises to those that maximized current profits ...." And, if "profits were high, they preferred to reinvest them in the enterprise rather than pay them out in dividends".[293]

How much has changed in four decades! Any unwritten social contract has been destroyed as layers of mid-level managers were shed because of the information revolution, and tacit guarantees of lifetime employment are no longer imaginable. The traditional concordance between managers and corporate interests has been largely obliterated. Managers have become focused on short-term personal gains, and increasingly, corporate compensation committees have tried, with mixed results, to link pay and performance.

In Good Company: How Social Capital Makes Organizations, published 24 years after Chandler's *The Visible Hand*, Don Cohen and Laurence Prusak criticize the mechanistic conception of business organizations that consist of free agents whose only common bond is the shared source of their paychecks.[294] As an alternative to the socially sterile view of business organizations in which everyone is a free agent out for personal financial gain, Cohen and Prusak promote the conception of organizations as potentially rich social networks.

Cohen and Prusak claim that the most effective modern organizations possess high levels of social capital, and that trustworthiness exists among managers. *Social capital* refers to a set of informal commitments or norms — which include joining in mutually beneficial reciprocal relationships, telling the truth, and meeting obligations faithfully — that binds groups together. Social capital enables members to trust one another, resulting in groups that operate more effectively and efficiently.[295] *Social capital* is a term from economics that likens it to the physical capital of firms and is comparable to *civic virtues* among an organization's employees. Cohen and Prusak make a strong case for the ability of senior executives to both create and destroy social capital. This situation is a far cry from the conception of the corporation as a nexus of contracts in which no social capital exists or is needed.

Jeff Skilling: Economic Samurai

In my use of the term *economic samurai* above, I apologize to the memory of actual samurai, who, like medieval knights of the West, had strict ethical codes. Choosing the executive who best exemplifies corporate free agency is a difficult task because there are so many strong contenders. Bernie Madoff, of Bernard L. Madoff Investment Securities, LLC, perpetuated the second largest fraud in US history, totaling $35 billion according to the *Forbes* website.[296] There were no principal–agent problems between executives and absentee stockholders because he was the sole owner.[297] Alternatively, the God-fearing leaders of Enron and WorldCom, Ken Lay and Bernie Ebbers, respectively, are good candidates for the dot.com era, and Richard Fuld, the Lehman CEO nicknamed "The Gorilla of Wall Street", seems an obvious candidate for the subprime era. However, I have chosen Jeff Skilling, Ken Lay's successor as Enron CEO, principally because so much has been written about him. He is currently serving a 24-year sentence in federal prison, but he was a real *kung fu kapitalist*.[298]

Skilling's classmates and the other neighborhood kids probably found it incredible that the quiet, physically unimposing boy they had grown up with was THE Jeff Skilling, rock star of the New Economy who appeared on television and magazine covers. He was one of four children in a family barely making it amid the ruins of central Pennsylvania steel mills. Skilling's family members might have been able to look back and see the budding qualities of his greatness, but these were not obvious early on.

Skilling had always worked hard to earn the money he needed. When his family moved to a working-class town outside Chicago, he worked as a janitor and handyman for a start-up television station. He learned to operate every piece of broadcast equipment and became production manager when the position opened. The first hint of his brilliance surfaced when he graduated 16th in his high school class of 600 students even though school was of little interest to him.

In addition to his willingness to work, Skilling displayed a high tolerance for risk and perhaps even an appetite for it.[299] He took his television station wages and borrowed money to invest first in stocks and then in bonds, going broke each time. His interest in investing was not deterred, even though his total losses during high school were almost equal to his first-year salary at the Houston bank where he worked upon graduation from college.

Skilling entered Southern Methodist University in Dallas as a freshman on an engineering scholarship. But again he showed little interest in school. That remained true until he began taking business classes to aid his investing and discovered his professional calling. It is likely he began formulating his Darwinian economic views during this period.

After working for a few years, Skilling applied to a single MBA program — Harvard's — despite his unexceptional grades from SMU. When asked if he was smart during an admissions interview, he responded that he was "f---ing smart". He proved he was f---ing smart by graduating as a Baker Scholar, one of the top 10% of his class. Unlike his time at SMU, Skilling came into his own at Harvard, demonstrating his brilliance, arrogance, and extreme economic views.

He believed the market was the ultimate judge of right and wrong, and that any government attempt at intervention was counterproductive. Although Skilling was later to deny the story, one classmate recounted his response to a question about what a CEO should do if the CEO thought a product might be harmful. Skilling said it was the CEO's duty to maximize shareholder value and it was the government's duty to do something if the product turned out to have problems. It was said his favorite book was *The Selfish Gene* by Richard Dawkins. The author was "mortified" to learn of Skilling's misguided views from a *Guardian* article.[300]

Skilling took a job with McKinsey & Company in Houston, where he worked on the Enron account. His high tolerance for risk and his brilliance brought about another life-changing event. He pitched his revolutionary idea for an "energy bank" to the top 25 Enron executives using a single slide rather than the customarily large set. It worked. Before long, Skilling left McKinsey to run Enron's energy bank, later becoming chair and CEO.

As Skilling rose quickly through the ranks, it was clear he had found a suitable home, and he was able to impress his personality and creed of greed upon an increasingly large number of individuals in the organization. His management philosophy was Darwinian, hiring the best people he could find and putting them in situations where they were forced to compete. He created groups in which the individuals did not get along, thinking it would increase their performance. Skilling told Enron's head of governmental affairs that loyalty was a commodity to be bought and sold: "I've thought about this a lot, and all that matters is money. You buy loyalty with money. This touchy-feely stuff isn't as important as cash. That's what drives performance".[301] This comment suggests that Skilling viewed Enron as a nexus of contracts, but a brutal one. Its winners were rewarded with vast sums of money and those found in the bottom 10% of employee reviews were shown the door.

Skilling transformed himself from a medium-sized, overweight, and balding man by losing 60 pounds, lifting weights, and using a hair restorative. He and a select group of Enron executives and customers went on daredevil expeditions. A photograph showing them on motorcycles wearing the appropriate headgear and body armor suggests a group of battle-ready samurai warriors.

Skilling was a brilliant visionary, but he had little interest in or ability to run a business. Individuals were rewarded handsomely for dreaming up grand projects projected to generate vast revenues. Using a forecasting trick that accountants refer to as *mark-to-market*, the anticipated revenues were reported as actual income even though the forecasts might never be realized. The massive debt incurred because of these ventures was hidden in *off balance sheet entities*. The price of Enron stock, along with bonuses for Skilling and his coconspirators, rose to astonishing heights until it hesitated like a rollercoaster at its apex and dropped like a dead weight.

Deregulation of energy markets was critical to Enron's success and Skilling held in contempt those who were slow to see the world as he did. He asked an Enron lobbyist how he could stand working with the idiots on Capitol Hill. Skilling told Texas Republican Joe Barton, chair of the House Energy and Power Subcommittee, that "You need to change your opinion" when complaining about the rate at which deregulation was taking place. Barton responded indignantly: "'I may not have as many millions as you do, but I am not an idiot'". Eventually Enron achieved some success in its efforts and the California electricity market was partially deregulated. Rather than taking advantage of the opportunity by reducing the cost of electricity, as Skilling had promised in a congressional hearing, Enron traders exploited every opportunity to increase their profits.

One former Enron executive stated that if California put in such a stupid system, it made sense to try to game it.[302] The energy traders studied the new California regulations and found flaws they could exploit to the firm's advantage. They could cause congestion and inflate the rates by transmitting electricity over low capacity rather than high-capacity lines. The traders could restrict supply by persuading power generation plants to shut down unnecessarily. And they could divert electricity out of state to create a shortage, and then bring it back to be sold at a higher price. They named such ploys Death Star, Get Shorty, and Ricochet.

The traders acted as self-appointed disciples of free-market capitalism who considered it their duty to punish Californians for their misguided ways. Recordings of their conversations reveal little concern for the impact high electricity prices had on Californians or for the outcome of California's test of the waters of deregulation:

"Yea, Grandma Millie, man".

"She's the one who couldn't figure out how to f...ing vote on the butterfly ballot".

"Now she wants her f...ing money back for all the power you've charged up her ass".

"It's kinda hard to say we shouldn't do this even though it's allowed because you know. I mean, that's what we do".

"The best thing could happen is a f...ing earthquake. Let that thing float out into the Pacific".

"Let 'em use f...ing candles".

Although the old ladies were indeed forced to use candles, Enron had made $1.33 billion in profits in 2000 from the California experiment and the top 200 Enron employees took home pay packages totaling $1.4 billion (an average of $7 million). At a conference in June 2001, Skilling joked: "You know what the difference is between the state of California and the Titanic?" His grinning answer: "At least the lights were on when the Titanic went down".

In a Hobbesian world of its own creation, a perpetual state of war existed among operations and individuals within Enron and between Enron and its customers and competitors. The only abiding truth was that Enron's stock prices and executive compensation had to keep going up. As CEO, Skilling perpetuated the illusion of Enron as a fount of exciting business deals, in reality many of them would never generate revenue and the phony accounting practices exaggerated revenues and hid debt. Less than 2 years after his Titanic joke, Enron sank out of sight with the lights on and Skilling went to prison shortly thereafter.

In 2006 Skilling began serving a sentence of more than 24 years, but he made a series of appeals including one before the Supreme Court. In June 2013 Skilling, the Justice Department, and prosecutors reached an agreement requiring him to turn over $41.8 million to victims of the Enron collapse and end his appeals in exchange for a reduced sentence of 14 years. At the hearing, a former Enron employee spoke of their betrayal by Skilling, but he refused his opportunity to respond. Employees and investors were, and probably remain, especially angry because he has never admitted guilt or expressed remorse.[303]

Pogo Economics and the Great Recession

Who were the culprits who brought about the subprime bubble and bust? Pogo, Walt Kelly's famous comic book character, has the answer: "We have met the enemy and he is us".[304]

First, the amateurs: Millions of us had been living extravagantly, taking out additional credit cards because the credit limit on our first card forced us to live within our means. The average household had 11 credit cards in 2008 and owed $11,211 in credit card debt, tripling the 1990 level of $3431.[305] Millions of us purchased houses that were more expensive than we could afford. Some were naïve first-time homeowners, but others were novice speculators who bought and fixed up houses they could never afford to keep. For a time, prices kept going up and houses could be flipped with a return on investment as high as 500%.

Second, the professionals: Some were real estate brokers who convinced the naïve to buy houses that were bigger and more expensive than they needed or could afford. Others were mortgage brokers who found willing lenders for such homebuyers. Still others were bankers and different lenders who made "desk approvals" or "liar's loans" earning their commissions and fees and then passing on the risks to firms demanding more and more mortgages. The real estate and mortgage brokers and the lenders all operated under the proverb: The bigger the loan sold, the bigger the commission will be. Once these mortgages were bundled and commoditized, those on Wall Street with MBAs and PhDs created and sold ingenious financial instruments appearing to turn mortgage lead into security gold, making millions in the process.

The alchemist's lead in this case was the "subprime" mortgage. These were not mortgages at an interest rate below the "prime rate", the low interest rate at which most solid businesses are able to borrow money. Rather, they would have been more aptly called "subgood" loans or high-risk mortgages. The sale of these high-risk mortgages and their commoditization created the serious economic risks that result when individuals make decisions without personally facing the possible negative consequences. In the present case, this *moral hazard*, as economists call it, amounted to profiting from the sale of houses, mortgages, or mortgage-backed securities, and passing along the risk to pension plans and other investors down the line. Those who profited most were investment bank executives who received huge bonuses because of risky bets they made with their firm's mostly borrowed money.

The regulatory agencies, rating agencies, stock markets, and public accounting firms were like inattentive chaperones failing to see the flasks of whiskey being passed around at the high school prom or perhaps taking a sip or two themselves. Yale professor of business and law, Jonathan Macey, uses reputation theory as a lens to examine the failure of these gatekeepers in *The Death of Corporate Reputation: How Integrity Has Been Destroyed on Wall Street.*[306] If their reputation for integrity were an invaluable asset for these organizations, then, according to the theory, they would not have abandoned their posts as protectors of the public interest.

There were three problems. First, public accounting firms were conflicted by what is called the *dual agency* problem in that their duty was to the public but the investment banks paid all of their fees. PriceWaterhouse accountants auditing Goldman Sachs books for 2013, as an example, probably spent more time at their client's offices than at their own and may have been conscious only occasionally of their fiduciary duties.

Second, perfect competition that might have set a very high standard of integrity does not exist among the public accounting firms. In fact, the Big Four accounting firms (Deloitte, PWC, Ernst & Young, and KPMG) constitute an oligopoly in which each firm is guaranteed a share of services performed for the large investment banks. The only real standard for integrity is that one's own firm should not be viewed as significantly worse than the others.

Third, these firms might strive to achieve the highest level of excellence, but this attempt does not mean that all of their accountants do so. The percentage of accountants who spend their whole careers with one of the Big Four is very small, so junior accountants may be looking more at their own exit strategy when they are auditing a potential employer's books. These ambitious professionals might also be taking the advice for politicians attributed to US House Speaker Sam Rayburn: "If you want to get along, you have to go along".

Variations on these themes also apply to the Big Three credit rating agencies (Moody's, Standard & Poor's, and Fitch) and the Big Two stock exchanges (New York and NASDAQ). The Securities and Exchange Commission also has had problems, according to Macey, because it has served as a steppingstone for employment with one of the big firms it is intended to regulate or as a path to elected office in the State of New York.

When homeowners began defaulting on their loans in increasing numbers, the house of cards came crashing down and the world found itself in a major recession. Doctrinaire individuals on the right and left offered as explanations their same old bromides. Those on the right maintained that the recession was caused by the government attempting to provide everyone with the opportunity to own a house whether they could afford it or not. Those on the left answered that it was caused by the failure of government to enact and aggressively enforce the regulation of financial markets. There is surely enough blame to go around in the era of Pogo economics where greed was evident on Main Street, Wall Street, and in between.

Barry Ritholt of *Barron's* offers a scathing analysis of the credit crisis, comparing the federal government's role to that of a bartender serving drunks.[307] In 2004, the Securities and Exchange Commission exempted five firms — Goldman Sachs, Merrill Lynch, Lehman Brothers, Bear Stearns, and Morgan Stanley — from margin requirements compelling them to have one dollar of assets for every $12 they took on in debt. These former investment banks leveraged themselves up to as much as $40 of debt for every dollar of assets they possessed. To put this in perspective, imagine a novice investor borrowing $400,000 to buy a "spec" home with no down payment and $10,000 in the bank.

Michael Phillips of *The Wall Street Journal* described the "food chain" for a subprime loan of $103,000 issued in 2007 for a 576-square-foot shack that would be condemned as "unfit for human occupancy" by the city of Avondale, Arizona, in 2009.[308] Most of the loan was used to pay off debts and the remaining $11,090.33 was used for home repairs and food. The borrower was 61-year-old Marvene Halterman, a recovering alcoholic who had not been employed for 13 years.

Ms. Halterman obtained the loan from Integrity Funding LLC, a local lender charging fees of $6153. An appraiser hired by Integrity valued the house at $132,000 and received a $350 fee. Integrity sold Ms. Halterman's mortgage to Wells Fargo Bank for the original price of $132,000 plus $3090 in fees. Wells Fargo sold her mortgage along with 4050 others to HSBC (Hong Kong Shanghai Banking Corporation) of London. The mortgages, more than 85% of which were subprime, were used as collateral for securities issued in July 2007. The Teachers' Retirement System of Oklahoma spent $500,000 on them. Although Standard & Poor's and Moody's Investors Services had given these securities their top AAA rating, the securities turned out to be worth about $15,000 or 3% of the original investment. Ms. Halterman's property was later purchased by her neighbors for $18,000 and torn down. We can all feel safer now because Barry Rybicki, the owner of Integrity, gave up his mortgage-broker license to work for a venture-capital firm.

Approximately $4.1 trillion in US mortgages were bundled in similar securities between 2005 and 2006. An estimated $1.6 trillion of this amount involved high-risk home loans. How much of this was simply a matter of "irrational exuberance" (a.k.a. unbridled greed), to use Alan Greenspan's understatement, and how much involved something more sinister continues to be determined by the courts. Operation Stolen Dreams began in June 2010 as an effort of President Obama's interagency Financial Fraud Enforcement Task Force.[309] The operation targeted 1517 criminal defendants and made 525 arrests. The losses due to fraud were valued at over $3 billion. Conspicuous in their absence are executives from the major Wall Street firms whose stockholders have paid out billions in fines without anyone admitting to criminal activity.

In its own investigation in 2009, the *Sarasota Herald-Tribune* identified 50,000 suspicious real estate flips and estimated the total value of the fraud to be $10 billion.[310] They identified Craig Adams, a local real estate agent, as "king of the Sarasota flip". They accused Adams of being the leader of a "daisy chain", the term describing a group of investors who flip houses among themselves to inflate their prices artificially. The group was involved in nearly $100 million in mortgage defaults, and Adams personally defaulted on more than $17 million. Others in the chain were his 70-year-old mother, who was involved in three deals, and his 82-year-old aunt, who participated in seven. After the investigation but before facing any criminal charges, Adams began helping cash-strapped borrowers avoid foreclosure.[311] In January 2012, he was sentenced to 3 years in federal prison and was hauled off without being able to say goodbye to his tearful wife.[312]

At the top of the subprime food chain were executives of investment banks who made millions by purchasing, bundling, and reselling mortgages to unsuspecting investors. Marvene Halterman, described earlier, was not at the bottom of the chain because she obtained a loan of $103,000 that she knew she could not repay. Instead, the bottom was occupied by hundreds of thousands of individuals like Gabriella Westfall, another resident of the Phoenix area, who played by the rules but was victimized by unscrupulous banks and a foreclosure processing company.

Westfall had served as a police officer for more than 25 years. By the time her story was aired on television in June 2013, she had spent 4 years worrying about losing her home and thousands of dollars from her savings for attorney's and court fees in the fight to keep her home.

She had been paying her mortgage faithfully when the amount of her monthly payment was increased without explanation. A bank employee told her she needed a loan modification and that she should stop payments for 3 months in order to receive one. At the end of the 3 months, she was told the bank would not renew her loan and that she was in default because she had not been making payments.

While examining her bank file, Westfall discovered a forged document that appeared to have been signed by someone named Linda Green. It turned out that tens of thousands of foreclosure proceedings contained the forged signature of Green. She had been an employee of DOCX, a mortgage document processing company, and the forged documents listed her as a vice president of dozens of banks. DOCX had created more than a million fraudulently signed and notarized documents that were the basis for illegal foreclosures causing hundreds of thousands of Americans to lose their homes. The company was forced to pay $190.6 million in lawsuits and settlements with the federal government, 47 states, and the District of Columbia.

Ms. Westfall contacted the Arizona attorney general about her plight but got no response. The attorney general told a television reporter in an interview for a June broadcast that fraudulent documents do not necessarily invalidate foreclosure proceedings like Westfall's.

I contacted Westfall by e-mail in March 2015 and obtained an update of her situation. She abandoned her home in December 2014 after being contacted by a representative of Homewood Residential Holdings, which had been formed by the private equity firm in 2007. She was told she should leave voluntarily or legal proceedings would be initiated that would result in her forcible removal. Since then, Westfall was contacted by a representative of Ocwen Financial Corporation which had purchased Homewood and approximately 422,000 mortgages with unpaid principal balances of over $77 billion.[313] Both Homewood and Ocwen were servicers responsible for collecting payments and performing other services associated with mortgages and mortgage-backed securities. Ms. Westfall plans to file a lawsuit against JP Morgan Chase for using documents forged by DOCX in her 2011 foreclosure proceedings. She believes the Bank of New York Mellon purchased her home at a trustee sale, but they deny owning it.

In an update in March 2016, Gabriella wrote that after losing battles in bankruptcy and federal courts, "I voluntarily moved out of the house in November of 2014; it recently sold in January of 2016. The house sat empty for a year. In the end although I did not win, I was happy to have stayed in the home almost 4 years after they foreclosed. Saw my kids graduate from high school and live in the same house. Watched my step daughter battle cancer and pass away in the living room. Good and bad memories; but relieved I go to bed at night and not worry that the next day I could be locked out of my home".

The investment banking executives, Marvene Halterman, and everyone in between contributed to the subprime bubble and bust. There had been some institutional changes that contributed to the problems. Bankers had begun to pass subprime mortgages like Ms. Halterman's and the risks associated with them on to others who would do the same. Investment banks had changed from partnerships in which they were investing their own money to corporations that gambled with stockholder money. But all parties in the food chain, except for Gabriella Westfall and others like her, displayed a wanton disregard for the welfare of others, and no institution or economic system except the federal government, it appears, can withstand such widespread abuse.

*　　　　*

The first section of Chap. 4, BGH and the Twin Pillars of Free-Markets, presented statements of the leading 20th-century economists demonstrating that neoclassical economics rests on the *twin pillars of free-market capitalism*. The twin pillars can be encapsulated in the belief traced to Adam Smith that the vice of personal greed is transformed into a public virtue of economic prosperity through the miracle of free markets.

This chapter has shown that the presence of personal greed and limited or ineffectual government regulation had catastrophic effects on our economy during the first decade of the 21st century. How could Adam Smith have been so wrong on such fundamentally important issues? The answer is he wasn't wrong. Rather, the brilliant economists cited earlier got Smith wrong and with disastrous consequences. Adam Smith wrote that a society "cannot subsist among those who are at all times ready to hurt and injure one another", and without justice "a man would enter in an assembly of men as he enters a den of lions".[314]

*　　　　*

It has seemed odd that so many brilliant economists have characterized the political philosophy of Adam Smith so incorrectly. It has been especially puzzling that Milton Friedman who seemed to identify himself with Smith and who wrote so beautifully about free market capitalism when he published *Capitalism and Freedom* in 1962 could make such contradictory statements on the Phil Donahue show 30 years later. It also seems inexplicable that the liberal economist Paul Samuelson knowingly perpetuated the cartoonish view of economic man proclaimed by conservatives.

The apparent explanation described in the following chapter is that economics became caught up in the hot war and the intermittently cold one beginning when Pearl Harbor was bombed on December 7, 1941 and ending when the Berlin wall was torn down on December 9, 1989.[315] A parallel struggle between supporters of an active government and those supporting free markets began in 1945 and continues today. The critical roles played by Friedrich Hayek, Milton Friedman, and George Stigler will be described.

Readers will find more detailed accounts of this history in *Masters of the Universe: Hayek, Friedman, and the Birth of Neoliberal Politics* by Daniel Steedman Jones; *Economists and Societies: Discipline and Profession in the United States, Britain, and France, 1980s to 1990s* by Marion Fourcade; and *The Road From Mont Pelerin: The Making of the Neoliberal Thought Collective* edited by Philip Mirowski and Dieter Piehwe.[316] If the melody underlying these works is the mobilization of argumentation against collectivism and socialism, then the fascinating counterpoint is the extent to which wealthy private interests used both the carrot and stick within university settings to support these efforts. As Friedman acknowledged: "In a capitalist society, it is only necessary to convince a few wealthy people to get funds to launch any idea ..." if they can foresee a good return on investment.[317] For some of these individuals and their representatives, investing in the Mont Pelerin Society and the Chicago School of Economics would see lower taxes and loosening regulation.

Chapter 8

Why has Radical Individualism been Promoted?

I was astonished and somewhat amused to see communist flags carried by demonstrators in Old Town Edinburgh a few years ago. At least in my eyes, the war against socialism and communism had been won so thoroughly and so long ago that the protestors seemed quixotic and even quaint, but that had not always been the case. After 7 December 1941, we were at war with the Japanese and Germans. When they surrendered, the Western democracies squared off against the Union of Soviet Socialist Republics and the People's Republic of China in the Cold War that followed. The conflict between China and the United Nations on the Korean peninsula ended in a stalemate only 3 years before the Pierson and Gordon–Howell reports were published. Communists and socialists were powerful forces in Europe and they are still prominent.

Many of the great economists cited in this book lived through the Great Depression and World War II and saw the Cold War. Some applied their skills as part of the war effort and continued to promote the ideal of political and economic freedom both at home and in the intellectual contest that ended with the fall of the Berlin Wall. This chapter describes how those who were devoted to advancing the science of economics while advocating for a particular political philosophy contributed to the unintended and unfortunate events described in the previous chapter.

Frederick Hayek and the Birth of Neoliberalism

The tragedy of the subprime bubble and bust and the Great Recession is that it was not inevitable, and capitalism, like all human institutions, is not inherently corrupt. US capitalism has seen better times than during the 21st century's first decade. How is it that the social disease of greed metastasized, causing great economic destruction and raising doubts around the world about the value of capitalism?

This search for answers begins with the darkest hours of World War II. As German bombs fell over London in September 1940, Austrian philosopher and economist Frederick Hayek (Nobel Memorial Prize 1974) contributed to the war effort in the best way he knew how, writing essays and beginning what would become one of the most influential books of the 20th century, *The Road to Serfdom.*

Britain, the only nation with even a slim hope of resisting the territorial aims and military power of Nazi Germany, was on its heels. The Soviet Union and the United States were sitting on the sidelines. The Soviets could not be trusted and the Americans, offering the only hope for victory in the massive conflict, watched ambivalently from their position of physical and political isolation.

Hayek's writings reveal that he saw a deeper meaning in the military conflict between the Allied and Axis powers. Underlying the military struggle lay an ideological one between the forces supporting the supremacy of the state and those who believed the state should be subservient to its citizens. Viewed from this perspective, the Soviet Union was closer to Germany and Japan ideologically than to Britain, and a probable consequence of an Allied victory would be war among the British and the Americans and the Soviets.

The future of *liberalism* in the 19th century British sense — economic and political freedom with minimal government involvement — appeared even bleaker than just described even if the Americans shifted the balance by entering the war. The United States, Britain, and other western democracies, according to Hayek, had been infected with *socialism* — the concentration of economic power in the hands of a strong central government. The Great Depression, beginning in 1930 and extending for more than a decade, raised serious doubts about the viability of free-market capitalism.

The English economist John Maynard Keynes published in 1936 *The General Theory of Employment, Interest, and Money* that presented a comprehensive and machine-like vision of an economy — an elegant macroeconomic theory. This theory promised that governments could utilize spending programs, tax policies, and the Federal Reserve (like the flight-control system of an airplane) to accelerate the rate of economic growth and end the misery of the seemingly endless depression. The result was President Franklin Roosevelt's New Deal. Additionally, the industrial mobilization required after the United States entered the war necessitated a command-and-control relationship between big business and government. Government spending as a percent of the nation's yearly expenditures on goods and services grew from 7.74% in 1900 to 19.84% in 1940 when Hayek began his book, and to 45.6% the year before its publication — approximately a fivefold increase over four decades.[318]

The Road to Serfdom — 1944

The Road to Serfdom was published in London in March 1944. A fellow Austrian refugee and friend of Hayek's showed the British page proofs to Aaron Director, a University of Chicago faculty member in economics before the war and in its law school afterward. Frank Knight, also a member in its economics faculty and leader of its more conservative members, received proofs as well and passed them along to the University of Chicago Press. The press released the American edition in April of the same year and the book continues to be sold in a special edition 70 years after its first appearance.

Hayek's provocative title and the book's dedication *To Socialists of All Parties* suggests an understandably black-and-white worldview. There is the libertarian ideal where governments protect rather than infringe upon individual rights. In contrast is the grim reality where western governments have adopted socialism in varying degrees and are descending the slippery slope toward totalitarianism. This descent, according to Hayek, was enabled by the illusion that the irreconcilable forces of collectivism and individualism — central planning and personal freedom — could be reconciled. Hayek's ideas were radical at the time but his radicalism was counterrevolutionary, as he wished to return to the liberalism of 19th-century Great Britain and the United States. He traced the origins of that liberalism to Christianity, the Greeks, and the Romans and to the Renaissance and the Enlightenment.[319]

The Intellectuals and Socialism — 1949

Hayek left his position at the London School of Economics, carrying the torch of neoliberalism to the United States. In a lecture at the University of Chicago, later appearing as an article entitled, "The Intellectuals and Socialism", he asserts that the success socialism had experienced in every country resulted from the increasingly dominant role of the movement's "more active intellectuals".[320] From them it had spread to "secondhand dealers": "journalists, teachers, ministers, lecturers, publicists, radio commentators, writers of fiction, cartoonists, and artists" who are professionals at conveying ideas but amateurs concerning their substance.[321] Through the work of secondhand dealers, the views once held only by socialist intellectuals metastasized (my term) — infecting the general public and becoming "the governing force of politics".[322] The socialists, he complained with grudging admiration, had been so successful in the Western world that "even the most determined opponents of socialism derive their knowledge from socialist sources on most subjects on which they have no firsthand information".[323] There is a remarkable similarity between this and Everett Rogers's theory of innovations discussed in Chap. 5 as the "more active intellectuals" correspond to "innovators" and the secondhand dealers to "opinion leaders".

*   *

Hayek's speech did not contain breaking news to the Chicago faculty because some had already been involved in organizing a small group of the "more active intellectuals" to serve as the *avant garde* in an ideological battle against more active intellectuals on the far left. Thirty-nine individuals attended an organizational meeting lasting from 1–10 April 1947. Seventeen were from the United States, eight from England, four each from Switzerland and France, and one each from seven other

European countries.[324] Academics, especially economists, dominated the group but other disciplines represented were law, history, political science, chemistry, and philosophy.

Hayek was elected president of the new society and reelected until 1960. His imprint upon it was profound. R. M. Hartwell, a former society president, describes Hayek's motivation:

> He wanted an authoritative reassertion "of these values on which European civilization was built": "the sacredness of truth ... the ordinary rules of moral decency . . . a common belief in the value of human freedom ... an affirmative action towards democracy," and "the opposition to all forms of totalitarianism, whether it be from the Right or from the Left".[325]

Adam Smith would surely have applauded such noble ambitions.

Hayek insisted that the organization should serve as a hothouse for all ideas consistent with these general principles and proclaimed that no official creed, doctrine, or policy statement should be adopted by the society and that no doctrinal litmus test should be used to determine its membership. Members should agree only in their rejection of socialism and were free to hold a variety of views concerning the role of government and the appropriateness of various governmental policies (e.g., protection of the small farmer).[326] Real or alleged problems with capitalism such as "economic instability, externalities, public goods and bads, resource depletion, environmental pollution, persistent poverty, and economic underdevelopment" were also debated.[327]

The society's membership was to be interdisciplinary and widely distributed internationally. It had no official headquarters and the usual annual meeting moved from one country to another across the globe. The group would remain informal, employing a clerical staff member but depending primarily upon the voluntary efforts of its elected officers. This approach was not intended to create a secret society, but the association did not promote its activities or the papers presented at its meetings — leaving political activism, and it was considerable, to individual members.[328] In a letter Hayek sent in 1946 inviting individuals to attend the first meeting, he proposed the group be called the Acton-Tocqueville Society, but the name "Mont Pelerin Society" was chosen to commemorate the site in Switzerland where it first met.

Hayek could never have imagined when he began working on *The Road to Serfdom* in 1940 that Milton Friedman (who was then beginning his teaching career with an MA at the University of Wisconsin) and his colleagues in the Chicago School of Economics would ultimately become the most active intellectuals leading the counterrevolution and driving socialists from the field.

Hayek passes the baton to Friedman

Chicago economists and their supporters were involved in the Mont Pelerin Society's formation and its evolution and growth into an unprecedentedly powerful intellectual and political force. Aaron Director, Milton Friedman, Frank Knight, and George Stigler attended the inaugural meeting. Eight months later, Director, Knight, and Charles Hardy (a Chicago graduate and economics teacher there) registered the society as an Illinois corporation — listing its address as the Chicago Law School.[329] The Earhart, Garvey Lilly, Olin, Relm, Roe, Scaife, Volkers, and Winchester foundations — as well as the Foundation for Economic Education — provided substantial and vital support.[330] Friedman was the society's first American president (1970–1972), followed by Stigler (1976–1978) and Gary Becker (1990–1992). Chicago faculty members Ronald Coase and Allen Wallis would also join, as would James M. Buchanan, a Chicago graduate who would also serve as society president (1984–1986).

Hayek joined the University of Chicago in 1950 as a professor in the Interdisciplinary Committee on Social Thought, where Frank Knight was a member. The committee remains today as an interdisciplinary version of the traditional discipline-based academic department with its own budget and PhD program.[331] Although Hayek and Friedman were friends and libertarians, they had fundamental disagreements and Hayek was not offered a position in the Department of Economics.[332]

Hayek's justification for limited government was not only a concern about its coercive power. It was, more fundamentally, the belief that neither legislators nor economists are capable of understanding the evolutionary and organic nature of human society and thus of representing the economy with simplistic models for the purposes of making economic policy. Not only does this ignorance prevent governments from passing effective laws, it also prevents economists from treating their discipline successfully as a science modeled after the natural sciences. Hayek claimed that individuals attempting to impose restrictive research methods on an infinitely complex reality were engaging in *scientism* rather than science. "The scientistic as distinguished from the scientific view is not an unprejudiced but a very prejudiced approach which, before it has considered its subject, claims to know what is the most appropriate way of investigating it".[333] This does not seem to be a popular view among American economists.[333]

Hayek handed over the reins to Friedman as the locus of Mont Pelerin Society activities shifted from Europe to the American Midwest, and faculty there incorporated the neoliberal political philosophy into what would become Chicago-style economics.

Milton Friedman and Neoliberial Ascendance

Milton Friedman received his undergraduate degree from Rutgers and his masters from Chicago. He received his economics PhD from Columbia University in 1946 and joined the Chicago economics faculty in the same year. He retired in 1976 but remained professionally active through the 1980s and 1990s.

Nobel Prizes in physics, chemistry, medicine, literature, and peace have been awarded since 1901. The Sveriges Riskbank Prize in Economic Sciences in Memory of Alfred Nobel — the Nobel Memorial Prize in Economics — was first awarded in 1969. Paul Samuelson won it at the age of 55 the following year, and Kenneth Arrow received recognition in 1972 at the age of 51. Milton Friedman was the third American-born economist to win when he received it in 1976 at the age of 64. The press release issued by the Royal Swedish Academy of Sciences announced that he was receiving the award "for his achievements in the fields of consumption analysis, monetary history and theory, and for his demonstration of the complexity of stabilization policy".[334]

A trained economist and journalist wrote: "Adam Smith is generally hailed as the father of modern economics and Milton Friedman as his most distinguished spiritual son".[335] Friedman lectured at Dartmouth University in 1976, addressing the question of whether progress had been made in the business system in the 200 years since *Wealth of Nations* was published.[336] He responded that Smith is usually regarded as a defender of the status quo, representing the existing institutions of his time. Friedman claimed that in reality, Smith was one of a small group of revolutionaries attacking the established economic and political order. He was partially right about Smith because while he was an economics revolutionary, he was very careful in avoiding criticism of the political order.

Friedman observed that the British government had almost as much control over economic affairs during Smith's time as the US government did at the time of his speech. He added that although Smith's book called for revolution in the conduct of economic affairs, he was not naïve and did not expect the revolution to succeed. Friedman expressed that he was in the same position 200 years after Smith.

The Methodology of Positive Economics — 1953

In the opening paragraph of his essay, "The Methodology of Positive Economics", Milton Friedman references a book by John Neville Keynes, British economist and father of whom he considered to be the infamous economist John Maynard Keynes. In that work, the elder Keynes distinguishes among the *positive science* of economics concerned with **what is**, the *normative or regulative science* focusing attention on what **ought to be**, and the art of legislation to establish rules for implementing economic policy. Keynes goes on to caution that "confusion between them is common and has been the source of many mischievous errors".[337]

After noting Keynes's warning, Friedman claims that disinterested citizens of the Western world, especially Americans, agree about their "basic values, the differences about which men can ultimately fight", but that they differ in their economic predictions.[338] Economists, for example, are concerned about the welfare of workers with limited skills but disagree whether a minimum wage increases or decreases their prosperity. Friedman fails to acknowledge that one basic value over which there has been considerable fighting and that continues to produce substantial disagreement is about the proper role of government and the appropriate degree to which it should impose restraints on individual freedom.

Friedman devotes most of his article to arguing that economists should accept the particular views consistent with his libertarianism: Individuals are assumed to maximize profits, markets are assumed to be perfect, research should involve the empirical testing of models based on those assumptions, and the quality of research should be judged solely by the predictive power of these models. Thus, the twin pillars of free-market capitalism, profit maximization and perfect competition, represent the core of his philosophical position. Sociologist Marion Fourcade of the University of California, Berkeley, notes in her discussion of Friedman's article: "It is among Chicago economists that the search for neoclassical purity has reached its peak, both at the level of the single individual and the level of the entire economy".[339] The Chicago School will be examined more fully in Chap. 8.

Friedman dismisses critics of the profit maximization assumption who make the exaggerated claim that it reduces a person to a "selfish and money-grubbing" creature. He counters with the controversial view that the assumption regarding individuals engaged in economic behavior is necessarily unrealistic because it employs a high level of abstraction. He jokes it would make no sense to include "the personal characteristics of wheat-traders such as the color of each trader's hair and eyes".[340] Similarly, he rejects criticism of neoclassical economic theory that claims the assumption of *perfect competition* provides a false and overly idealistic view of reality. The very lack of realism of these assumptions makes them useful, according to Friedman. Incidentally, their functional form determines the predictive power of economic models rather than the labels that may or may not be attached to them.

In his defense of profit maximization and perfect competition, Friedman equates the science of economics with a single methodology that employs simple mathematical models of buyers, sellers, and markets that are incapable of capturing their essential complexity. These models do ignore the color of wheat farmers' eyes but they also fail to consider that farmers buy their seed wheat on credit and wait months before they know what their final cost and revenue per bushel will be. Farmers are more like high-stakes gamblers whose yearly income is based on a throw of the dice than people with perfect information and the ability to respond to it instantly.

Friedman claims that the ultimate purpose of a positive science is to produce "valid and meaningful ... predictions about phenomena not yet observed", and that predictive power "... is the only relevant test of a hypothesis ...".[341] Predictive power, however, is one of many criteria used for evaluating research results. Toward the end of the paper, Friedman adds two more, "clarity" and "precision", as criteria.[342] A fourth criterion Friedman employed is referenced in Chap. 4, where he criticizes Harry Markowitz's dissertation despite empirical support for the value of diversified investment portfolios because his findings were not based on theory.

Predictive power is obviously beneficial when the goal is to anticipate future events, but explanatory power is often necessary if the goal is to alter those events. The hypothesis that poisonous swamp vapors cause malaria had great predictive power during the middle ages; people with malaria lived near swamps. Our modern understanding of the germ theory of disease and the role of mosquitoes in spreading malarial parasites offers predictive power and also strong explanatory power that directs the treatment of the disease and the prevention of its spread.

Predictive power is always important but is rarely considered sufficient in the social sciences where elaborate explanations of human behavior are deemed necessary, and the isolation of cause-and-effect relationships is of paramount importance. Consider the research problem in marketing, dismissed by mainstream economists: Why do individuals buy what they do and how do they go about doing it? Skimming the index of any textbook on consumer psychology reveals dozens of factors contributing in small, but statistically significant ways to both the prediction and understanding of purchase behavior. These factors deal with characteristics of the buyer as an individual or organization, the product, and the purchase and consumption situations. Researchers conduct controlled experiments meeting the highest scientific standards to examine a variety of predictor variables and to determine their interrelationships and relative importance.

Although the stated purpose of Friedman's article is to promote positive economics, he does so by defending a very narrow conception of individuals, markets, research methods, and the judgment of research quality. The article's actual purpose appears to be to repudiate the emerging theory of monopolistic competition on the grounds that it is unscientific despite its realistic assumptions and relative theoretical complexity (a more detailed discussion appears in Chap. 10).[343]

The theory of monopolistic competition not only differs from the neoclassical economics Friedman defends, it is downright antithetical to it. The assumptions of monopolistic competition are opposite those of neoclassical economics: transaction costs, imperfect information, differentiated products, and so forth. Monopolistic competition offers a rich understanding of the economic world but does not lend itself to precise predictions of economic outcomes using mathematical models, relying instead on controlled experiments. To dismiss the theory for not being *scientific* or *economics* requires new narrower definitions of both terms.

Edward H. Chamberlin, who coined the term *monopolistic competition*, used the experimental method to demonstrate that imperfect markets did not become perfect ones, as conventional theory had predicted.[344] Vernon L. Smith, recipient of the Nobel Memorial Prize in 2002 for his pioneering work in experimental economics, published his first paper on the topic in the University of Chicago's *Journal of Political Economy*. He altered Chamberlin's experimental design and found that markets became increasingly competitive, as might be expected, because some markets in the real world are competitive and others are not.

It is also clear that monopolistic competition is not based on either of the twin pillars. Sellers are depicted as complex organizations rather than as one-dimensional individuals. Innovations commonly drive rapid expansion of markets and contribute to wide fluctuations in economic activity — defying, at least in the short and intermediate runs, the pressures toward equilibrium. The theory is silent concerning the proper role of government. Finally, monopolistic competition lacks rigidity and is capable of adapting to and coexisting with research findings from various business disciplines.

*   *

What Friedman excluded from his reference to Keynes's cautionary words about mingling positive and normative economics is as revealing as what he included. Keynes continues by declaring that neither the *laissez-faire* nor socialist political philosophies "can form an internal position of the positive science of political economy".[345] This situation exists, he says, because the standard of excellence by which each group evaluates research quality is biased in favor of the extent to which the findings support its conflicting creeds.

Keynes grants that the leading British economists — Smith, Malthus, and Mill — have favored *laissez-faire* policies in their applied work. However, "they do not regard it as an axiomatic and inexorable formula by which all particular proposals may be tested, but as a practical conclusion whose validity in every case depends on particular circumstances". Keynes concludes this portion of his book by stating that both *laissez-faire* and socialist economists have conflated their political philosophies with the science of economics. He declares that the quality of a group of economists should be measured by the extent to which its members avoid this pitfall.

If Keynes is correct to assert that Smith did not regard *laissez-faire* policies as being suitable in every circumstance, then he places Smith among conservatives within the vast ranks of economists who believe in the superiority of an alloy over pure *laissez-faire* or pure socialism. The problem is that getting the proportions right is immensely difficult. There is a prayer for those who try: God, grant me the serenity to accept markets that are working effectively, the courage to promote government intervention for those that are not, and the wisdom to know the difference.

Capitalism and Freedom — 1962

Friedman published *Capitalism and Freedom* in 1962, the year Hayek returned to Europe. The book is an equally important companion to Hayek's *The Road to Serfdom* appearing 18 years earlier. Friedman states he and others constituted a "small beleaguered minority regarded as eccentrics by the great majority of our fellow intellectuals".[346] They were worried about the welfare state and Keynesian ideas that threatened both freedom and prosperity.

Friedman lays out the principles of liberalism in this work and examines instances where the federal government has departed from those principles in dealing with economic and social issues such as free trade and income inequality. He writes eloquently about these principles, making a strong case for free markets. Although he was not an anarchist, he fails to spell out in this book and elsewhere a detailed explanation of the role government should play.

Friedman presents a nuanced picture of human nature in this work. He notes that claiming individuals follow their own interests does not imply "narrow self-regarding interests". Rather, they "include the whole range of values that men hold dear and for which they are willing to spend their fortunes and sacrifice their lives".[347] He proclaims that society rests upon a consensus concerning the rules governing their behavior, but "no set of rules can prevail unless most participants most of the time conform to them without external sanctions...".[348] Nevertheless, a "major aim of the liberal is to leave the ethical problem for the individual to wrestle with".[349] Friedman uses the term *liberal* in the British sense of freedom from the strictures of government, which is counter to the American usage that indicates support for what would be for him an overreaching government.

Concerning the role of government, Friedman states the scope of government must be limited to two functions: protecting "our freedom both from the enemies outside our gates [with armed forces] — and from our fellow-citizens [with a justice system] and to preserve law and order, to enforce private contracts, to foster competitive markets".[350] Concerning the need for a justice system, he contends that "we cannot rely on custom or on this [social] consensus alone to interpret and to enforce the rules; we need an umpire".[351] The "liberal conceives of men as imperfect beings" and that the "the liberal regards the problem of social organization to be as much a negative problem of preventing 'bad' people from doing harm as of enabling 'good' people to do good...".[352]

Friedman says that in addition to these two functions, the "government may enable us at times to accomplish jointly what we would find it more difficult or expensive to accomplish severally". Economists refer to these accomplishments as *public goods*.[353] However, by relying primarily on voluntary cooperation and private enterprise, private citizens place a "check on the power of the governmental sector and an effective protection of freedom of speech, of religion and of thought".[354] Unfortunately, Friedman does not provide concrete guidance concerning how these noble aims are to be carried out.

The Social Responsibility of Business is to Increase Profit — 1970

In 1970, Milton Friedman published a widely read and highly controversial article in *The New York Times Magazine*. His first thesis is that profits are evidence that corporations are being socially responsible when they are conforming to "… the basic rules of society, both those embodied in law and those embodied in ethical custom".[355] I cannot imagine a good counterargument.

His second thesis is that executives must not spend corporate resources for "… providing employment, eliminating discrimination, avoiding pollution and whatever else may be the contemporary crop of reformers". This position is problematic.

Readers might expect Friedman to criticize CEOs' diversion of corporate resources on the grounds that they are violating their fiduciary duty to stockholders that is established in law and ethical custom. In other words, executives should not spend corporate funds on their pet social projects, lavish redecorations of their offices, or their own undeserved bonuses. Readers discover that Friedman never mentions fiduciary duty and criticizes only what he calls "pet projects". He then makes the stunning statement that corporate executives who follow the preaching of social reformers are advancing the cause of "… pure and unadulterated socialism".

Friedman differentiates among three cases. First, it is legitimate for all private individuals, including stockholders, to spend their personal funds on social causes. Second, it is also legitimate that some individuals form nonprofit corporations for the sole purpose of supporting social causes. Third, it is illegitimate for executives to divert corporate funds to social causes because shareholders are interested only in maximizing their dividend payments.

How can Friedman claim that expenditures on social causes are bad because all stockholders wish to maximize dividends when he does not claim it is a violation of the executives' fiduciary duty? His attempt to justify this claim is faulty on two grounds.

First, it is false to conclude executives must always fulfill the wishes of those stockholders who own enough shares to control the company. For example, stockholders might ignore ethical custom by demanding that manufacturing plants operate only in countries with no effective child labor laws or sell harmful products abroad even though they are illegal in the United States. Stockholders' desire for something does not mean that it is either ethical or legal. Anyone who believes this to be true is committing the *naturalistic fallacy* (discussed in Chap. 5) because shareholders demand that the value of the stock they own be maximized; therefore, it is right and good that the value of their stock be maximized no matter what other effects these actions may have.

Second, the suggestion that all or most stockholders want to maximize dividends is a matter of fact, not speculation. Friedman's only support of this claim, however, is that Adam Smith stated two centuries earlier that he never saw much good come from "those who affected to trade for the public good". This is a very narrow and misleading interpretation of Smith's views. It is true Smith wrote famously: "It is not from the benevolence of the butcher, the brewer, or the baker that we expect our dinner, but from their regard to their own interest".[356] They do so out of the prudent desire to take care of themselves and their families. But Smith never implied that the butcher did not, or should not, give a mutton joint to a needy family. Smith praised acts of benevolence in his ethics book *Theory of Moral Sentiments*. He wrote in this great work that wise and virtuous men always sacrifice their own interests to those of the greater society.[357]

Further, firms focusing exclusively on the maximization of shareholder wealth appear to be in a distinct minority. Stockholders have not abandoned corporations such as Whole Foods, Target, Bank of America, and hundreds of others that contribute to charity directly or through foundations they have established expressly for that purpose.[358] It is also true that not all libertarians agree with Friedman on this point. John Mackey founded Whole Foods on the principle that the company would contribute a portion of its earnings to charity and treat its employees, customers, suppliers, and other stakeholders as partners rather than targets of cost-reduction programs.[359]

The unstated motive prompting Friedman's argument probably has nothing to do with shareholders' wishes and everything to do with the perceived threat posed when America's largest and most powerful businesses allocate resources for purposes other than maximizing profits. Such social engineering is socialism when the government does it and according to Friedman, it is tantamount to socialism when businesses do.

Despite the weaknesses of Friedman's arguments, they have given credence to agency theory. Michael Jensen uses something called a *production function* to demonstrate a mathematical truth in a *Journal of Applied Finance* article: When corporations must maximize one variable, shareholders' wealth, they must necessarily minimize all others.[360] When taken to its extreme, this perspective indicates that when shareholders' wealth is maximized, the cost of producing products is zero and workers are not paid anything. A sophisticated view is that shareholders' wealth is maximized because corporations spare no expense in producing the best products available and handsomely paid workers take personal pride in the good reputation of their employer and the products it sells. In other words, stockholder wealth is maximized when the expenditures on a corporation's other stakeholders are optimized.

Free to Choose — 1980

Friedman retired from Chicago in 1977 and became senior fellow at the Hoover Institute, a Stanford University public policy think tank.[361] He and his wife Rose published *Freedom to Choose: A Personal Statement* in 1980. The book's theme is that the government's role during the 19th century was only "… to serve as an umpire to prevent individuals from coercing one another …" but it was abandoned during the 20th century and the role of government became that of "… a parent charged with the duty of coercing some to aid others".[362] Its first chapter discusses virtues of markets, and the next eight enumerate problems caused when the federal government attempts to reshape the natural social and economic order. The book concludes with a chapter discussing signs of what appear to be a return to free markets, the cause Milton had begun fighting for as a young man.

The period of free markets in America actually began when the colonists threw off strictures of Britain's mercantilist policies in the 1770s. Government regulations increased around the turn of the 20th century and increased profoundly during the Great Depression. The Friedmans' description of the golden age of liberalism is more narrowly focused on the period of rapid economic growth that occurred in the late 1800s and early 1900s, the last third of the 150-year period when there was little government regulation, or need for it, and no efforts to deal with what today we call "social justice".

The Friedmans are dismissive of the "… myth that has grown up in the United States that paints the nineteenth century as an era of the robber baron, of rugged, unrestrained individualism".[363] They reject this characterization of the great entrepreneurs of the period, attribute the great economic growth of the period to them, and fail to acknowledge any harm they caused. Their rejection of the "myth" is dubious on three grounds. First, the extraordinary economic growth during the last third of approximately 150 years of liberal government was caused principally by the industrial revolution and opportunities it created.

Second, John Jacob Astor, Jay Gould, Cornelius Vanderbilt, and a score of others did not bring about the industrial revolution by themselves; these entrepreneurs rode the great wave, but they did not create it. Rather, they symbolize a great historical era just as Daniel Boone, Meriwether Lewis, William Clark, and Davy Crocket did for the opening of the West. Many of us have ancestors now lost in history who worked in steel mills, laid railroad tracks, and farmed using the latest equipment and technology of their time. Adam Smith's description of economic growth in 18th-century Britain provides us with a superior understanding of what happened in the United States a century later:

> … capital has been silently and gradually accumulated by the private frugality and good conduct of individuals, by their universal, continual,

and uninterrupted effort to better their own condition. It is this effort, protected by law and allowed by liberty to exert itself in the manner that is most advantageous....[364]

Friedman expressed views very similar to that of Smith in *Capitalism and Freedom* but they are conspicuously absent in *Free to Choose*.

Third, arguments for free markets in the nineteenth century were undermined by the pernicious political philosophy of Social Darwinism. The origins of the link between human competition and what would be Darwin's theories appeared before the publication of Darwin's *The Origin of the Species* in 1859 or *The Descent of Man* in 1871. Herbert Spencer, the most famous proponent of Social Darwinism, wrote in 1851: "The poverty of the incapable, the distresses that come upon the imprudent, the starvation of the idle, and those shoulderings aside of the weak by the strong, which leave so many 'in shallows and in miseries,' are the decrees of a large, farseeing benevolence".[365]

Spencer supported *laissez-faire* government where the inevitable advancement toward the perfection of the human race was not impeded by misguided social programs, such as public education that supported the unfit.[366] He considered taxes beyond those necessary to protect property rights, a violation of those rights. Spencer, not Darwin, coined the term *survival of the fittest* in 1897.[367]

John D. Rockefeller, entrepreneur and founder of the University of Chicago, expressed Spencerian views in a Sunday school class where he explained his guiding philosophy in creating the Standard Oil monopoly: "The growth of a large business is merely a survival of the fittest.... The American Beauty rose can be produced in splendor and fragrance which bring cheer to its beholder only by sacrificing the early buds which grow up around it. This is not an evil tendency in business. It is merely the working-out of a law of nature and a law of God".[368]

The intellectual legacies of both Smith and Darwin were abused to support the radical individualism of the Gilded Age. Smith never praised greed. Darwin never supported human predation and wrote that

Ultimately a highly complex sentiment, having its first origin in the social instincts, largely guided by the approbation of our fellow-man, ruled by reason, self-interest, and in later times by deep religious feelings, confirmed by instruction and habit, all combined, constitute our moral sense or conscience.[369]

Finally, it should be noted the natural history of government intervention to be discussed in Chap. 10 was introduced in *Free to Choose*. Although the Friedmans do not say so, the theory also explains the global rise of socialism and communism in response to the "real or fancied evils" of industrialization and the emerging class of capitalists. Additionally, the increase in government regulation, especially of banking, was a response to the "real or fancied evils" widely believed to have caused the collapse of US housing and financial markets during the mid-2000s. This extended view of the natural history suggests a pendulum of government intervention swinging exaggeratedly from the left to the right and back again. What is not clear is whether there is a point of equilibrium where a just and efficient division of labor between government and privately owned institutions is to be found.

Friedman: The last prophet

The Mont Pelerin Society strayed profoundly from Hayek's original vision over its first five decades. Fears that society had become far too Anglo-Saxon and too dominated by the Chicago School of Economics had been realized in the eyes of some.[370] Both these trends were reinforced by the fact that Friedman, Stigler, Buchanan, Becker, and Coase were Nobel laureates and the first four had served as society presidents. The result was a potent force reshaping the academic and political worlds. The marriage of neoliberalism and neoclassical microeconomics gave birth to the Chicago School of Economics that emerged in the late '40s and grew to dominate the academic disciplines of economics, business, and law. Neoliberalism reached its political apex when Margaret Thatcher became British prime minister in 1979 and Ronald Reagan was elected as the US president in 1981.[371] The press for deregulation was relentless, however, and the ascendency of neoliberalism among intellectuals continued.

R. M. Maxwell noted: "By 1990 it seemed that much of what the founding fathers had formed the Society for had been attained and that the

Society's specific aims had been achieved".[372] Hayek, who died in 1992, might have revised a statement of fact he made before the Chicago faculty in 1949 with two word changes: "even the most determined opponents of *neoliberalism* derive their knowledge from *neoliberal* sources their knowledge on most subjects on which they have no firsthand information".[373]

But I wonder whether he had any nagging doubts about the Chicago School's promotion of radical individualism, and the apparent disappearance of any concern for "the ordinary rules of moral decency" that he viewed as a critical component of neoliberalism.[374]

In *The Chicago School*, a history Friedman praised as "thorough and extraordinarily well-informed", author Johan van Overtveldt declares with arguable understatement, "Friedman is probably one of the most enthusiastic and articulate supporters of a free market system that has ever lived".[375] Nobel laureates are given star status even though few members of the general public understand why a particular economist received the award. This is most likely true concerning Friedman, who will be remembered as the laureate who trashed socialism, identified greed as the engine of free-market capitalism, and was dismissive of the harm caused by some of the rugged individuals of the 19th century.

Paul Samuelson, a professional rival and personal friend of Friedman, commented: "Now I don't think Milton is a charlatan ... He believes what he says anytime he says it. But he also has a very healthy respect for his audience. If you are a yokel, he gives you a hokum answer. If he is giving his presidential address, he states it more guardedly, and more carefully ... It's simply a matter of the style of the person".[376] Samuelson's characterization helps us understand why Friedman employed an intellectual version of Mohammed Ali's "rope-a-dope" routine on Phil Donahue, his ill-equipped and ill-prepared television host.

Samuelson told an interviewer shortly before his death that Alan Greenspan, former chair of the Federal Reserve, also defended free-market capitalism by ignoring its faults: "But the trouble is that he had been an Ayn Rander. You can take the boy out of the cult but you can't take the cult out of the boy. He actually had instruction, probably pinned on the wall: 'Nothing from this office should go forth which discredits the capitalist system. Greed is good'".[377]

Friedman, and Greenspan for that matter, would have served the cause of free-market capitalism better if they had offered something like this economic equivalent of Winston Churchill's description of democracy: "Many [economic] systems have been tried and will be tried in this world of sin and woe. No objective thinker pretends that [free-market capitalism] is perfect or all-wise. Indeed, it has been said that [free-market capitalism] is the worst form of [economic system] except all of those other forms that have been tried from time to time".[378] Instead, Friedman's vast learning, humor, and eloquence, plus his status as a Nobel Prize-winning economist, enabled him, probably inadvertently, to help introduce a creed of greed into the American consciousness.

Mischievous Errors of The Chicago School

Libertarian economists have enjoyed a dominant position extending far beyond their imperial seat at the University of Chicago. The university's website indicates that of the 74 Nobel Memorial Prize laureates in economics as of 2013, 26 are or have been affiliated with the university, and five of those received their awards during the past 10 years.[379] I can imagine presidents of rival universities wishing for an National Football League (NFL)-like system for economics, with salary caps and a draft allowing the weakest department to make the first pick each year from among the discipline's emerging superstars. Those wishing to compete with Chicago might also wish to emulate them by being able to place economists in their business schools, law schools, and elsewhere on campus.

The distinction between neoclassical or mainstream microeconomics and the Chicago School of Economics has not always been made clear in my readings. The terms *neoclassical economics* or *the neoclassical synthesis* appear to rely on the classical economists' model of markets but incorporate a better understanding of demand and the recognition of macroeconomics.[380] Economists, characterized in this manner, span the spectrum from liberals on the left to libertarians on the far right, where Friedman and many of his Chicago colleagues have resided.

There is, of course, no formal Chicago School of Economics. The Department of Economics is part of the university's Social Sciences Division. Not every economist at Chicago has agreed with the tenets of this so-called school, and not everyone who has agreed with them has resided in the Department of Economics. Others are found in the Chicago Booth Graduate School of Business and its Law School, and many are found at other universities.

The definition of the school used here is taken from an article in *The Elgar Companion to the Chicago School of Economics* that identifies it as an informal group of economists who share the following characteristics: "a deep commitment to rigorous scholarship and open academic debate, an uncompromising belief in the usefulness and insight of neoclassical price theory, and a normative position that favors and promotes economic liberalism and free markets".[381] Obviously, this definition does not require a professional affiliation with the University of Chicago.

This classification also reveals a mischievous conflation of the libertarian political philosophy and positive economics to which Milton Friedman alerts us in his 1953 article. The warning is not that economists who conduct research with scientific objectivity should refrain from making policy recommendations. In fact, it is important that economists contribute to policy discussions in areas where they have expertise. Rather, the mischief Friedman references occurs when the influence goes the wrong way up a one-way street, when supposedly scientific research is shaped by value judgments that predetermine research methods and findings as well as specific policy recommendations. Such a situation seems to this outsider to be all too common among economists. Liberals tend to see market failures everywhere and recommend the nostrum of government intervention while conservatives see government failures everywhere and recommend the natural cure of *laissez faire* policies.

If Friedman's reasoning is sound concerning problems caused by conflating normative and positive economics, then it can be used in examining the definition of the Chicago School presented previously. The first clause, "a deep commitment to rigorous scholarship and open academic debate", should characterize all academic departments in every discipline (so long as no blood is drawn), and the Chicago School distinguishes itself with its deep commitment to these principles.

The second clause notes "an uncompromising belief in the usefulness and insight of neoclassical price theory". In his article on positive economics, Friedman defends perfect competition as the centerpiece of price theory, but he, Stigler, and others have focused more recently on "modern price theory", with the price mechanism as its central feature. Stigler identifies three premises of this revised theory in his memoirs published in 1988. First, the pursuit of "efficiency is pervasive in economic life, where efficiency means producing and selling goods at the lowest cost (and therefore the largest possible profit)".[382] Second, "it is virtually impossible to eliminate competition from economic life", and third, efforts to impose competition through government regulation tend to be counterproductive. These premises imply that even natural monopolies are or will be sufficiently competitive to ensure adequate competition.

The third clause in the Chicago School's definition, "a normative position that favors and promotes economic liberalism and free markets", is an extension of the second if we accept Stigler's description of modern price theory. The "uncompromising belief" in price theory and its constituent assumptions are problematic. If assumptions may or may not be true while maxims are self-evident truths, then the twin pillars of free-market capitalism — economic man and market perfection — are maxims, at least for true believers. As considerable attention has already been devoted to economic man and agency theory, the maxim of market perfection is examined here more closely.

The Nobel Memorial Prize ceremony for economics in 2013 resembled a wedding where an uninvited ex-spouse showed up. Chicago economist Eugene Fama received the prize for his contributions to the *efficient market theory*, and Yale economist Robert Shiller received it as well for his contributions to what might be called the *inefficient market theory*. In 1988, Shiller and a colleague examined the relationship between stock prices and the financial performance of the corporations issuing those stocks. They discovered that stock market price fluctuations accounted for 27% of the corresponding fluctuations in stock dividends. Other researchers utilized a different time period and found the estimate to be 15%.[383]

What does Shiller's number mean? If the market were perfectly efficient, then this number should be 100% or close to it, but 73% of the price fluctuations remained unaccounted for in his test of the efficient market hypothesis. It is very rare for a meaningful study to explain a high percentage of variations in human behavior when a single variable is employed, and 27% is impressive by this standard. However, the fact that 73% of the

variation in stock prices were unaccounted for means that a rival to efficient market hypothesis would need predictive power of only 28% to
displace it as **the** explanation.

Adding a second independent variable to a model would likely
improve its predictive power and could never hurt it. Shiller contends that
an important portion of stock market price fluctuations is attributable to
booms and busts unrelated to corporate performance. These fluctuations
are better explained by mass psychology and herd mentality than the
rational calculation of perfectly informed individuals. He contends that
booms are produced by irrational exuberance.

Fama seems to share a version of Jensen and Meckling's belief quoted
previously: "All markets are almost always in equilibrium, and all forces
must almost always be in balance at almost all times".[384] The Federal
Reserve Bank of Minneapolis published an interview with Fama just a
month before the housing boom drove the stock market boom to its peak
in December 2007. He said, "The word 'bubble' drives me nuts. For example, people say 'the Internet bubble'.... How many Microsofts would it
have taken to justify the whole set of Internet valuations? I think I estimated it to be something like 1.4". The Internet bubble reached its peak in
March 2001, and the market hit bottom in October 2002.

In his Nobel Memorial Prize acceptance speech, Fama attributes
"bubbles" and busts to "fluctuations in business conditions" but does not
explain why these conditions vary so radically over relatively short peri-
ods or why they are not merely reflections of the irrational exuberance of
speculators and others induced to buy houses as their prices rose to his-
toric levels.[385] He also states that *bubbles* are defined as price increases
followed by predictably strong decreases, but he claims that no one has
been able to make these predictions.

Fama declared in the interview that the stock market crashes of 1929
and 1987 were the only two bubbles that occurred during the 20th century
and that they provided the market with needed corrections.[386] He did not
indicate why perfect markets need correcting in such a dramatic fashion
rather than having continuous adjustments brought about as new perfect
information is accommodated. The National Bureau of Economic Research
reports one economic contraction (recession) that ended in December
1900 and twenty other expansions and contractions that occurred during

the 20th century.[387] Michael Lewis's book *The Big Short: Inside the Doomsday Machine* or Gregory Zuckerman's *The Greatest Trade Ever: The Behind-the-Scenes Story of How John Paulson Defied Wall Street and Made Financial History* tell of how Wall Street investors timed the bust with sufficient accuracy to make billions.[388]

It should be clear by now that not everyone holds the maxims that economic man is antisocial and amoral, that the price system achieves perfection almost universally, or that the price system is sufficiently perfect to counter the destructiveness of the economic men who comprise it. Additionally, it seems the support for the maxims cannot be more than equivocal if all the evidence is examined.

*   *

A reunion occurred after Allen Wallis returned from Stanford in 1946 and George Stigler returned from Columbia in 1958 to join their old classmate Milton Friedman at the University of Chicago. Wallis taught statistics there until his appointment as dean of the Graduate Business School (GSB) in 1956.[389] The GSB had been floundering and the university administration was considering its elimination. Wallis convinced the president, as part of his job package, to double the school's budget and transfer the Walgreen Foundation and its substantial endowment from the Division of the Social Sciences to the GSB.[390] Wallis had served previously as a consultant and staff member for the Ford Foundation, and the GSB would receive $2.9 million in Ford grants between 1954 and 1964 — the second largest amount given by Ford to any school.[391]

Wallis utilized this increased wealth to hire other free-market economists, among the most prominent being Merton Miller and George Stigler. Miller, a pioneer in the field of financial economics, joined the GSB in 1961 and would go on to win the Nobel Memorial prize.[392] Wallis, Stigler, and Friedman were also members of the Mont Pelerin Society; Stigler became its president. Friedman was the public face of the Chicago School and the neoliberal political movement in the United States, while Wallis and Stigler were administrators with lower public profiles but they would have great influence nationally.

Some outsiders doubted whether the GSB would embrace the inter-disciplinary approach to business education promoted by the Ford Foundation. Robert Gordon, coauthor of the Gordon-Howell report, wrote to a foundation project director declaring: "Emphasis on the economic ingredient of the curriculum (and probably of a traditional Chicago mold particularly if George Stigler accepts the Walgreen professorship) might override the other social science elements".[393]

Gordon's concerns were fully realized after Stigler accepted the position. The prevailing attitude at Chicago was that there might be other social study disciplines but economics was the sole social science and that the others could become more scientific if they adopted the theories and methods promulgated by the Chicago School. Stigler devoted himself to articulating and supporting the "Chicago way" within the economics department, the GSB, the law school and elsewhere across the nation.

Stigler accepted the Walgreen Chair and dispensed over 100 Walgreen Foundation grants between 1958 and 1980. He was highly critical of the Johnson Administration's efforts to establish economic performance guidelines, considering them dysfunctional government interventions. He organized a conference on the topic in 1966 funded by the Walgreen Foundation. One outcome was the publication of *Guidelines, Informal Controls, and the Marketplace* edited by two economists on the GSB faculty, George Schultz and Robert Aliber.[394] Schultz, another free-market economist, had succeeded Wallis as GSB dean in 1962 and later went on to serve as the US Secretary of Labor, director of the Office of Management and Budget, US Secretary of the Treasury, and US Secretary of State.

Another outcome of the conference was its immediate and direct impact on federal economic policies. Stigler wrote to his patron, Charles R. Walgreen, Jr.: "This was a very successful affair ... the heavy attacks on the guidelines program have had a very good effect upon [Chair of the Council of Economic Advisors for the Johnson Administration] Gardner Ackley".[395]

Stigler organized a conference in 1972, a decade after the Food and Drug Administration required a more demanding process for approving prescription drugs. Pfizer, G. D. Searle, Merck, Sharp and Dohme, Upjohn, and Smith, Kline, and French provided financial support in addition to that of the Walgreen Foundation.[396] The University of Chicago

Center for Policy Study published the conference proceedings and one contributor testified on the subject before a Senate hearing. The Center's director notes in the volume's preface that controversy had surrounded the conference before the proceedings appeared in print, and claims it is not a treatise but rather a contribution to the debate on an issue of public importance not unlike, in his words, "a postcard portraying a volcano".[397]

Today's readers might identify as red hot magma Stigler's introductory remarks criticizing socialists — and John Kenneth Galbraith specifically — for promoting the growing intrusion of the federal government and spotlighting the ineffectuality of industry-specific regulations. He also proposes that the enforcement of FDA statutes would be done more cost-effectively if the process were privatized. Anyone detecting a violation could take the culprit to court. He offers as a model the Justice Department which allows private actions to be brought under the Sherman Antitrust Act with the promise that attorneys may collect triple damages.[398]

Stigler went on to establish the Center for the Economy and the State that enabled him to promote neoclassical economics and neoliberal public policy on an unprecedented scale. The center relied on a substantial stream of donations from major corporations and private foundations. It has published over 200 working papers, summaries of which have appeared in *Capital Ideas* magazine published by the GSB. Stigler was a major contributor to the center with his work promoting the complementary premises of robust markets and dysfunctional regulation, and he was the first of seven GSB faculty members to receive the Nobel Memorial Prize.[399]

The center, renamed the Stigler Center for the Study of the Economy and the State upon his death in 1991, remains strong. The Center began with six affiliated faculty members, but that number grew to 22, of whom 15 are members of what is now the Chicago Booth Graduate School of Business according to its 2013–2014 annual report.[400]

*   *

No one has yet risen to assume the mantle of neoliberalism that Milton Friedman wore so brilliantly. Perhaps this void exists because no young neoliberal has possessed the passion of Hayek or Friedman, who lived through the trials of the Great Depression and World War II. When Hayek wrote "The Intellectuals and Socialism" over 65 years ago, the neoliberals were isolated and marginalized. Four decades later, Stigler wrote in his memoirs that his fear of growing totalitarianism had not been realized since the publication of *The Road to Serfdom*. Although the role of the state has expanded in the United States and other western countries he observed, the loss of personal freedom has not accompanied it. In fact, the range of economic choices presented to Americans has expanded because of the spread of higher education and the rise of real incomes.[401] Another way of putting it is that poverty is tyrannical and tends to coexist with political tyranny. In any case, it is clear that the positions have been reversed, and the socialists (at least in the United States) have been isolated and marginalized.

Not all members of the Chicago School were sanguine about the success of the neoliberal counterrevolution. In 1990, 2 years after Stigler's memoirs were published, James M. Buchanan gave a lecture in Sidney, Australia, bearing the provocative title "Socialism is dead, but Leviathan lives on". In it he writes:

> With no overriding principle that dictates how an economy is to be organised, the political structure is open to maximal exploitation by the pressures of well organised interests which seek to exploit the powers of the state to secure differential profits.[402]

Friedman's spoken and written statements were more consistent with Buchanan's than with Sigler's.

Although Friedman's motives for promoting a distorted and destructive characterization of economic man seem consistent with his political philosophy, it is a puzzle why other great economists representing various positions along the political spectrum did so as well. Perhaps, some insight can be found in Paul Samuelson's characterization of the political environment soon after World War II when he introduced his textbook. He notes that the term *Keynesian-Marxist*, popularized by Herbert Hoover, was used to brand professors attempting to incorporate macroeconomics into college textbooks. Those at many colleges "came under attack by regents and alumni visiting committees who had been alerted to the heresies being imposed on innocent college youth".[403]

This situation occurred before the Joseph McCarthy era of witch-hunts for communists among government officials, professors, and members of the clergy. Sociologist Marion Fourcade describes campaigns across the nation that were undertaken to discredit economics professors thought to have Keynesian-Marxist leanings, and reports that a dean at the University of Illinois was removed from his position in 1951 for recruiting such faculty members.[404]

Board members and businessmen who had graduated from MIT attacked drafts of Samuelson's textbook, *Economics*, fiercely. One of them made a list of 100 "heresies" he had found in the manuscript and declared that Samuelson's reputation could be preserved if the text were vetted by a classical economics authority at Yale. The MIT president intervened on Samuelson's behalf and he was able to publish the uncensored version of his work. It was a phenomenal marketplace success because he "considered it good business [and I would argue good economics] to articulate carefully just when and why an unorthodox paradigm might make sense under certain conditions, whereas at other times orthodox paradigms would commend themselves". Perhaps he thought that the choice of labels attached to the mathematical model for the seller really did not matter in the larger context of economic predictions and policy recommendations. If so, he was wrong because they have turned out to matter a great deal.

*   *

I must confess I have often had difficulty in determining what writers mean by the term *socialism*, because it appears to have three usages. First, it refers to situations where the government controls, or interferes with, the operation of free markets. By this definition, even a *laissez-faire* government is socialistic because, at minimum, it raises taxes to support the chief of state, who oversees the systems of defense and justice. Second and third, *socialism* refers to cases where a government goes too far in owning the means of production or too far in controlling them through regulations. The problem with the last two of the three usages is that economists seem to differ concerning what they believe is "going too far". However, it brings some comfort to know that most American economists seem to agree unanimously that going too far is bad.

*   *

To summarize, the neoliberal movement began in the 1940s as a response to the totalitarian threats of Germany and Japan and to the popularity of socialism in the Western democracies. The locus of the movement shifted from Europe to the United States and its leadership from Frederick Hayek to Milton Friedman. As this essentially political movement settled in the University of Chicago's Department of Economics, it became conflated with positive economics as it focused on promoting deregulation. The resulting nexus of professional economists and supportive institutions became the Chicago School of Economics.

Friedman aligned himself with Adam Smith and became widely recognized as his greatest disciple. This association changed Smith more than it did Friedman. Smith came to be viewed as the father of *liberalism*, although the term in the contemporary sense was unknown to him. The widely held misrepresentation of Smith's doctrine was that individuals should pursue their own interests without regard for the welfare of others and that markets should operate without encouragement or interference from government.

Friedman appeared on the Phil Donahue show to defend free-market capitalism, but he denied its shortcomings and any positive role the government might play in economic affairs. These were hyperbolic statements concerning public policy, but the implications for those seeking to rationalize destructive behavior were unfortunate. He was dismissive of the harmful and destructive nature of greed and the importance of ethical behavior. Friedman intimated that greed is the fuel of capitalism and gave it respectability. It enabled one successful businessman applying for the position of lecturer in the marketing department to tell me with apparent pride that his business philosophy was "greed is good".

One need only accept what Friedman wrote in *Capitalism and Freedom* to refute the implausible idea that greed is good. The creed of greed cannot be traced to Smith's works. In fact, he devoted considerable effort to refuting the contention that greed is good, and he would certainly have been horrified to read the attributions made to him that are found in the first section of Chap. 4.

Two points need to be emphasized here. First, a social science discipline, even one based upon mathematics and statistics, cannot be a positive or value free social science if the research outcomes it produces support consistently a particular political philosophy — whether it be from the left or the right. Second, Friedman remarked that free-market capitalism works only to the extent that a sufficient number of participants play by the rules without questioning them. To the degree that they cannot be trusted, then, it is the vital role of the government to maintain law and order. Otherwise, there will be anarchy. Government regulation may be crude and heavy handed but it can be critical because, as Adam Smith wrote, entering a society in which individuals are out to harm others is like entering a den of lions. Thus, promoting radical individualism and *laissez faire* government simultaneously undermines free-market capitalism.

Adam Smith never used the term *laissez faire* and students in my seminar on the life and works of Smith have struggled with pigeonholing him into our modern categories of liberal, conservative, and libertarian. Rightfully so, because some of the policies he recommended will never be incorporated into the Democratic, Republican, or Libertarian parties' platforms. He supported existing policies and proposed new ones that included: providing universal education for children, supporting the state church, capping interest rates, utilizing progressive taxation, subsidizing fishing and imposing wage supports for the common laborer, and requiring Catholics to pay double the taxes paid by Protestants.

Chapter 9

Would Smith Agree with the Twin Pillars?

George Stigler wrote in his memoirs that Jacob Viner, a Chicago economics professor of an earlier generation, told him "that the average modern reference to classical economics is so vulgarly ignorant as not to deserve notice, let alone refutation".[405] The preceding chapters should make clear modern errors concerning Adam Smith have been harmful and deserve both notice and refutation.

Any accurate depiction of Adam Smith's views concerning commerce and the role of government must place them in the context of his four-part course covering natural religion, ethics, public policy, and jurisprudence. *Theory of Moral Sentiments*, representing the first two sections of his course, was foundational to Smith's public policy views expressed in *Wealth of Nations*. A fair reading of Smith's published works and the student notes on jurisprudence reveal arguments against the twin pillars of free-market capitalism that are stronger and more pervasive than those in favor of it.

Invisible Hand Not About Selfishness or Greed

The term *invisible hand* appears only once, several hundred pages into *Wealth of Nations*. It is false to declare, as many have, that selfishness or greediness in the marketplace is commonplace and desirable because the invisible hand will compensate for any damage caused. Nowhere in *Wealth of Nations* did Smith praise selfishness or greed. Nor did he justify selfishness and greediness because they result in good economic outcomes. The word *greed* appears only once in *Wealth of Nations*, in reference to the dietary habits of hogs.[406] Smith used *avarice*, his preferred synonym for *greed*, six times in describing heads of state, landowners, grain merchants, and the rich.[407] He described the destructive nature of avarice in all these cases. When commenting on landowners, he proclaimed: "[A] varice and injustice are always short-sighted".[408] Smith did not equate *self-interest* with *selfishness*, and described *selfishness* as *self-interest* "vulgarly understood".[409]

Adam Smith also used the term *invisible hand* once in *Moral Sentiments* to describe the behavior of the rich. Here he developed the term's meaning while devoting two full chapters to repudiating the idea that greed is good. While *Wealth of Nations* offers no evidence supporting the idea that Smith believed selfishness or greediness is good, *Moral Sentiments* makes clear he rejected this idea.

Adam Smith's invisible hand was a metaphorical reference to the deistic God of the 18th century Enlightenment. He believed we are designed by God to care for others, as we care for ourselves, in the marketplace and elsewhere, but modern scholars have ignored the religious foundations of Smith's economics.[410] Their inclusion here is done so readers are able to see his full system and to understand **why** he believed in free markets.

Contemporary scholars often ignore beliefs integral to historical works that clash with their own. Sir Isaac Newton , a purported founder of the godless, materialistic, and deterministic view of modern science,[410] wrote in *Principia*: "The most elegant system of the sun, planets, and comets could not have arisen without the design and dominion of an intelligent and powerful being.... And because of his dominion he is called Lord God...".[411] Philosopher Susan Neiman noted that Newton "... viewed his work as testimony to the glory of God, and no eighteenth-century admirer would have disagreed".[412] Adam Smith was one of these advisors and his views were similar and he attempted to be the Newton of moral philosophy.

The Invisible Hand of God

Smith wrote in *Moral Sentiments* that God designed the great machine of the universe to give us happiness and to ensure our species' continuation.[413] Each of us plays a small, positive role in God's great plan when our consciences dictate our behavior. We declare ourselves God's enemies when we interfere with this plan by acting unethically.[414] These statements indicate Smith believed that malicious greed (greed harming others) was vicious, not virtuous.

The invisible hand metaphor in Smith's theory is not about selfishness or greediness. Rather, it is about our inability to understand the small parts we play in God's great plans. We should focus on our own modest roles that have consequences we could never anticipate but that are nevertheless part of God's great plan. This is not a deterministic view of the world because individuals choose whether to advance or impede this plan.

Unintended consequences

Smith compared the design of the universe to that of a watch in which each part serves its narrow purpose in contributing to the greater purpose of keeping time. The watch's mainspring could not perform its narrow function more effectively if it could somehow understand its ultimate purpose. Concern for the ultimate purpose rests with the watchmaker. Likewise, we would never suggest our vital organs are aware of their vital role in keeping us alive.[415]

Human beings, mainsprings, vital organs, and everything else have been designed by God to perform their specific functions. He alone is responsible for operating the universe and for ensuring the happiness of humankind, according to Smith. Our responsibilities and abilities are infinitely smaller. Our duty is to look after our own happiness and that of our family, friends, and country.[416] Only human beings in all creation are rational, but we are no better at comprehending the great and unintended consequences of our behavior than a mainspring or a vital organ.

Unintended consequences play a profound role in Smith's view of things. The single appearance of the invisible hand metaphor in *Moral Sentiments* is where Smith observes the "selfishness and rapacity" of the wealthy and the great who spend money extravagantly on palaces when the poor might have benefited from their generosity. However, the poor are paid to build these palaces and produce their contents, thus the rich:

> are led by an invisible hand to make nearly the same distribution of the necessities of life, which would have been made, had the earth been divided into equal portions among all its inhabitants, and thus without intending it, without knowing it, advance the interest of the society, and affords means to the multiplication of the species.[417]

The editors of *Moral Sentiments* noted that "… Smith writes disparagingly of the 'natural selfishness and rapacity' of the rich, but this does not mean that he regards all self–interested action as bad in itself. It can have beneficial unintended consequences".[418]

Not all unintended consequences discussed in *Wealth of Nations*, however, were positive. The feudal estate, essentially a military organization without military purpose, had by the 18th century morphed into a commercial enterprise. The once great feudal lords had become landlords and the vassals their tenants. Kinship, loyalty, and mutual protection were replaced by money as the tie binding rural society. The landlords hired others to manage their estates while they lived in London engaging in the brutal combat of high fashion. The tenants had beaten their broadswords into plowshares, their spears into pruning hooks, and manly virtue declined in Scotland.

> To gratify the most childish vanity was the sole motive of the great land-owners who began extracting cash rents from tenants to pay for their luxuries [Smith complained]. The merchants and craftsmen, much less ridiculous, acted merely from a view to their own interest and in pursuit of their own peddler principle of turning a penny wherever a penny was to be got. Neither of them had either knowledge or foresight of that great revolution which the folly of the one, and the industry of the other, was gradually bringing about.[419]

Smith identified three unintended consequences of this shift to a market economy. The first was the improvement of the agricultural sector that Smith considered to be the primary contributor to the increasing wealth of

Britain. This agricultural transformation, however, resulted in the gradual decay of "...the martial spirit of the great body of the people ...".[420] The second was the decline in the number of citizens able to serve in the armed forces resulting in smaller militias and necessitating a larger standing army. Thirdly, Smith spoke contemptuously of the deformity of cowardly citizens no longer capable of defending themselves in war or maintaining their reputations in peace. Smith might have explained this last unintended consequence by implying that even God had to make tradeoffs and he valued prosperity more than a martial citizenry.

Notice the variety of motives found in these examples: The domestic investor was prudent, the rich and great were selfish and rapacious, the poor worked to eat, the landowners were vain, and the merchants and craftspeople were industrious. Buyers and sellers in these examples entered into transactions voluntarily and considered themselves to be better off for having done so. They were unaware they were improving the domestic economy, redistributing wealth, and improving agricultural productivity. In criticizing mercantilist policies, Smith made a telling remark about the relationship between buyers and sellers: "Commerce, which ought naturally to be, among nations, as among individuals, a bond of union and friendship, has become the most fertile source of discord and animosity".[421] (Unfortunately, these bonds were not always apparent during the first decade of the 20th century.)

These examples do not point to selfishness and greed. Adam Smith never denies the existence of selfishness and greediness. *Wealth of Nations* is full of examples of such motives, but he considered them as rust and debris obstructing the great machine of commerce.[422] Smith believed human beings must be guided by their moral principles for the machine to work smoothly.

What motivates butchers, brewers, and bakers

One of the most famous and widely misinterpreted quotes from *Wealth of Nations* is as follows:

> It is not from the benevolence of the butcher, the brewer, or the baker, that we expect our dinner, but from their regard to their own interest. We

address ourselves, not to their humanity but to their self–love, and never talk to them of our own necessities but of their advantages. Nobody but a beggar chooses to depend chiefly upon the benevolence of his fellow–citizens.[423]

The *Oxford English Dictionary* identifies two meanings of *self-love*.The first is "… regard for one's interests or well-being; chiefly with definitely opprobrious [shameful] implication, self centeredness, selfishness". The second is: "Regard for one's own well-being or happiness, considered as a natural and proper relation of a man to himself". The modern equivalents of these usages might be *narcissism* and *self-esteem* respectively.

Smith also saw self-love from these two points of view. Smith declares in *Moral Sentiments* that "self-love may frequently be a virtuous motive of action".[424] On the other hand, he observes in *Wealth of Nations*: "It is the interest of every man to live as much at his ease as he can … [and to neglect] some very laborious duty … at least as interest is vulgarly understood…".[425] Smith praised self-love in the first sense and criticized it in the second.

Such usage of self-love was not uncommon. Alexander Pope, the British poet, published *An Essay on Man* in 1734 in which he declares:

So two consistent motions act the Soul;

And one regards Itself, and one the Soul;

Thus God and Nature link'd the gen'ral frame,

And bade Self-love and Social be the same.[426]

Smith was certainly aware of these verses. He owned a 7-volume set of Pope's work and quoted *An Essay on Man* in one of his own essays.[427]

If Smith had used *prudence* in his famous comment about butchers, brewers and bakers, instead of *self-love*, the history of economics might have been very different. *Prudence*, the term I have chosen as the proper synonym for *self-love* is the theoretical linchpin connecting *Moral Sentiments* and *Wealth of Nations*. Smith states in *Wealth of Nations* that we each work to utilize our own capital most effectively. We seek our own benefit rather than that of society, but our success in utilizing our talents and resources also benefits society.[428] Although some spend more than they own, we can assume most do not. Not everyone acts prudently, but almost everyone does.[429] Here Smith offered a more complex, nuanced and benign version of what has become known as "economic man".

For Smith self-love was only one motivation for engaging in commerce. He provided a second: "we desire wealth because of the admiration we receive from others. We spend extravagantly because of vanity rather than because of the pleasure we enjoy from the objects we acquire".[430] According to Smith, there is a dark side to an inordinate concern with one's place in society. The great source of human misery arises from over-rating the difference between one position in life and another.

Avarice exaggerates the benefits of wealth over poverty. Ambition exaggerates the benefits of a public life over a private one. Vanity over-rates the benefits of popularity over obscurity. Those controlled by these emotions tend to be miserable and often harm society in their efforts to acquire what they do not possess.[431] Smith stated that the vices of greed, ambition, and vanity often harm society and the individuals possessing them:

> Examine history and search your memory to recall the great misfortunes of public or private life and you will discover that most human tragedies occurred because the fallen were not satisfied when they were well off. Their lives would have ended more happily had they been content with their situations. The inscription on the tombstone of the man who tried to improve good health by taking medicine — "I was well, I wished to be better; here I am" — may generally be applied with great justness to the distress of disappointed greed and ambition.[432]

Wealth of Nations offers the "trucking [or trading] disposition" of human beings as a third explanation for the human tendency to engage in business. Smith observed that individuals trade the surplus goods they produce, and this has resulted in the unintended consequence of bringing about the division of labor and increased productivity. This trucking disposition could be a human trait or the result of reason and speech, but it is common to all human beings and does not exist in animals.[433]

Finally, Smith identified the strong and almost universal desire among human beings to "better our condition". Although the "passion for present enjoyment" may be violent and difficult to restrain, "... the principle of frugality seems not only to predominate, but to predominate very greatly". This is the desire to better our condition and it "... comes with us from the womb, and never leaves us till we go into the grave".[434] For example, the common laborer, when able to live above the subsistence level, exerts his strength to the utmost level with the "... comfortable hope of bettering his condition, and of ending his days perhaps in ease and plenty...".[435]

Thus, prudence, vanity, the trucking disposition, and the desire of most everyone to better conditions are activated when feudal and mercantilist restraints on human liberty are removed. The invisible hand of God orchestrates the dual nature of self-love for the common good. Business becomes what philosopher Charles Griswold calls the process through which you give me what I want and I give you what you want in an economic world organized on the basis of "mutual sympathy".[436]

Smith would reject the concept of economic man

The roots of the concept of radical individualism and the belief that private vices are transformed into public virtue can be traced to Thomas Hobbes in the first case and to Bernard Mandeville in the second. Clearly, however, these views of human nature and economic man reached the 20th century despite Adam Smith's efforts rather than because of them. These efforts reside in two chapters of *Moral Sentiments*.

Smith disassociated himself from Hobbes and his followers in a chapter entitled "Of those systems which deduce the Principle of Approbation [seeking approval] from Self-love". He stated that Hobbes believed that "... man is driven to take refuge in society, not by any natural love which he bears to his own kind, but because without the assistance of others he is incapable of subsisting with ease or safety".[437] Smith claimed, instead, it is the God-given attachment human beings feel for each other that is the basis upon which society was formed.

Smith rejected the idea that society was established through an informal social contract among warring parties who agreed to stop fighting. Instead, he believed society arose out of the sympathetic feelings shared naturally among individuals. He illustrated sympathetic feelings by saying he would enter into the grief of a parent who had lost a child rather than imagine how he would feel if he had lost a child. He concluded by saying that this system "... which deduces all sentiments from self-love ..." fails to realize that sympathy is not "... in the least selfish". Greedy and amoral individuals, the embodiment of economic man, do not contribute to a harmonious society.

In the second chapter entitled "Of licentious Systems", Smith rejected Bernard Mandeville's assertion that all good deeds are motivated by vanity, and are thus vicious. Mandeville's overly broad definition of vice includes those acts which have good outcomes but which are motivated by self-satisfaction or pride. Smith disagrees, arguing that self-love may frequently be a virtuous motive of action, declaring that the love of virtue is "... the noblest and best passion in human nature".[438] To discourage what Mandeville called vice "... would be pernicious to society, by putting an end to all industry and commerce, and in a manner to the whole business of human life".[439]

Moral animals

If there is a paragraph capturing the meaning of *Wealth of Nations*, it is this:

> In the midst of all the exactions of government, this [nation's] capital has been silently and gradually accumulated by the private frugality and good conduct of individuals, by their universal, continual, and uninterrupted effort to better their own condition. It is this effort, protected by law and allowed by liberty to exert itself in the manner that is most advantageous, which has maintained the progress of England towards opulence and improvement in almost all former times, and which, it is to be hoped, will do so in all future times.[440]

If Smith believed God had designed the universe and all its parts to work in concert and bring about human happiness, what design characteristics did God give human beings for this purpose? He devoted much of *Moral Sentiments* to answering this vital question.

Just as God implanted our physical appetites and our sense of pleasure and pain to encourage us to take care of ourselves. Smith said he also implanted in us the emotion of sympathy so we are born caring about others and what they think of us. After all, we are helpless and could not survive without the cooperation and support of others.

Smith believed that from birth we learn the difference between right and wrong by watching how others behave and are treated in response. Through socialization, as the process is called today, we acquire a number of human virtues — qualities of moral excellence. "Our reverence for morality is part of our nature and confirmed by our reason and philosophy. The important moral rules and commands are laws of God who ultimately rewards the obedient and punishes the disobedient".[441] The four virtues identified by Smith as vital to a happy and prosperous society are prudence, justice, benevolence, and self-command.

The religious doctrine Smith learned as a child was that human beings are inherently selfish and disobedient because of original sin. Smith's innovation was in proposing that prudence — looking after one's self is a virtue. Looking both ways before we cross the street, going to work or school when we don't feel like it, and brushing our teeth are prudent behaviors, not selfish or greedy ones. No one would ever claim looking both ways or brushing one's teeth are selfish or greedy acts.

Justice is the virtue of acting fairly and causing no harm to those around us. In today's terminology it is a negative virtue; we are virtuous when we refrain from causing harm to others. Thus, justice is the virtue that keeps us from being selfish or greedy. Smith stated that society does not leave this virtue to our discretion, and it may be imposed upon us by force.[442] If one person defrauds another of £10, the injured party can reclaim the money through legal action. Smith wrote:

> Hurting our neighbor cannot be justified. There is no reason to do evil to another person that can be justified in the eyes of others except in retaliation for an evil action taken against us. No impartial spectator can approve of a person's actions that cause unhappiness to someone else only because it brings happiness to himself, nor should he take something of value from someone else because it is of equal or greater value to himself. We must view our actions as they appear to others rather than as we tend to view them ourselves.[443]

Where injustice is commonplace, we must deal with the unscrupulous as if we had entered a den of lions.[444] Thus, according to Smith, capital punishment may be appropriate if it removes the unjust individuals from society and terrifies others by their example.[445]

Benevolence is a positive virtue, so we are virtuous when we are generous. Smith wrote that wise and virtuous men always sacrifice their own interests to those of the greater society.[446] He linked personal virtues with civic virtues. Nonetheless, he declared a society would be less pleasant but would not collapse if love and affection did not motivate its members to help one another. No harm is done when merchants engage in mutually beneficial transactions without love or affection as long as they are just.[447] However, Smith believed that while a just society can survive, one that is also benevolent would thrive.

Smith noted that from birth we naturally desire to please others and to avoid displeasing them.[448] It is pleasing for us to see signs of happiness and prosperity around us. We are disturbed by a dysfunctional society because our own happiness and prosperity is tied to those of society. We condemn those things that destroy society and are willing to go to any length to stop them.

The virtue of self-command or self-control moderates the other virtues. Without it, the virtue of thrift taken to its extremes becomes the vice of either miserliness or extravagance. Likewise, prudence in excess becomes selfishness.

Smith contended society cannot survive if its members are always willing to harm one another. When selfishness and greed dominate, all social ties are broken, society is fractured, and its parts are scattered. Even criminal gangs must refrain from robbing and murdering their members. Sympathy for others, however, leads us to understand the importance of morality, which in turn leads to prudence, benevolence, justice, and self-command. To use Smith's metaphor, benevolence is the building's ornament. Justice is its foundation. Society will "crumble into atoms" when justice disappears.[449]

Adam Smith's Philosophy was Not Laissez–Faire

"Let events go ahead and happen as they might" (*laissez-faire, laissez passer*) is a phrase attributed to a merchant responding to a question about the proper role of the French king in dealing with business and trade.[450] The term *laissez-faire* became widely used in the 18th century, and Smith likely heard it during his lengthy visit to France. He never used the term, but some claim incorrectly that his invisible hand metaphor indicates Smith's endorsement of the laissez-faire position.

The term *laissez-faire* has two potentially contradictory interpretations. First, the merchant might have been arguing for the status quo, declaring that things, including existing regulations, should be left as they are. Clearly Smith did not take this position; he was a reformer promoting the elimination of feudal and mercantilist policies. The second and much more popular interpretation is that the merchant was asking that business not be regulated. Because *Wealth of Nations* is largely an attack on existing regulations, it is commonly assumed that Smith supported the second version of laissez-faire.

Using distinctions made by Ludwig von Mises, the first interpretation of the statement would be one supported by conservatives, and the second by 20th century libertarians but not by 19th century liberals.[451]

Smith's views were often more nuanced than his quotable rhetorical statements have led readers to believe and he did not oppose government regulation. For example, he compared the requirement of firewalls between adjoined buildings to the banking regulations he supported. He admitted that restrictions on bankers are necessarily "… a manifest violation of that natural liberty which it is the proper business of law, not to infringe, but to support".[452] But in the following sentences he stated that the exercise "… of the natural liberty of a few individuals, which might endanger the security of the whole society, are, and ought to be, restrained by the laws of all governments…". Smith's friend David Hume and the jokester of the two might have quipped "Smith giveth and Smith taketh away".

Smith believed in free markets. However, his faith in the invisible hand was qualified, as he also believed in what we refer to as *public goods*. His trust was further qualified by his recognition of what we call *market failures* — instances where the invisible hand needs help in remedying socially undesirable market outcomes.

Free markets

Smith wrote that a system of natural liberty will reestablish things as God intended them if all governmental efforts to encourage or restrain individuals are removed.[453] Everyone, he declared, should be completely free to employ his or her efforts and capital in competition with everyone else, as long as they behave justly and obey the law. Thus, heads of state should not be so deluded as to believe they can direct the efforts of private individuals more effectively than individuals can direct themselves.

Smith's inclination toward dramatic over-statement may have been intended to keep readers awake. It would have been better had he written that a system of natural liberty will establish itself when government efforts to encourage or restrain individuals are *minimal*. This revised statement is more consistent with his other statements. Later in the same lengthy paragraph, he identified three functions appropriate for the state: to provide for the nation's defense, to maintain a system of law enforcement, and to establish public works and institutions that cannot be provided by individuals but are of great value to society.

Infrastructure and institutions

Smith wrote extensively about the need for armed forces and considered the relative merits of a militia versus a standing army. He recognized the considerable expenses associated with national defense and recommended these expenses be covered by taxes. While he did not acknowledge it explicitly, Smith enlarged the scope of this function to include the protection of Britain's global business interests.

Smith emphasized the importance of a justice system to the proper functioning of society. He discussed many British laws, especially in *Lectures on Jurisprudence*, but wrote very little about the organization of the justice system or crime prevention. During the 18th century, law and order were maintained by an evolving patchwork of state, church, feudal, and urban jurisdictions. Smith believed the state's justice system should be supported through usage fees and general revenues.

The primary purpose of *Wealth of Nations* was to attack mercantilist policies and the remnants of medieval institutions and laws. However, a close examination of it and his *Lectures on Jurisprudence* reveals that Smith's view of the proper role of government was quite expansive; he argued that as societies improve and become increasingly complex, "… the number of their laws and regulations necessary to maintain justice, and prevent infringements of the right of property…" increases.[454]

Smith recommended public works and institutions to support commerce and to educate the nation's youth and its citizens of all ages; he also supported public expenditures to support the dignity of the king. He identified the construction of public works such as roads, bridges, canals, and harbors as examples of infrastructure supporting commerce. He declared public works deserved public funding, but noted they may generate their own revenue. Highways, bridges, and canals were supported with tolls, and duties on the tonnage of shipping provided revenues to maintain harbors. These charges are ultimately borne by consumers, but are more than offset by the reduction in distribution costs enabled by improvements in infrastructure. Additionally, Smith considered minting coins from the bullion of private citizens and delivering the mail as important government functions. In many countries, he observed, the fees charged for these services produced surpluses contributing to the state's general revenue.[455]

Smith recommended tolls and other fees be charged to maintain public works,[456] and observed that public services were performed most effectively when the public servant's rewards were based on performance.[457] Smith commented "that tolls for the maintenance of a high road, cannot with any safety be the property of private persons",[458] but he also questioned the diligence of public officials assigned to oversee the use of these revenues. Thus he proposed courts of "inspection and account" be established to supervise the use of toll revenues.

Smith complained that paying for road repairs with taxes on vehicles proportional only to their weight was biased in favor of the rich because tolls are "chiefly supplied at the expense of the poor, not of the rich; at the expense of those who are least able to supply it, not those who are most able".[459] His concern for the poor is revealed more fully later in this discussion.

Smith did not discuss the use of private lands for purposes of public infrastructure. He condemned *purveyance* — the ability of the crown to appropriate private lands.[460] However, most pathways, roads, river crossings, and waterways had probably been used by the public since ancient times and were recognized in common law as *public rights of way.*[461] It appears Smith supported the state's role in providing infrastructure for public rights of way and requiring users to pay for their maintenance.

A second category of public goods consists of institutions to educate all children and adults. Smith proclaimed that educational institutions, like public works supporting commerce, justify public support, and generate sufficient revenues to cover their expenses.[462] Schools for the education of children and churches for the edification of adults were operated and funded by taxes imposed at the local or parish level in 18th-century Britain. Customarily, students paid a fee or honorarium to their teachers (Smith received them), but many university professors were supported principally by income from private endowments (a practice he criticized). Smith justified education as a public good; "some attention of government is necessary in order to prevent the almost entire corruption and degeneracy of the great body of the people".[463]

While public schools and universities were for the young, religious instruction should be provided, in Smith's view, for people of all ages. The object of this instruction was "not so much to render the people good citizens of this world, as to prepare them for another and better world in the life to come".[464] The Crown was head of the Church of England, while the Church of Scotland was state sponsored. The local or parish churches were funded through taxes and the income from private endowments.

Although Smith recognized the importance of religious instruction, he objected to the doctrinal monopolies of established churches. Competition among religious sects might "reduce the doctrine of the greater part of them to that true and natural religion".[465]

Smith observed the divergent interests of church and state. He proclaimed the revenue of every established church, excluding revenue associated with particular lands or manors, should be included in the general revenue of the state. His rationale was that land taxes — tithes — collected by the church, for example, reduced landowners' contributions to the defense of the state.

Smith declared that the state might support two remedies to offset the "… unsocial or disagreeably rigorous … morals of all the little sects into which the country was divided".[466] The first remedy was to make the study of science and philosophy a prerequisite to the practice of liberal professions and candidacy for any "honourable office of trust or profit". The second remedy was to allow "entire liberty" to those who without "scandal or indecency" entertain the people with painting, poetry, music, and dancing. The Church of Scotland considered these activities frivolous and prohibited them.

Smith rejected the theology of 18th-century Presbyterianism to which he was born, but he may not have rejected all prejudice then associated with it. He believed the private acts promoting Catholicism should no longer be treated as treasonous, but "it might be reasonable to discourage it by imposing double taxes or such like penalties... on any one as silly as to prefer the Roman Catholic to the Protestant religion".[467] This statement, found in student notes from Smith's jurisprudence lectures, may have been one of his rare jokes.

Finally, Smith believed in maintaining the Crown's, or chief magistrate's, dignity. London — with the wealth and splendor of the court and Parliament, its imposing government buildings and public spaces, and martial public events — spoke loudly of Britain's power and authority. Ambassadors and ministers were agents of the Crown, requiring financial support proportional to their high station. "Lands, for the purposes of pleasure and magnificence, parks, gardens, public walks", with significant maintenance costs and no offsetting revenue, should belong to the Crown, according to Smith.[468]

The Invisible Hand Needs a Hand

Those on the political right, especially individuals taking the *laissez-faire* position, tend to minimize the importance of instances where markets fail to solve important social problems and thus require intervention. These *market failures* take the form of *externalities*, or the side effects of economic activity, as when mining pollutes the ground water. They also exist when markets do not arise to provide adequately a vital product or service. For example, pharmaceutical companies may not find it cost-effective to develop a drug treating a tropical disease afflicting primarily the poor.

Smith never used the term *market failure* and may not have conceived of the concept clearly, but there are a number of instances where he indicated government intervention was needed, either to aid the poor or stabilize otherwise competitive markets. Smith demonstrated his concern for the poor in several ways. Most banknotes were in large denominations and were intended for exchanges between businesses, while consumers made purchases with coins. King George III prohibited in 1765 the issuance of notes valued at less than £1. When banknotes in small denominations were allowed, the poor set up what Smith called "beggarly banks" that would often fail, leaving the poor with worthless notes.[469]

Modern conservatives have criticized several of Smith's policy recommendations. One was his suggestion of the need for a minimum wage when hardship is brought about because of the decline in demand for labor or because of the decline in the purchasing power of silver coins.[470] Smith noted that the supply of labor in any field responds to what we call now the laws of supply and demand. When the demand for workers in a high-paying field declines, some of them are forced to take lower-paying jobs. When the demand for manual laborers declines, however, the number of lower-paying jobs is insufficient and some individuals are unable to support themselves or their families. Smith proposed a minimum wage for inferior servants under these circumstances. Additionally, if the purchasing power of silver declines, the wages of manual laborers are insufficient to pay for their necessities. When this happens, their pay should be increased sufficiently to allow them to purchase their necessities. Smith did not discuss how this program might be administered or by whom.

Elsewhere, he argued that if a heavy tax is placed on grain, the wages of the laboring poor should be augmented to enable them to educate and bring up their children so as to ensure population growth. On the other hand, Smith realized this augmentation would restrict the number who could be hired and thus slow the nation's economic growth. The debate over this trade-off remains heated today.

Smith supported the controversial idea of progressive taxation. He noted the poor had difficulty obtaining food and that they spent most of their income getting it. Most of the expenses of the rich, in contrast, are to obtain a splendid house with the "luxuries and vanities" to fill it. A tax on houses would seem appropriate; it "… is not very unreasonable that the rich should contribute to the public expense, not only in proportion to their revenue, but something more than in that proportion".[471] This progressive tax is consistent with Smith's general principle that subjects should contribute to the state in proportion to "the revenue which they respectively enjoy under the protection of the state".[472]

Smith also argued that a subsidy of herring fishing "might contribute a good deal to the relief of a great number of our fellow-subjects, whose circumstances are by no means affluent".[473]

Smith condoned maintaining reserve limits for banks.[474] He also agreed with limiting the amount of copper and silver in coins to prevent them from being melted down and sold as metal.[475] He did not object to the law requiring that coins minted by the Crown be accepted in financial transactions.[476] Also, he supported legislation to prevent the manipulation of stock prices.[477] Another of his most controversial views was that the government should cap interest rates.[478]

Smith's recommendations reached the point of micromanagement in one instance. He noted that some landlords were so conceited in their own knowledge of farming that they required tenants to engage in specific, often ill-advised, methods of cultivation. He recommended that higher taxes be imposed to discourage these practices.[479]

Maintaining an empire

Mercantilist policies resulted in a heavy-handed attempt to dominate international trade and necessitated a strong army and navy. Monopolizing international trade meant colonization, and the British army was needed to protect private commercial interests from the hostile actions of other European nations and from native states and populations. The navy was necessary to ensure privately owned British ships could sail the world without interference, and to deploy British troops on foreign shores. In fact, governmental and private interests were confused, both in Parliament and in British colonies. The line in the 18th-century anthem "Rule Britannia! Britannia rule the waves" might have been "Rule Britannia! Britannia rules international commerce".

Smith was highly critical of both English colonial policies and colonial administrations, but he was not critical of the existence of British colonies. Desperate American colonies issued paper money as legal tender that could not be redeemed for gold or silver for several years and did not pay dividends like bonds. These notes were discounted substantially in trade and their real value declined considerably over time. Debtors gained unfairly at the expense of creditors — often the British — when this currency was used. Smith approved of an act of Parliament forbidding its use. He would certainly be astonished to find that modern nations back their paper money with their questionable reputations rather than with gold. We can only speculate about whether he would agree with some on the right who believe the world should return to the gold standard.

Smith's colonial policy recommendations were both negative and positive in nature. On the negative side, he wrote "The act of navigation, therefore, very properly endeavours to give sailors and shipping of Great Britain the monopoly of the trade of their own country, in some cases, by absolute prohibitions, and in others by heavy burdens upon the shipping of foreign countries".[480] The American colonists were not so dismissive of the navigation acts, and the Boston Tea Party was not held to celebrate them. Smith also noted that the British prohibited the production of steel and iron bars in the American colonies.[481]

On the other hand, some of the colonial policies were beneficial to colonial interests. Smith indicated that the extension of fisheries to the American colonies increased the shipping and naval power of Great Britain.[482] He recommended, additionally, the state's maintenance of forts, garrisons, fortified counting houses, and storehouses in the colonies.[483]

Smith encouraged international trade, reasoning that just as individuals should specialize and exchange their surpluses for mutual advantage, so should nations. He preferred free trade, but approved of certain trade agreements. He supported trade restrictions in retaliation to those imposed by foreign nations. And he recognized that granting temporary monopolies to international trading companies enabled them to offset the great expense and risk they faced.

*   *

No one can argue that interest rate caps, minimum wages, progressive taxes, and the use of military forces to protect private commercial interests around the world reflect the laissez-faire philosophy. Nor are *laissez-faire* views consistent with providing state-funded schools or a state-sponsored church to ensure a pious and civic-minded citizenry.

The lesson for those who declare something is true or good because Adam Smith said so should be wary of what other ideas will fall under his mantle of authority. Part of what Smith wrote was either incorrect or ill considered, and arguments will continue concerning what truths comprise the remaining part.

*   *

Economics is a highly diverse discipline and I have used the works of numerous economists to support my criticism of mainstream economics. Robert H. Frank has written several books that have been helpful and my favorite is *Passions within Reason: The Strategic Role of Emotions*.[484] Jerry Evensky's *Adam Smith's Moral Philosophy: A Historical and Contemporary Perspective on Markets, Law, Ethics and Culture* is also excellent.[485]

A third such author is Amartya Sen (Nobel Memorial Prize 1998), who received recognition for work in welfare economics. In *The Idea of Justice* (1988), *On Ethics and Economics* (2009), and other writings, Sen displays a deep understanding of the works of Adam Smith and cites *Moral Sentiments, Wealth of Nations*, and *Lectures on Jurisprudence*.[486] While Smith's theory of justice concerned personal morality, Sen has expanded Smith's theory to include an array of human rights far broader than those considered by the Enlightenment thinkers of Smith's time, including the rights of the ill, the handicapped, and the uneducated. Injustice, as Smith discussed it, is remediated through the judicial system, while injustice discussed by Sen is addressed principally by the legislature.

Sen laments that "the assumption of the completely egotistic human being has come to dominate much of mainstream economic theory…" and that it has been adopted in the fields of politics and law.[487] He recognizes the "breathtakingly narrow reading" of Adam Smith's writings in which

Smith has often been "... wrongly thought to be a proponent of the assumption of the exclusive pursuit of self-interest in the form of the so-called 'economic man'".[488] Sen argues: "While some men are born small and some achieve smallness, it is clear that Adam Smith has had much smallness thrust upon him".[489] He argues that the venal conception of economic man is too narrow and offers considerable evidence in support of his views, including the work of economist Robert Frank.

Frank has dedicated much of his career to correcting the deformed view of economic man and to its negative impact on our society. In *Passion within Reason*, he wrote:

> ... our beliefs about human nature help shape human nature itself. What we think about ourselves and our possibilities determines what we aspire to become; and it shapes what we teach our children at home and in the schools. Here the pernicious effects of the self-interest theory have been more disturbing. It tells us to behave morally is to invite others to take advantage of us. By encouraging us to expect the worst in others, it brings out the worst in us: dreading the role of chump, we are often loath to heed our nobler instincts.[490]

Chapter 10

What are Alternative Views
in Economics?

The economics discipline is broad, diverse, and dynamic, and many of its premises, theories, and findings are inconsistent. Research within the mainstream and its growing eddies has enabled me to see the shortcomings of mainstream economics. Four examples follow. First, I discuss the use of games as a metaphor for commerce, employed by both Adam Smith and Milton Friedman. Second, Friedman's concept of the natural history of government regulation reveals the importance of trust to the success of free markets. Third, the disagreement concerning whether the most essential trait of free market capitalism is competition or cooperation is considered. Finally, I argue that monopolistic competition is far superior to perfect competition as the primary theoretical foundation of business school curricula.

The Sport of Business

It was raining heavily and our East Lansing High School PE teacher had to come up with something for us to do indoors. He was brand new with lots of good ideas, but one of them was not what he called "marine basketball". After we had gathered in the gym, he introduced us to this interesting sport. About 50 of us were divided into two groups and given a ball. He said that the game had only one rule: If your team gets the ball in the hoop, you score a point. He blew the whistle, watched us with growing horror, and blew the whistle again almost immediately. I had no idea where the ball was, but I had a friend from the other team in a headlock. Fortunately, only feelings were hurt and our teacher survived to spend his career there at ELHS, but no one ever got to play marine basketball again.

Sport as a metaphor for business is commonplace. In *Moral Sentiments*, Adam Smith wrote: "In the race for wealth, and honors, and preferments, he may run as hard as he can, and strain every nerve and every muscle, in order to outstrip all his competitors. But if he should jostle, or throw down any of them, the indulgence of the spectators is entirely at an end. It is a violation of fair play, which they cannot admit of".[491] In *Capitalism and Freedom*, Friedman observes that within a legal framework, the day-to-day activities of business are like a game: Players accept the rules and there is an umpire to interpret and enforce them.[492] Neither Smith nor Friedman claimed that points scored or rewards received should be shared equally among the contestants. Rather, their intent was to illustrate that games, like free markets, must have rules and those rules must be followed.

While it is dangerous to push a metaphor too far, it is worthwhile to consider this one further. Its usefulness depends in part upon the sport used in the comparison. Obviously, business is not like boxing, where the goal is to reduce the opponent to unconsciousness. Professional golf is the best metaphor for my purposes. Golfers are fiercely competitive and the stakes are high, but they play directly against the course and only indirectly against each other, like two websites competing for the same customers in a life-and-death struggle. The top players at a Professional Golfers' Association (PGA) tournament are usually on different parts of the course at any one time; they can't see each other, and they keep their own scores so the temptations to cheat are great. Officials are noticeable only at major events and even then there may not be enough to watch all the players.[493]

The beauty of the PGA tour is in the sportsmanship shown by players like Brian Davis. He came in second at the Verizon Heritage at Hilton Head Island in 2010. His club brushed a reed during his backswing on the first hole of his playoff with Jim Furyk. He called a two-stroke penalty on himself, although no one else saw this violation of PGA rules and it was virtually impossible to detect it in a video of the event shown later on television. Davis probably didn't pause to calculate the $411,000 he was giving up because of his scrupulous honesty.[494]

Because of self-regulation PGA officials are virtually invisible and it is exceedingly rare for a call to change a tournament's outcome. In this sense professional golf is an ideal metaphor for a free-market economy with *laissez-faire* government.

Now consider basketball, although either football or hockey would do. It is a sport somewhere between boxing, where victory is achieved by injuring the opponent, and golf, where the players have no direct physical contact. In the boring old days of basketball, a defender could try to block the path of an opponent or block the ball, but intentionally touching an opponent was considered a foul. Today hand checks and body checks, as long as they are more discreet than those in hockey, are commonplace. It is the official's job to decide when one player touching another constitutes a foul, and players push the limit to see how closely a particular game is being officiated. There appear to be constraints self-imposed by the players, although it is not uncommon for one who has given in to temper to be restrained by teammates. As a consequence, National Basketball Association (NBA) officials are highly visible and have a significant impact on the outcome of every single game. Professional basketball is a great sport with great moments, but it is not an admirable one in the sense that professional golf is.

Imagine if golf adopted the tactics of professional wrestling. A player in the rough sneaks to improve the lie of his ball or place an opponent's ball behind a tree. A player on the green "talks trash" to break the concentration of another who is about to putt, and the ineffectual official cannot stop it. The players' words become heated. Tempers flare, fighting erupts, and one golfer is taken to the hospital. A drunken fan taunts a player's wife and the player rushes into the gallery swinging his putter. Attendance and television ratings might increase, but most of those who love and respect the sport would likely turn to something else.

Professional as opposed to collegiate wrestling is theater rather than a true sport. Ironically, it is like golf because the wrestlers show brilliantly disguised self-restraint and officials do not determine the match's outcomes. Those big, powerful men can dish out more than they can take, and without restraint the losers would be routinely taken to the hospital. An uncle of mine was a professional wrestler who played the role of bad guy. In the old days, wrestlers sat on stools between rounds like boxers still do and his worst injury occurred when a female fan climbed ringside and hit him in the face with the stool he had been using.

The Natural History of Government Intervention

Milton Friedman blames the destruction of what he considers to be the magnificent period of *laissez-faire* economic policy during the late 19th century on federal regulation reacting to public outcry over the "real or perceived" injustices of those labeled robber barons.[495] Richard Posner, an economist and federal judge who some believe is the most influential legal thinker in the country, is dismissive of the media's "silly" and "ignorant" denunciations of 'Wall Street' for greed and extravagance" in the wake of the subprime bust. "What did reporters think businessmen were like?" he has asked.[496] Are injustices of robber barons of the 19th and 21st centuries, like industrial accidents, one of the prices society must pay to enjoy the fruits of free-market capitalism?

Some may be philosophical about the exploits of Jeff Skilling, Bernie Madoff, Richard Fuld, and others who were brought down by their misdeeds rather than by ineffectual federal regulators or law enforcement officers who arrived too late on the scene. After all, it is argued, the cost of regulating businesses and the resultant expenses imposed upon law-abiding firms far outweigh the victims' losses. Even if this view were true, this interpretation does not tell the whole story for several important reasons.

First, the cost of government regulation and the expenses incurred when businesses comply with them are borne by virtually everyone. In contrast, individual investors in Enron, Madoff Securities, Lehman Brothers, and similar firms experienced devastatingly large losses. Additionally, hundreds of thousands of those at the bottom of the food chain lost their homes after the collapse of the housing market. If Adam Smith is correct that the "first and chief" purpose of government is to preserve justice among members of the state, protecting the rights of some from the violations of others, then these events represent a serious failure of government.[497]

Second, Friedman offers his conception of the "natural history of government intervention" in *Free to Choose*. First, "real or fancied evils" led to public outrage.[498] In response to some perceived injustice, public outrage occurs and the political process takes over, the public is appeased, and the resulting regulation turns out to benefit the special interests involved in its writing. It is hard to imagine a strong counterargument to the reality of Friedman's natural history of government intervention although the validity of the alleged abuses and the responses to them may be disputed. Adam Smith wrote: "What institution of government could tend so much to promote the happiness of mankind as the general prevalence of wisdom and virtue? All government is but an imperfect remedy for the deficiency of these".[499] The presumption is that the greater the deficiency the greater is the remedy needed.

Third, if freedom is treated as a license to harm others then anarchy will likely result in the absence of government intervention. In *Trust: The Social Virtues and the Creation of Prosperity*, political scientist Francis Fukuyama writes, "Law, contract, and economic rationality provide a necessary but not sufficient basis for both the stability and prosperity of postindustrial societies...".[500] When the ability of citizens to trust strangers is added to law, contract, and economic rationality, however, both the necessary and sufficient conditions are met, enabling a society to achieve stability and prosperity.[501] Sociologist Wayne Barker contends that confidence and interpersonal trust are essential to the success of democratic societies and large, complex organizations.[502]

To the extent trust is lost because of past violations, transaction costs are imposed on the parties involved and on society as a whole. When a handshake does not suffice, attorneys, written contracts, and witnesses are required. When a contract will not do, a vigilant civil and criminal justice system become necessary. When the justice system fails, aggrieved parties begin to take matters into their own hands, and society drifts towards anarchy.

As our ability to trust strangers varies, so must the role of government (Fig. 1). Anarchy exists when strangers cannot be trusted and government is ineffectual or nonexistent. Somalia, designated as S, is a good example of an anarchy candidate because it does not have a functional government and disputes are settled with guns. *The Economist* declared it the worst

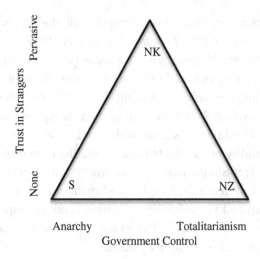

Anarchy   Totalitarianism
Government Control

Figure 1:   Trust and its alternatives.

country on earth in 2009 and Transparency International declared it the most corrupt, using their Corruption Perceptions Index for 2014.[503] It is thus positioned at the left of the pyramid's base. Totalitarianism describes conditions where the strong hand of government, as in Thomas Hobbes's *Leviathan*, is a terrible substitute for a society's reliance on trust. Think of the Socialist Republic of Yugoslavia after Tito and Iraq after Saddam Hussein. North Korea (NK) holds the worst score, using the 2015 *Index of Economic Freedom* developed by the Heritage Foundation, as North Koreans possess neither economic nor political freedom.[504]

Laissez-faire government is feasible when the ability to trust strangers is pervasive. New Zealand (NZ) is in strong contention for an award in this category.[505] It ranked second as the least corrupt nation according to the *Corruption Perceptions Index 2014* and has the third highest score on the *2015 Index of Economic Freedom*.

Adam Smith wrote in *Theory of Moral Sentiments*:

> "Society … cannot subsist among those who are at all times ready to hurt and injure one another. The moment that injury begins, the moment that mutual resentment and animosity take place, all the bands of it are broke asunder, and the different members of which it consisted

are ... dissipated and scattered abroad by the violence and opposition of their discordant affections. If there is any society among robbers and murderers, they must at least ... abstain from robbing and murdering one another".[506]

A nation's position within the trust/control pyramid can change, and Hobbes and Smith painted very different pictures of Britain. The English Civil War was under way and King Charles I had been beheaded when Hobbes wrote about a continual state of war in which "every man is the enemy to every man" and life is "solitary, poor, nasty, brutish, and short".[507] (One might wonder: When life is solitary, poor, nasty, and brutish, what's wrong with short?) Smith published *Wealth of Nations* 125 years later, when Britain was enjoying a period of internal peace and stability.

While my students have tended to agree in class discussions concerning the locations of New Zealand, Somalia, and North Korea in the trust/control triangle, positioning the United States has posed considerable difficulty. Students have agreed that a nation's position can change, but are uncertain about where the United States should be located and whether it has moved in recent history. Francis Fukuyama offers strong evidence in his provocatively titled book, *The Great Disruption: Human Nature and the Reconstruction of Social Order*, that Americans' ability to trust strangers declined over the period from the 1960s to the 1990s.

Fukuyama's use of the term disruption refers to decline in morality at the individual level and in social capital at the societal level. He views the principal cause of such disruption to be technological changes we have experienced and "the very scale and diversity of [our] contemporary society ...".[508] Its effects include an increase in the breakdown of families, chronic poverty, crime, drug abuse, gains in wealth resulting in greater inequality, and the rise of the modern welfare state. Parallel to these changes has been "a broad cultural shift that has included the decline of religion and the promotion of individualistic self-gratification over community obligation".[509] These differences have also been accompanied by superior economic growth, innovation, technology, and a denser civil society.[510]

Fukuyama affirms Adam Smith's belief that human beings are problem-solving creatures who depend upon each other for care and adapt to evolving circumstances in society.[511] Smith could not, however, have anticipated the technological changes that have burgeoned since his death nor the scale of social disruptions they continue to cause. Smith's belief in a benevolent creator might have led him to share Fukuyama's tentatively optimistic views that social capital is beginning to be restored in America.

Fukuyama's book, published in 2000, obviously does not include statistics for either white-collar or blue-collar crime occurring since its publication. Major changes in information and financial technology during this period after the turn of the century contributed to the dot.com and subprime bubbles and busts, which then caused the loss of jobs, homes, and prospects for millions of Americans. This series of events would suggest there should be a corresponding upsurge in the incidence of blue-collar crime.

Some of the statistics I have reviewed, however, imply a less optimistic view than Fukuyama proposes: They indicate beneficiaries of the two booms and busts committed fraud on a magnitude dwarfing that of blue-collar crime. Consider the single incident of Bernie Madoff, who was said to have embezzled $35 billion.[512] The 408,217 robberies reported by the FBI for 2009 amounted to only 1.45% of the losses for those who invested with Madoff.[513] Alternatively, if the level of losses due to robberies remained constant, it would take until 2078 for the cumulative losses to equal those attributed to Madoff. And these numbers are dwarfed even by net losses to stockholders and taxpayers because of the malfeasance of individual investment bankers. It makes as much sense to blame the banks themselves as the getaway car of a bank robber. Robert Shiller's *Finance and the Good Society* provides a description of the valuable services provided by investment banks and other financial institutions.[514]

Paradox of the Invisible Hand

Free-market capitalism is viewed widely as essentially a process in which buyers compete among themselves to maximize their utility, sellers compete among themselves to maximize their profits, and buyers and sellers compete with each other to gain the most favorable outcome from each transaction. This view is reinforced when metaphors of Darwinism, criminal activity, and war are invoked to promote book sales. Richard Dawkins chose the provocatively misleading title *The Selfish Gene* for his best-selling but serious work supporting the view that natural selection occurs at the individual rather than group level. Although genes are obviously brainless, he wrote, "Like successful Chicago gangsters, our genes have survived, in some cases for millions of years, in a highly competitive world".[515]

Other sensational book titles include: *Xerox: American Samurai*; *Sun Tzu: War and Management*; *Marketing Warfare*; *The War Lords: Military Lessons for Business Strategists*; and (my personal favorite) *Scotland's Malt Whisky Distilleries: Survival of the Fittest*. Unlike criminal activity and war, evolution can be a useful metaphor for business but it won't sell many books. Consider the fictitious *Corporate Kudzu: How Amazon is Smothering Authors and Publishers*.

Competition is vital to understanding free-market capitalism but it does not explain by itself how universal selfishness and indifference to the welfare of others results in anything other than chaos or that the price mechanism does not work when there are no property rights. The metaphor of the invisible hand can only be understood when the complementary role of competition and cooperation is recognized.

Elinor Ostrom received the Nobel Memorial Prize in 2009 and posed the following question during her awards presentation: "Are rational individuals helplessly trapped in dilemmas?" She noted that the answer provided by conventional economic theory is "yes" but countered that this response is not always true because "...the reality is that cooperative behavior is widespread, although far from inevitable".[516]

Ostrom's research focused on *the tragedy of the commons*, the term inspired by English farmers whose sheep overgrazed and destroyed the pasturage they used in common. The groups of Asian farmers and fishers she studied formed three categories. The first included groups in which all members had used as much water as they wanted or caught as many fish as they could and depleted the resources — behavior consistent with a strong version of conventional theory. In the second category, some group members were free riders who used the limited resources extravagantly — behavior consistent with a weak version of the theory. In the third, groups were comprised of members who used their proper

shares of the common resources and protected them for future use —
behavior contrary to conventional theory.

Ostrum found groups that were successful in conserving their precious resources without outside intervention. Group members monitored each other's behavior and punished those who were greedy. The performance of self-regulating groups was superior to that of groups reliant on government enforcement of responsible behavior. In an analysis of 47 irrigation systems and 44 fisheries, Ostrom found that over 72% of farmer-managed systems were successful in allocating space, time, and technology in their conservation efforts.[517] In contrast, only 42% of government-regulated irrigation systems had equivalent levels of success, even when they possessed superior engineering capabilities. Ostrom observed that group-enforced norms tended to persist, but when discipline was external to the group, good behavior deteriorated when it was no longer monitored. You will recall the comparison of professional golf and basketball.

Ostrom studied whether individuals will cooperate in utilizing a shared resource, while the research described in Chap. 6 utilized the prisoner's dilemma, ultimatum, and dictator games to address the same question experimentally. Both bodies of research found that individuals are likely to cooperate and to punish players who do not. The studies employing games were conducted under strict experimental controls (strong internal validity) but there is some question about whether results using such methods are applicable to natural settings (questionable external validity). By contrast, Ostrom's research was observational rather than experimental (questionable internal validity), but the observed behavior took place in its natural habitat in which group members maintained strong, long-term relationships because of the resource they were forced to share, and the outcomes of their interactions were life-shaping (strong external validity). When considered as a body, this research suggests that the superiority of *Homo reciprocans* (reciprocal man) over *Homo economicus* (economic man) is found in many settings.

Reciprocal man is a modern elaboration of an old concept. Smith distinguished between *self-interest* and *selfishness,* describing the latter as self-interest "vulgarly understood" in *Wealth of Nations.*[518] Alexis de Tocqueville, the French political thinker, included a chapter entitled "How the Americans Combat Individualism by the Principle of Self-Interest Rightly Understood" in *Democracy in America*. He writes:

> The Americans . . . are fond of explaining almost all actions of their lives by the principle of self-interest rightly understood; they show with complacency how an enlightened regard for themselves constantly prompts them to assist one another and inclines them willingly to sacrifice a portion of their time and property to the welfare of the state.[519]

He offers additionally that Americans tend to dismiss their own altruistic behavior because "they are more anxious to do honor to their philosophy than themselves".

Public affairs professor Hugo Heclo argues that de Tocqueville's insight remains an aspect of American exceptionalism because we are more likely than citizens of other nations to assume challenges through voluntary association rather than relying on the government.[520] Consider our nation's fire departments, which exemplify such voluneerism. Of the nation's 30,052 fire departments, 19,807 (66%) rely exclusively on volunteers and another 7768 (26%) utilize some volunteers. Volunteers account for 786,150 (69%) of the nation's 1,140,750 firefighters, and 95% of them work in communities with fewer than 25,000 inhabitants.[521]

Problems with free riders arise for volunteer fire departments that rely on contributions or assessments to support their operations. A friend described the case of newcomers to a small New England town who discovered that a can of kerosene and a book of matches had been left on their front porch as a friendly reminder that they hadn't contributed to the fire department. A family in South Fulton, Tennessee, ignored a less subtle message when someone else's house was allowed to burn because its owners had not supported their fire department.[522] The family did not appreciate the message fully until they saw the firefighters stand by as their house burned because they had not paid their $75 annual fee.

*   *

Remarkably, Smith uses the word *cooperation* only once in *Wealth of Nations* but he devotes its opening passages to the cooperative efforts necessary for the division of labor that is foundational to civilized society.[523] He begins by noting that a solitary individual is unable to provide for himself or herself the food, clothing, and housing enjoyed by the poorest peasants in every civilized society, and the common laborer in these societies enjoys luxuries denied to savage princes with a thousand subjects.

Smith illustrates his point with two vivid examples. First, an individual working alone can produce as many as ten straight pins daily. But when the task is divided into eighteen distinct operations performed by ten individuals working as a team, the daily output for the average worker can reach 4800 pins.[524]

The second example describes the incomprehensibly large and complex supply network necessary to make a common laborer's coarse woolen coat. Versions of this story can be found in *Wealth of Nations*, an early draft of this great work, and the two sets of jurisprudence notes.[525] He begins with the wool:

> The shepherd, the sorter of the wool, the wool comber or carder, the dyer, scribbler, the spinner, the weaver, the fuller, the dresser, and with many others, must all join their different arts in order to complete even this homely production.[526]

He continues by describing the acquisition of the dye from overseas, the manufacture of shears to cut the wool and the metal used to make shears, the transportation required at various stages in the process, and the material needs of the workers employed throughout. If we consider the workers who maintained the roads, the civilian sailors who brought the dye to Britain, the British sailors who protected commercial shipping, and employees of the royal mint who made the coins used in the many transactions, then it is difficult to identify anyone who had not helped in some way to make the humble coat.

Although Smith used *cooperation* only once in *Wealth of Nations* and not at all in *Theory of Moral Sentiments*, he used *competition* 134 times in the first work and four in the second. This imbalance does not suggest the relative importance of the two characteristics of free markets, in Smith's view, because he believed competition and cooperation must be balanced if free-market capitalism is to work effectively. Smith's intentions in this regard are expressed in one of his most eloquent and succinct statements: "Every man, as long as he does not violate the laws of justice, is left perfectly free to pursue his own interest his own way, and to bring both his industry and capital into competition with those of any other man, or order of men".[527] Justice differentiates a pirate from a sailor, a swindler from a business promoter.

Smith's discussion of justice in *Theory of Moral Sentiments* addresses what may appear to be an overemphasis of competition in *Wealth of Nations*. The personal goals of individuals and the ways they fulfill them vary greatly, but the system of free-market capitalism operates effectively if these individuals act justly and the state is able to catch and punish transgressors. Thus, individuals use their energy, talents, and resources prudently in competitive markets, but they must restrain themselves or be restrained by the justice system. You will recall that Smith declared that a society without justice will "crumble into atoms".[528]

The views Friedman expressed in *Capitalism and Freedom* are consistent with Smith in these matters. The Austrian libertarian Ludwig von Mises expressed similar views in the early pages of *Liberalism: The Classical Tradition*, first published in 1927: "Human society is an association of persons for cooperative action.... In the absence of the division of labor, we would not be in any respect further advanced today than our ancestors of a thousand or ten thousand years ago".[529] Morality is required for social existence and "must be demanded of each member of society".[530] "Life in society will be quite impossible if the people who desire its continued existence and who conduct themselves accordingly had to forgo the use of force and compulsion against those who are prepared to undermine society by their behavior".[531] Von Mises notes that liberal and *laissez-faire* economic policies are not the same and that "we cannot do without the apparatus of government in protecting and preserving life, liberty, property, and health of the individual" as long as it does not discriminate between one group and another.[532]

Imperfection as an Ideal

Stigler's *The Theory of Price* and selections from Edward Chamberlin's *The Theory of Monopolistic Competition* and Joseph Schumpeter's *Capitalism, Socialism, and Democracy* were assigned reading for my

MBA studies at Michigan State University.[533] Stigler's work represents the neoclassical tradition while Chamberlin's book, along with Joan Robinson's *The Economics of Imperfect Competition*, offers a radical departure from that tradition, as is suggested by their book titles.[534] Both the economics of perfect competition (neoclassical economics) and the economics of imperfect competition (monopolistic competition) played major but potentially irreconcilable roles in business school curricula throughout my career.

Although the influence of neoclassical economics overshadows monopolistic competition in both the economics and business disciplines, these conflicting perspectives' coexistence is evidenced in the business lexicon.[535] The saying that Britons and Americans are two peoples separated by a common language applies to economics and business professors as well. Important terms shared by the two fields are defined in different and contradictory ways. One such term is *profits*. According to economics professors, *profits* are the revenues remaining after deducting expenses, including the cost of the buildings and equipment needed to operate a firm.[536] It would be more lucrative for the owners to cease operations and invest their funds elsewhere if these capital costs could not be recovered.

Firms do not earn profits under conditions of perfect competition by definition, and profits appear where markets are imperfect, as in the case of oligopolies and monopolies.[537] In other words, economic profits are desirable to sellers for obvious reasons, but undesirable to buyers because they indicate market inefficiency and should rightfully go to buyers in the form of lower prices.[538] Economic profits are commonly referred to as *excessive profits* to distinguish them from business profits.

According to business professors and the IRS, however, *profits* are the *revenues* remaining after a firm has paid its *expenses*, with the meaning of these terms determined by the federal tax code, which seems to vary yearly. Using this definition, profits can be made even if an unhealthy business does not recover its capital costs. Business profits are desirable to sellers, and buyers express their approval of them implicitly by paying a premium for a superior product; those purchasing a Samsung Galaxy S6 without an annual contract from AT&T for $1015 are rejecting a *Nokia Lumia 625* priced at $85. To say that economics professors view excessive profits negatively and business professors view them positively is an understatement; profits are the lifeblood of free-market capitalism in the eyes of business professors and professionals and not a measure of inefficiency.

Economics and business professors also disagree concerning the meaning of *competition*. For economics professors, the conditions under which competition is found in its purest form are labeled unambiguously: *perfect competition* — that is: large numbers of buyers and sellers, identical products, perfect information, no excessive profits, and no government intervention except for the provision and protection of property rights. Perfect competition is considered desirable for individual buyers and for society because its existence guarantees the most efficient allocation of resources, at least by economists' standards.

The only decision for a seller under conditions of perfect competition is to act like a thermostat: turning off the production switch when the right quantity of goods has been produced. Accordingly, no complex decision-making is required and no trained managers are needed to make them. Consider what it would mean to students seeking careers in marketing if perfect competition prevailed.

We teach that every product is comprised of a *marketing mix*, and the *Four Ps* is often used as a mnemonic for the concept. *Product* includes the good and the package containing it, as well as its accessories, labels, and instructions. *Place* refers to the distribution of products through wholesalers and retailers (Barnes & Noble) and the Internet (barnesandnoble.com), with the aid of shippers such as USPS. *Price* encompasses the sales price, coupons, markdowns, and use of credit cards or installment plans. Finally, *promotion* refers to personal selling, sales promotion, advertising, and publicity used to inform and persuade potential customers.

All products and their prices would be identical within each market if perfect competition prevailed. Distribution would not be required because sellers and buyers would interact directly and without cost or effort. Promotion would be unnecessary because customers would have perfect information. Additionally, firms could not innovate or expand their operations because they would not have the retained earnings needed to finance these activities.

The peculiar circumstances of perfect competition are exceedingly rare. Consequently, plenty of opportunities are available for business school graduates to apply their knowledge and skills. When they do encounter conditions approximating perfect competition, however, their job may well be to eliminate it by replacing price competition with non-price competition. Consider the options available to firms with quantities of 24-karat gold to sell. Those without entrepreneurial spirit or speculators sell it as a commodity at its spot price. Others charge a premium by transforming it into gold leaf and gold wire for artists. Still others manufacture gold-plated or gold-filled jewelry or utilize its conductive and noncorrosive properties in smartphones and other electronic devices.

Perhaps best of all, Tiffany & Co. produces a diamond engagement ring in 18-karat gold with their brand name engraved inside the band. It is placed in a black suede clamshell and wrapped in a Tiffany Blue box tied with a white ribbon. A suitor might be able to buy a virtually identical ring at a pawnshop for an amount far less than Tiffany's price. Or the suitor could buy a gold-plated ring with a cubic zirconia if the would-be fiancé might be pleased with such an efficient use of limited resources (unless the difference were spent on, say, a set of golf clubs).

Chamberlin gave the name *product differentiation* to the major strategic tool utilized under conditions of monopolistic competition.[539] A product is differentiated when buyers value goods or services for their distinguishing characteristics, whether they are "real or fancied".[540] These characteristics may reside in the product itself, such as patented features, trademarks, brand names, or distinctive packaging, coloring, design, or style. They also exist in the manner in which a product is sold through a retail store, including its location, physical appearance, quality of staff, and services provided. Monopolistic competition, based on non-price competition, is congenial to concepts such as *brand recognition, recall, preference, loyalty, loyalty programs, lifetime value of a customer,* and *brand equity*. These concepts have no meaning in neoclassical economics.

This exercise can be undertaken with other business sub-disciplines. For example, there would be no need for CPAs because perfect information exists. There are no supply chains to optimize because there are no intermediaries between the manufacturer who is maximizing profits and the consumer who is maximizing utility. Additionally, the stock market and stock traders would not exist and there would be no transaction costs (principally the cost of information) to prevent individuals from investing directly in manufacturers.

Neoclassical economic theory presents a static (photo) image of economic activity while monopolistic competition presents a dynamic (video) image of it. Neoclassical theory presents a mechanical view of economic activity while monopolistic competition presents an organic view. This evolutionary perspective is evocative of Schumpeter's concept of *creative destruction.* "The fundamental impulse that sets and keeps the capitalist engine in motion comes from the new consumer goods, the new methods of production or transportation, the new markets, the new forms of industrial organization that capitalistic enterprise creates".[541] He used the continued industrialization of agriculture as a case in point.

The history of the automobile illustrates the point that technical innovation has been the most significant basis for product differentiation. A steam-powered automobile was invented in France before the American Revolution. Since then over 100,000 US patents have been granted for its improvement and there is no end in sight.[542] The addition of internal combustion engines, steering wheels, inflatable tires, starter motors, enclosed passenger compartments, air conditioners, and disk brakes have differentiated the innovator's product temporarily and increased its profitability while competitors sought to copy it or gain an advantage of their own.

The market for steam-powered automobiles was destroyed and replaced by the market for automobiles powered by internal combustion engines. Batteries or fuel cells are likely to make internal combustion engines and gasoline obsolete. Automobiles will become more completely automatic as we turn over their control to computers.

Other examples of this creative destruction include the markets for pharmaceuticals, medical diagnostic devices, airplanes, satellites, smart phones, smart watches, computer hardware and software, data storage and transmission systems, and financial instruments. Some may remember data stored on paper tapes and may have entered data on IBM punch cards and sorted them on machines designed solely for that purpose.

Marketing segmentation is a second strategy employed under conditions of monopolistic competition. It is based on the recognition that customer demand is never homogeneous and markets may be deconstructed into smaller ones, each with their own distinctive requirements.

Toyota offers the battery-powered Yaris for around $18,000 and Tesla focuses on the particular market segment of automobile customers who are willing and able to spend $80,000 to save the planet while going from zero to 60 miles an hour in 3.9 seconds. Even something so simple as table salt exists in great variety, with prices varying accordingly: fine, coarse, rock, sea, iodized, kosher, and seasoned salts that are found in a variety of dispensers and package sizes.

The perfectly competitive market is portrayed by a supply curve that slopes upward and to the right and a demand curve sloping downward and to the right. By contrast, each product has its own supply and demand curve when products are differentiated and markets are segmented. The successfully innovative firms sell products that are in high demand at premium prices as long as they can maintain their differential advantage. A prime example is the Ford F150 series of pickups, second among all the best-selling vehicles in US history and the only pickup in the top ten list.[543] The company has sold 35 million F150s over six decades.

Ford Motor Company offers twenty-nine vehicles on its website and each has its own supply-and-demand curve that fluctuates to show locations and slopes in a constantly updated graphic portrayal. No mathematical model can capture this complexity or incorporate the varied, complex, and ever-changing characteristics of Ford's target customers. This complexity has caused neoclassical economists to employ mathematical models containing only a few variables, but this is not an option for Ford executives who must utilize research and development and marketing research to make risky bets that determine their company's fate. It is the role of engineering, business, design, and other academic programs to help them meet these challenges.

It is the drive for a monopoly position and the resulting profits rather than the achievement of that position that motivates firms in high-risk industries because such a position is fleeting. Both *Nokia* and *Blackberry* were once dominant players in the mobile phone market but have been relegated to the sidelines. This rosy picture of imperfect competition that rewards good behavior is not meant to suggest that problems cannot exist. Would-be competitors collude. The lack of perfect information can conceal fraud and shoddy workmanship because of the great complexity of so many products and services.

The version of monopolistic competition that has emerged from the work of Chamberlin, Robinson, and Schumpeter and that now underpins business curricula possesses four distinct qualities. First, markets are driven by a succession of innovations, often with no end in sight. Second, even when the real costs have fallen, as in the case of computers, the primary battlefront remains on enhanced design and performance.

The third distinctive characteristic is that the use of monopolistic competition in business schools has not been constrained by a reliance on the mathematical models of buyers, sellers, and markets.[544] Although these models have been challenged for their ability to predict uncertain economic events, the point here is that they do not provide enough information to be useful enough by themselves to inform decision-makers, especially in the fields of marketing and management where human behavior adds such great complexity.[545]

For example, whole courses are devoted to consumer behavior (a.k.a. consumer psychology) and to corporate strategy. Leaders of successful corporations make decisions incorporating a complex and dynamic view of their internal operations and the environments in which they compete. Some decisions, like reordering inventory, can be reduced to simple decision rules but such methods cannot extend very far in aiding executives competing in the uncertain world of monopolistic competition.

Fourth, the business version of monopolistic competition does not rest on the twin pillars of free-market capitalism. Concerning the first pillar, the premise that everyone is an economic man leads to the view, that a corporation a nexus of contracts among employees who are focused exclusively on their own material gain is sterile and destructive. Additionally, the concept of a production function that specifies the optimal combination of inputs to maximize output may represent an assembly line effectively, but the modern corporation is more than an assembly line and the stock price is not the sole measure of its success. The production function cannot explain why Apple stores I have visited are bustling with scores of loyal employees and customers while Microsoft stores are virtually empty.[546]

The organic view of the firm presented by the book *In Good Company*, quoted in Chap. 7 and represented in the first (1990) and third (2012) statements by the Business Roundtable, provide superior representations of corporations, stakeholders, and the individuals comprising them. When the Roundtable vacillated concerning the purpose of the firm, its senior members may have recalled words management professor Peter Drucker wrote in 1955:

> ...profitability is not the purpose of business enterprise and business activity, but a limited factor of it. Profit is not the explanation, cause or rationale of business behavior and business decisions, but the test of their validity.... If we want to know what a business is we have to start with its *purpose*. And its purpose must lie outside of the business itself. In fact, it must be in society since a business enterprise is an organ of society. There is only one valid definition of business purpose: *to create a customer.*[547]

Wharton graduates or former marketing students associated with the Roundtable may remember the views of marketing professor Wroe Alderson, who declared in 1957:

> A business firm or any other operating organization can be analyzed in terms of inputs and outputs. The primary output of the typical business firm is a flow of salable products. It is this output which justifies the existence of the enterprise and from which are derived such secondary, but highly essential outputs as profits, wages, and payments to suppliers.[548]

Concerning the second pillar of free-market capitalism, monopolistic competition is not based on any preconceptions about the proper role of government and the CEOs working in technology-driven industries are probably highly ambivalent about the issue. On the one hand, most CEOs will likely complain about the costs of regulatory compliance. On the other, government-sponsored research in medicine and public health, microelectronics, aerospace engineering, the Internet and related technologies, and other industries reflects the profound impact of government-sponsored research and development on technology-driven industries. One astonishing result is that I am able to obtain a bird's eye view of Adam Smith's grave using a weather application on my iPhone.

We business professors have done a disservice to our students by our failure to articulate the appropriate domains for the application of the economics of perfect competition and that of imperfect competition. Because of that inaction, we have also failed to indicate the hazards that occur when economic theories are misapplied, especially when those theories rest on toxic assumptions.

*   *

We have traveled a long way as I have shared my journey in search of the true Adam Smith. It began when I could not find the twin pillars of free markets in what I had always been taught were their headwaters — Adam Smith's *Wealth of Nations*. I learned afterward that the economics taught in business schools as an ostensibly value-free science is laden with the value judgments that greed is the engine of capitalism and that markets regulate themselves without governmental involvement. Later it became clear that a creed of greed has been perpetuated as a shadow curriculum in business schools which can help explain the reckless and destructive behavior of leaders of some of our nation's largest corporations. A review of Smith's complete works and alternative economic theories and methods has demonstrated that the twin pillars were built on sand. Just behavior is required for any society to prosper and if it is not self-imposed by its members, then it must be imposed upon them by the government.

If this idea is true, why did brilliant people promote the disastrous myth of the twin pillars? I believe they were used as weapons to combat collectivism and socialism without appreciating that individuals looking for justification of their greedy and often destructive acts might adopt them in forming a creed.

Chapter 11

What Lessons Can be Learned?

Since the decline and fall of Enron, I have thought deeply about whether business school graduates are prepared to respond appropriately to the important and complex ethical decisions they will inevitably face. Are there indications that business students have received the proper training? It doesn't seem so.

Resisting Groupthink

Enron was the embodiment of the new capitalism, America's corporate favorite, and its profile was very high at the McCombs School of Business at the University of Texas at Austin. The firm was expanding rapidly and hiring many of our best graduates. There were plaques in our building complex recognizing Enron's generosity. Across the street from campus, Ken Lay, the company's founder, was temporarily immortalized on a large limestone block in the lobby of the Bullock Texas State History Museum.

I was excited when Rick Causey, Enron's chief accounting officer, agreed to speak to my class. His secretary called the day before, informing me that Rick had to attend an emergency board meeting in New York and that she had scheduled an excellent replacement. The substitute speaker did a fine job, but one of the students asked some tough and rather puzzling questions about what was going on inside the company. Although I did not know it then, the New York meeting was the beginning of the end for Enron, and Rick Causey would be in federal prison before long.

The real Enron turned out to exemplify *vulture capitalism*, a term used during the 2012 presidential election to describe firms that cause great harm to others in the name of profits. It was largely a financial illusion conjured by executives transferring hundreds of millions of dollars from the pockets of its employees and other stockholders into their own.

I organized a conference on business ethics the year after Rick canceled his visit. The featured speakers were William Powers, former special investigative board member of Enron and until recently president of the University of Texas at Austin, and Sherron Watkins, Enron whistleblower and *Time* Magazine person of the year for 2002.

The remarkable backdrop for the conference was that both Watkins and Causey held degrees from our undergraduate and graduate business programs. Causey's image around the school, like that of Watkins, was of a fine individual even after Enron's collapse. It was hard for those who had known him for years to absorb the terrible news from Houston.

The plaques and the limestone block are long gone, but questions remain. Why did top executives, generously rewarded for Enron's initial successes, go on to destroy the firm and the lives of many, including their own? How did Watkins avoid the problems that beset so many of her fellow executives?

Is there anything in Causey and Watkins's experiences at the University of Texas, Austin that could explain their differing fates? I wonder if our university faculty, staff, and administration have an obligation to prepare our students to recognize and make ethical decisions, or is it simply enough to provide them with excellent technical skills to be used for either good or bad?

Identifying What is Legal but Unethical

In 2012, I asked a distinguished finance professor whether Bain Capital had engaged in *vulture capitalism* when it bankrupted Ampad, a paper manufacturer, and made millions. He responded that the deals of private equity firms increase economic efficiency and that their principals and investors make money when the firms they help operate make money. Not long afterward, I asked the founder of a private equity firm about the remarkable returns of Bain Capital. He said his own investors expected very high returns and if his firm passed up a good opportunity, a rival firm would take it. Neither of the men I spoke with acknowledged that individuals working in private equity firms might encounter investments promising high returns that involved unethical or illegal behavior.

I later wondered if the private equity principals and investors felt any ethical constraints as they pursued massive returns for themselves and, in theory, reallocated resources so that they would be used more efficiently. It is magnificent when private equity firms and venture capitalists earn vast returns after investing in and nurturing start-ups. With the help of Bain Capital, a young firm like Staples grew from a one-office supply store in 1986 to more than 22,000 stores operating in 23 countries in 2012.[549] Surely many of Staples's inefficient competitors had been driven out of business, but that is only the indirect result of Staples's actions because customers brought about their demise by purchasing Staples's superior offerings. This process of creative destruction, by which inferior products and services are replaced by superior ones, explains why we no longer ride in horse-drawn buggies but instead enjoy a host of transportation choices that were nonexistent a decade ago.

However, the positive outcome for anyone other than the principals and investors of Bain Capital is less obvious in the case of Ampad. Bain Capital purchased Ampad from Mead in 1992 for $5 million. Ampad's revenues grew from $107 million to $573 million, a four-fold increase in just 7 years because of business acquisitions and cost-cutting efforts. But its debt rose from $11.3 million to $392 million, a 33-fold increase over the same period. In other words, Ampad took on an immense debt burden relative to its ability to pay it off.

Ampad stock was offered for sale to the public in 1996 and the firm then experienced a brief period of profitability. Soon, however, workers were laid off and plants were closed.[550] Ampad filed for bankruptcy protection in 2000 and its assets were sold off the following year. The bad news for Bain principals and investors was that they had lost their initial investment of $5 million. The good news according to the *Boston Globe* was that prior to the bankruptcy, Bain extracted $19.5 million in fees, $60 million from money borrowed to finance the acquisitions of related businesses, and $50 million when Ampad's stock was sold to the public — a total of $124.5 million.[551]

Following the logic of the finance professor, Ampad went out of business because it was inefficient and the office supplies industry provided greater value to the public without it. However, this explanation does not seem accurate for this particular case because the company has been reincarnated and its products are once again selling under the Ampad brand. A more likely explanation for Ampad's bankruptcy and liquidation is the great debt burden imposed on it by Bain Capital. Was an equivalent debt burden imposed on Staples and did Bain withdraw proportionally large fees from it? Probably not, but in either case, Bain's principals and investors were positioned to succeed whether Ampad went bankrupt or not.

Does any of this matter? The president of Ampad met his fiduciary duties requiring him to place the interests of Bain Capital investors and principals above his own, but did he meet those duties to investors purchasing stock in the company after it was made available to the public or to future Ampad investors? Did Bain Capital as majority stockholder have any fiduciary duties to the minority stockholders when it extracted so much money from the company? Does it matter that Ampad's unionized workers were fired when Bain took over, rehired as nonunion workers, and lost their jobs again when the company liquidated? What were the long-term effects of this sad history on the communities where Ampad's plants were located? Could the cumulative effects of such events across the country help account for the decline in our nation's industrial base? How is it that individuals who might never have lied, cheated, or stolen engage in such activities with little apparent thought or remorse?

Is anyone asking these questions? Not likely in classrooms, where it is stated or implied that the only stockholders who matter are the private equity firms, their principals, and their investors. Never mind that they extract massive returns for themselves, while other stockholders, banks, employees, and communities suffer as a firm plunges into bankruptcy.

Working in a Bad Barrel

A team of Certified Public Accountants (CPAs) sat around a conference table wrapping up a major client's project. The senior partner in charge of the account had not been able to work on it and did not attend this final meeting. The partner leading the meeting stated it would be very embarrassing if the senior partner's time sheet indicated he had not worked on the project as expected. The partner announced he would give the senior partner some of his own hours. He then looked down the conference table at my former student, the only undergraduate intern in the room. He passed around the table to her the senior partner's time sheet and asked her to fill it out. (I have since been told it is not uncommon for young accountants and consultants to be asked to "adjust" their own time sheets.)

Imagine what must have gone through the head of my former student as all eyes were turned to her. It may have been something like this: "I remember learning in accounting that falsifying time sheets is fraud. Is there something here I don't understand? The hours were actually worked, but they will be billed at the higher rate of the senior partner. I have really enjoyed working with these people, and they may offer me a full-time job. I don't want to let them down. Why did he ask me to fill out the sheet? Are they testing my honesty? Are they asking me because I am in a weak position to refuse or because the 'mistake' if caught could be blamed on an inexperienced intern?"

The young woman took the time sheet and waited until the meeting was over and she was alone with her supervisor. She passed it to him saying she could not fill it out. She turned down their offer and took a job with a strategic consulting firm — a good apple found a good barrel.

Why did the young woman show such "grace under pressure", as Hemingway described *courage*? What, if any, obligation do I have to the fine young men and women in my classes to prepare them for such challenges? I don't need to know about deontological (rule-based) and teleological (consequence-based) ethics to tell them they may be put in situations where they will be encouraged to engage in unethical or illegal acts. I could use the examples of Sherron Watkins and my former student who felt alone at the end of the conference table, and say that I hope I would have made the same decisions if I had been in their shoes.

*   *

The results of the Stanford simulation and the two business experiments discussed in Chap. 5 suggest that ordinary young men and women may be induced without any expectation of reward to assume the role of a malicious guard or a corporate board member who takes the lives of unsuspecting customers.[552] Others may act like rational, selfish economic man if they have any hint that a stranger will do the same. It is obvious that none of these actions took place in real settings where the expectations and rewards and punishments are made clear, but that seems to make the findings more ominous rather than less. Why did the young men and women behave as they did when the stakes were so low and they could have gotten up and left whenever they wanted to? Whatever the explanation, these studies and hundreds of others illustrate how vulnerable all of us are to group pressure and other situational influences that influence us to behave in ways that are contrary to our better selves.

*   *

Lester Thurow, economist and at the time Dean of MIT Sloan School of Management, is dismissive of business ethics in a 1987 *New York Times* article. He observes: "Injunctions to 'be good' don't sway young men and women in their mid- to late 20's". Accordingly, he concludes: "In the final analysis, what we produce is no worse than what we get".[553] Thurow's observation is correct because no graduate program can be expected to plant the seeds of good behavior on soil barren for more than two decades. He is wrong, however, to reject any responsibility for the behavior of Sloan graduates. On the one hand, business school faculties should acknowledge and repudiate the creed of greed that inhabits the shadow curriculum prevalent in business schools and recognize that it may undermine the best intentions of susceptible students. On the other hand, faculties should enable students to construct survival guides before they enter careers where the temptations are great and the damage caused by misdeeds spread across an industry, as they often are, and can be measured in trillions of dollars.

The Federal Bureau of Investigation (FBI) reported 408,217 robberies in 2009 that accounted for $508 million in total losses.[554] The $35 billion embezzled by Bernie Madoff is 69 times these 2009 losses but is inconsequential compared to the more than $4 trillion some claim were the financial losses caused by the sub-prime and dot.com bubbles and busts.[555]

Business school faculties should play an important role in helping students choose a suitable career path and learn how to traverse a potentially hazardous one. Students could benefit by considering one manager's observation: "What is right in the corporation is not what is right in a man's home and church. What is right in the corporation is what the guy above wants from you. That is what morality is in the corporation".[556] Could a job be so attractive that students would want to work for this company? If students take such a job with it, could they resist the extraordinary and often subtle pressures to engage in unethical and illegal acts?

Criminologists Neal Shover and Andy Hochstetler observe that a feature of many white-collar criminals is that they believe in the conventional standards of right and wrong except when operating in a no ethics zone of their own creation. They are vulnerable because they conceive of themselves as good law-abiding citizens and thus whatever they do is ethical and legal. At the crime scene, typically a well-appointed office or conference room, they engage in what outsiders condemn as socially deviant behavior in part because "they [and their co-conspirators] define the act of stealing in a way that enables them to maintain a favorable self-concept". Street criminals, in contrast, do not tend to engage in such rhetorical niceties.[557]

Where People Are the Bottom Line

Several years ago, I took a team of highly capable undergraduates to a case competition in Copenhagen, Denmark. Executives from a global manufacturer headquartered there presented a problem they had faced to teams invited from around the world. The team offering the most satisfactory recommendations for solving the firm's problem would win the competition. The executives stressed that moving their manufacturing "off shore" was an unacceptable response to the threat of low-cost Asian manufacturers.

My students insisted in their presentation that the only viable course of action was to open a manufacturing plant in Asia. They did not make it beyond the semifinals, despite their polished presentation and careful analysis. Their mistake was in not listening carefully to their "client". My mistake was that I had taught them à la Milton Friedman that the only criterion they should use in analyzing such cases was the extent to which their recommendations increased shareholder wealth.

I had not chosen for my class cases addressing ethics or corporate social responsibility: issues such as adulterating products, laying off workers, shutting down plants, or polluting the environment. I had, however, thoughtlessly given them a decision-making model focused on increasing the effectiveness and efficiency of operations that did not include considerations of ethics or social responsibility. What I had done was the equivalent of placing future pilots in a flight simulator under conditions where they did not experience the challenges of bad weather or mechanical difficulties. The Danish executives demanded of my students a solution to a much more complex problem than I had taught my students to consider: How can a manufacturer maintain its domestic factories and workers and still compete effectively with low-cost competitors elsewhere in the world?

I realized in retrospect that I was supporting the creed of greed. Mea culpa.

What Next?

Business education was transformed in the 1950s because of interventions by the Ford and Carnegie foundations. Visionaries inside and outside of academia believed the nation's economic potential was not being fully realized. This was important for the well-being of Americans and because our powerful military and political presence was vital in the epic struggle against communism. Additionally, our institutions served as a standard of excellence against which other nations compared themselves. A key to our nation's success in these endeavors was a cadre of highly competent managers leading our nation's corporations. But the visionaries acted because they believed America's business schools had come up short.

A second period requiring a thorough examination of business education is at hand for similar reasons. The quality of business students and faculty and the depth of the technical skills being imparted have never been better. However, the narrowness of that training and the biases it contains has undermined the prosperity of many of our citizens, weakened our nation in its continued struggle against totalitarianism, and tarnished our image as a global standard of excellence. The failure of business schools to provide students with a complete education imparting the moral vision and sense of responsibility required of those leading our economic institutions has contributed to these unfortunate circumstances.

The fundamental problem is the existence of a shadow curriculum that contaminates business programs by advocating the unethical and illegal behavior of managers and denigrating governmental efforts to protect the safety and property rights of those unable to defend themselves. An examination of the dot.com and subprime bubbles and busts and more recent instances of corporate predation reveal the devastation caused by the small percentage of business school graduates and others who have adopted this creed of greed. The creed's unseen and undesirable presence in business schools is analogous to antibiotic-resistant staph infections afflicting a small percentage of hospital patients.

The loss of jobs due to globalization and technological changes has occurred for decades and will continue inevitably. However, there is an added reason for the suffering of millions of Americans. During the first decade of the 21st century, millions of homebuyers, retirees, investors, and taxpayers were deprived of trillions of dollars because of the predatory actions of the leaders of some of the nation's largest and most powerful corporations. The continuation of this trend is not inevitable, but the likelihood that it will continue should worry even those who have benefited most from this massive transfer of wealth.

While millions of workers and their families have managed to survive, the erosion of faith in our economic and civic institutions has been profound. Gabriella Westfall, the police officer from Arizona who worked hard and played by the rules, lost her home because of the unscrupulous behavior of a nexus of businesses she had once trusted. Americans have had a relatively high tolerance for economic inequality during much of our history because we have been optimistic about our prospects and those of our children. This optimism and the basis for it appear to be vanishing for vast numbers.

Business schools, supported by their alumni, have responded to the crisis by increasing the resources devoted to the teaching of ethics and corporate social responsibility. Such efforts are admirable but can only contribute marginally because they run counter to the shadow curriculum contaminating economic models and their assumptions that are being taught in core and tool courses. The assumption that individuals are rational and selfish may be appropriate for research purposes but it can also act as a toxin leading students and practitioners to believe that greed, power and wealth are the only virtues in the Darwinian world of business.

My hope is that the analysis and conclusions found in previous chapters will enliven the debate on a variety of topics. One issue seems worthy of mention here. Do business professors have any duties to their students, the organizations hiring them, and the public at large? Should they exercise due diligence when presenting their students with economic theories and models such as those reviewed in this book? In other words, are professors acting unethically when they fail to inform their students of the limitations of these theories and models and the great harm that may result when they are used to make business decisions?

I sincerely hope that business faculty and administrators will address this and the other serious issues raised herein or that one or more organizations will lead an intervention as the Ford and Carnegie foundations did so effectively six decades ago.

Afterword

The Enron Corporation, my former place of employment, is now the byword for mega corporate scandal. We live in the post-Enron era with new legislation aimed at preventing a repeat of the corporate meltdowns of the early 2000s: Enron, WorldCom, HealthSouth, Adelphia Communications, and Tyco, among others. The Sarbanes-Oxley Act of 2002 was meant to protect shareholders from manipulated financial statements. Yet we endured a far worse meltdown in 2008 with the collapse of Bear Stearns, Lehman Brothers, and the whole financial sector. The Dodd-Frank Act was passed in 2010 as the purported answer to prevent risky business by the banks. It too proved inadequate in preventing JP Morgan Chase Bank from losing $6.2 billion in 2012 in a flawed trading activity dubbed the "London whale scandal".

Over a decade after Enron's collapse, I am still paid to speak to global audiences about my experiences there. Audiences are concerned about the future of our capitalist system. One of the underlying causes of Enron's collapse was misaligned executive compensation incentives combined with weak checks and balances in our watchdog groups. This broken system continues today and the fear of another meltdown keeps me gainfully employed.

I am often asked about the importance of teaching business ethics classes in our business schools. Audiences are concerned about the generations of future leaders who enter the business world with the firmly rooted idea that greed is good and markets correct for unethical behavior.

I have actually heard Enron used as a positive example of the corrective role of markets. If we are relying on bankruptcy as a check and balance, then we truly are in dangerous waters.

In *Seeking Adam Smith: Finding the Shadow Curriculum of Business*, Eli Cox explains how we ventured into these dangerous waters where chasing the almighty dollar and acquiring ever bigger homes, luxury vehicles, and exotic vacations became the goal of far too many of our business graduates. Where and when did we lose our bent toward fairness, cooperation, and altruism and begin embracing the "greed is good" mantra?

Dr. Cox provides a thoroughly satisfying discourse starting with a deep dive into Adam Smith's work and legacy, the origin of the business school in our modern universities and then continuing with the driving forces of capitalism and the colonization of business schools by the economics discipline. *Seeking Adam Smith* explains how we ended up in a system that seems unfair at best and rigged at worst. I came away with a better provocative question to pose to my corporate audiences: Should we do away with the business degree and by extension, the business school? The shadow curriculum Dr. Cox exposes is probably doing us more harm than good as a society.

Cox quotes Adam Smith, "Every man, as long as he does not violate the laws of justice, is left perfectly free to pursue his own interest his own way, and to bring both his industry and capital into competition with those of any other man, or order of men". Cox observes, "Justice differentiates a pirate from a sailor, a swindler from a business promoter". Enron's electricity traders were morally bankrupt as they took advantage of California's deregulated energy markets between 1997 and 2000, yet they rationalized their behavior, admitting they were abusing the flawed system California had instituted but claiming by doing so, they were benefiting other states who would learn from California's mistakes. Clearly, Enron's traders were pirates coming up with Jack Sparrow-worthy yarns insisting they were just sailors.

Dr. Cox has a distinguished 47-year career as a business professor, primarily educating at my alma mater, The University of Texas at Austin. Rick Causey, Enron's Chief Accounting Officer, is also a graduate of UT-Austin. Dr. Cox takes ownership of our education, wondering how we faced the ethical challenges at Enron and landed in different camps, one opposed to the accounting, one rationalizing it.

I believe *Seeking Adam Smith* is a vitally important book, starting a much-needed dialogue about the goal of business schools in the western world. I can't help but notice the growth in Faith and Culture centers at Yale, Princeton, and the University of St. Thomas, Houston, to name just a few. One of the more popular courses at Yale's center is titled *Life Worth Living*, and UT now offers a course called *Gameplan for Winning at Life*, with success not measured in salary and assets but in connection, resilience, and influence.

Seeking Adam Smith is not an anticapitalism book. Eli Cox is clearly a champion of business who not only explains how our business schools and fast-paced new economy companies ended up producing too many pirates and swindlers and not enough sailors and business promoters, but also offers lessons learned and a pathway back toward valuing those goals in life which truly produce contentment for the individual and betterment for society.

Sherron Watkins, Enron Whistle-blower,
Time Person of the Year 2002.

Notes

1. Egan, "2008: Worse than the Great Depression?"
2. Middleton and Light, "Harvard Changes Course."
3. A more complete list of the assumptions of perfect competition includes: (1) infinite number of sellers who are price takers; (2) infinite number of buyers who are price takers; (3) pairings or buyers and sellers occur at random; (4) homogeneous product; (5) buyers and sellers have perfect information; (6) no transaction costs except for fully maintained property rights; (7) freedom of entry and exit for buyers and sellers; (8) no collusion or governmental restraints except for those relating to the recognition and protection of property rights; (9) no economies of scale; (10) all inputs are homogeneous; (11) all resources are mobile; (12) all resources are utilized; (13) all resources are utilized most efficiently; (14) no impact on third parties (i.e., externalities); (15) economic activity is represented as temporary disruptions of equilibrium; and (16) equilibrium provides the ideal allocation of scarce resources.
4. Jevons, *The Theory of Political Economy*, 277.
5. Stewart, "Account of the Life and Writings of Adam Smith, L.L.D", 268–69.
6. Rae, *Life of Adam Smith*, 5.
7. Stewart, "Account of the Life and Writings of Adam Smith, L.L.D," 326.
8. Ross, *The Life of Adam Smith*; Hirst, *Adam Smith*; and Rae, *Life of Adam Smith*.
9. Stewart, "Account of the Life and Writings of Adam Smith, L.L.D," 274.
10. Haakonseen, "Natural Jurisprudence and the Theory of Justice"; Rae, *Life of Adam Smith*, 434; and Ross, *The Life of Adam Smith*, 404–05.

Seeking Adam Smith: Finding The Shadow Curriculum of Business

11. The first set of notes was discovered in 1895 and the second in 1958. See introduction to Meek *et al.*, eds., *Lectures on Jurisprudence*, 4, 9.

12. Smith, *Essays on Philosophical Subjects*, 49; *The Theory of Moral Sentiments*, 184; *An Inquiry into the Nature and Causes of the Wealth of Nations*, 456.

13. Samuelson, *Economics: An Introductory Analysis*.

14. The other seven, listed in the bibliography were written by Campbell and Skinner, Farrar, Fay, Hirst, Phillipson, Rae, and Scott.

15. Mossner, *The Life of David Hume*.

16. CBS News, "Ebbers Sentenced to 25 Years."

17. "Top Gun for Hire," 32.

18. Dash, "Former Chief Will Forfeit $418 Million."

19. Pitts, "Justice Falls Victim to Jail Privatization"; Hurdle and Tavernise, "Former Judge Is on Trial in 'Cash for Kids' Scheme."

20. Cassin, "Oscar Wyatt Founder of Coastal Corporation, Pleads Guilty to Iraq Bribes."

21. Will, "Greed Does Have Its Saving Graces."

22. Smith, *An Inquiry into the Nature and Causes of the Wealth of Nations*, 14–15.

23. O'Day, *The Professions in Early Modern England, 1450–1800*, 11.

24. http://www.bestmedicaldegrees.com/30-of-the-oldest-medical-schools-in-the-world/

25. "About William and Mary Law," https://law.wm.edu/about/index.php and "School of Medicine: A Brief History" http://www.archives.upenn.edu/histy/features/schools/med.html

26. Frankel, *Trust and Honesty*, 140.

27. This review of fiduciary duties is drawn from Frankel, *Fiduciary Law*; *Trust and Honesty*.

28. Frankel, *Fiduciary Law*, 80.

29. See Fan, "Can China Stop Organ Trafficking?"

30. Heath, *Morality, Competition, and the Firm*, 102–15.

31. Frederick Taylor University, "Frederick Winslow Taylor."

32. Taylor, *Principles of Scientific Management*, 10.

33. Ibid., 20, 100.

34. Ibid., 83.

35. Ibid., 25, 26.

36. Ibid., 59.

37. Ibid., 126.

38. Bourke, "Mayo, George Elton (1880–1949)."

39. Donham, "Foreword," viii.
40. Mayo, *The Social Problems of an Industrial Civilization*, xvi.
41. Gordon and Howell, *Higher Education for Business*, 21.
42. Pierson *et al.*, *The Education of American Businessmen*, 36.
43. AACSB International, "Accreditation Standards."
44. Gordon and Howell, *Higher Education for Business*, 289–90; 445–49.
45. Byrne, *The Whiz Kids*, 29.
46. The federal government's sustained interest in data analysis contributed to the emergence and development of the field of management science.
47. Byrne, *The Whiz Kids*, 40, 49.
48. Khurana, *From Higher Aims to Hired Hands*, 263.
49. The Carnegie Foundation issued a similar report and exposé of medical education in 1910. See Flexner, *Medical Education in the United States and Canada*.
50. See for example, Brossard and Dewhurst, *University Education for Business*; Hofstader and Hardy, *The Development and Scope*; American Association of Collegiate Schools of Business, *Faculty Requirements and Standards in Collegiate Schools of Business*.
51. Khurana, *From Higher Aims to Hired Hands*, 270.
52. Pierson *et al.*, *The Education of American Businessmen*, 218–19.
53. Ibid., 36, 40.
54. Gordon and Howell, *Higher Education for Business*, 5.
55. Pierson *et al.*, *The Education of American Businessmen*, 47.
56. Ibid., 65.
57. http://www.chicagobooth.edu/about/history and http://www.hbs.edu /about / facts-and-figures/Pages/history.aspx
58. Gordon and Howell, *Higher Education for Business*, 3.
59. Ibid., 166.
60. Ibid., 201–03.
61. Ibid., 200–01.
62. "Economist George Leland Bach, Founding Dean of Carnegie-Mellon Business School, Dies at 79," Thursday, September 1, 1994, http://news. standford.edu/pr/94/940930Arc4114.html
63. Felton, ed., *Carnegie Mellon 1900–2000*, 155.
64. Khurana, *From Higher Aims to Hired Hands*, 236.
65. Bach, "Managerial Decision Making," 319–54; Gordon and Howell, *Higher Education for Business*, viii.
66. Bach, "Some Observations," 351.
67. Felton, *Carnegie Mellon 1900–2000*, 155.

68. Bach, *Economics*.
69. "Economist George Leland Bach, Founding Dean of Carnegie-Mellon Business School, Dies at 79," Thursday, September 1, 1994, http://news.standford.edu/pr/94/940930Arc4114.html
70. http://www.gsb.stanford.edu/stanford-gsbexperience/leadership/history/balanced-excellence-george-leland-bach
71. Bach *et al.*, "Economics in the Curricula of Schools of Business," 563.
72. Bach, "Some Observations on the Business School of Tomorrow," 354–58.
73. Bach *et al.*, "Economics in the Curricula of Schools of Business," 563.
74. Simon, "Constructing a University," 3.
75. They included Richard Michael Cyert, Charles Holt, James Gardner Marsh, John Frasier Muth, and Allen Newell. See Felton, *Carnegie Mellon 1900–2000*, 155.
76. John Frasier Muth did foundational work on the theory of *rational expectations* that is employed by the efficient market hypothesis and Herbert Simon developed the concept of *bounded rationality*. See: Muth, Rational Expectations"; Simon, *Models of Man*.
77. Curtin, "Operations Research," 925–31.
78. Simon, "Constructing a University," 5.
79. Mintzberg, *Managers Not MBAs*, 31.
80. Gordon and Howell, *Higher Education for Business*, 21, 27.
81. Ibid., 23.
82. Augier and March, *The Roots, Rituals, and Rhetorics of Change*.
83. Skousen, "The Perseverance,"137. The Samuelson book is still in print. The 19th edition with William Nordhaus came out in 2010. http://shop.mheducation.com/search.html?search Query=economics+samuelson
84. Samuelson, *Economics: An Introductory Analysis*, 37. Also see Samuelson, *Economics,* 10th ed., 43; Samuelson, and Nordhaus, *Economics,* 14th ed., 35. I have added **bold** for emphasis in this and other quotes in this section.
85. The complete paragraph from *Wealth of Nations* with the portions kept by Samuelson printed in bold: "But the annual revenue of every society is always precisely equal to the exchangeable value of the whole annual produce of its industry, or rather is precisely the same thing with that exchangeable value. As **every individual**, therefore, **endeavours** as much as he can both to employ his capital in the support of domestick industry, and **so** to direct that industry **that its produce may be of the greatest value**; every individual necessarily labours to render the annual revenue of the society as great as he can. **He** generally, indeed, **neither intends to promote the publick interest, nor knows how much he is promoting it.** By preferring the

support of domestick to that of foreign industry, **he intends only his own security**; and by directing that industry in such a manner as its produce may be of the greatest value, he intends **only his own gain, and he is in this**, as in many other cases, **led by an invisible hand to promote an end which was no part of his intention.** Nor is it always the worse for the society that it was no part of it. **By pursuing his own interest he frequently promotes that of the society more effectually than when he really intends to promote it.** I have never known much good done by those who affected to trade for the publick good. It is an affectation, indeed, not very common among merchants, and very few words need be employed in dissuading them from it." See Smith, *An Inquiry into the Nature and Causes of the Wealth of Nations*, 456.

86. Specifically, the paragraphs preceding the full quote indicated that individuals choose to invest domestically when the returns are equal or nearly equal to foreign investments. Their motive is that domestic investments are less risky. Although their motivation is not a nationalistic desire to support domestic industry, such investment "... puts into motion a greater quantity of domestic industry, and gives revenue and employment to a greater number of the inhabitants of the country, than an equal capital employed in the foreign trade of consumption." See Smith, *An Inquiry into the Nature and Causes of the Wealth of Nations*, 455.

87. Ibid., 457. Underlining added to the original.

88. Samuelson, *Economics*, 39. Also see Samuelson, *Economics,* 10th ed., 41; Samuelson and Nordhaus, *Economics,* 14th ed., 34. Emphasis added.

89. Schlefer, "Today's Most Mischievous Misquotation," 16–19.

90. Samuelson, *Economics: An Introductory Analysis,* 36.

91. Arrow and Hahn, *General Competitive Analysis*, vi, vii.

92. Arrow, "Discrimination in the Labour Market,"124. Emphasis added.

93. Baumol, "Smith Versus Marx," 117.

94. Ibid., 119.

95. Ibid., 117. Emphasis added.

96. Stigler, "Economics — The Imperial Science?," 304.

97. Ibid., 304.

98. Ibid., 3, 6.

99. Ibid., 7.

100. This perspective was first received with skepticism by about 20 University of Chicago economists, but its influence has been profound, resulting in the creation of the cross-disciplinary field of *law and economics*. Richard Posner (economist, federal judge, and leader in the field) offers stronger

212 *Seeking Adam Smith: Finding The Shadow Curriculum of Business*

support for Stigler's position than did Stigler himself. Posner argues that while economists do not include considerations of fairness and justice in their analyses, they can assess the long-term economic consequences of alternative decisions being considered by a judge. Posner suggests further that from this long-term and generalized perspective, the economic and legal views will often result in similar outcomes. See Stigler, *Memoirs of an Unregulated Economist*, 75–79. See Posner, *Economic Analysis of the Law*.

101. Becker, "Crime and Punishment," 176. Emphasis added.

102. Black, *A Dictionary of Economics*, 135. Emphasis added.

103. Stiglitz, *Making Globalization Work*, 189–90.

104. The lecture was given in Kirkcaldy, Scotland, in June 1973 at a gathering celebrating the 250th anniversary of Smith's birth. It appeared in print in two books. See Galbraith, "The Founding Faith"; Galbraith, "The Founding Faith," 152–68 (159 quoted).

105. This version of Phil Donahue's interview of Milton Friedman was uploaded on July 14, 2007, and had been viewed 2,377,843 times by March 8, 2015, www.youtube.com/watch?v=#6652A9

106. Buchanan, *The Collected Works of James M. Buchanan*. Emphasis added.

107. Samuelson and Galbraith were not libertarians.

108. Very interesting and pleasing discoveries in this journey have been the existence of the sociology of business and the self-examination that has taken place within the field of management.

109. Cournot, *Recherches sur les Principes Mathematiques de la Theorie des Richesses*.

110. Columbia Business School, "The Power of Possibility."

111. The economics department is located in the business school at Carnegie Mellon. See http://www.tepper.cmu.edu/doctoral-program/fields-of-study/financial-economics/.

112. Jovanovic, "The Construction of the Canonical."

113. Ibid.

114. Overtveldt, *The Chicago School*, 201–09.

115. Sargent, "Rational Expectations," 432–35.

116. Underlying rational choice is the "methodological precept" of *methodological individualism* that claims the behavior of organizations and institutions must be seen and examined as the collective action of individuals. See Heath, "Methodological Individualism."

117. Hutcheson, *An Inquiry into the Original*, 114.

118. See Mill, *Utilitarianism*; Persky, "Retrospectives."

119. Friedman, "The Methodology of Positive Economics," 30.
120. Marshall, *Principles of Economics,* 78.
121. Marshall, *Principles of Economics*, 8th ed., 5.
122. Young, ed., *Rational Choice Theory and Religion.*
123. Feddersen, "Rational Choice Theory and the Paradox of Not Voting," 99–112.
124. de Waal, *The Age of Empathy*, 175.
125. Ross, "Game Theory."
126. http://www.rankingthebrands.com/The-Brand-Rankings.aspx?rankingID= 37&year=857
127. Noe, "A Survey of the Economic Theory of Reputation."
128. Shapiro, "Premiums for High Quality Products."
129. Kingsbury, "Apple Is Now More than Double the Size of Exxon."
130. 901 F.2d at 629 as quoted in Prentice, "The Case of the Irrational Auditor," 136.
131. Milgrom and Roberts, "Predation, Reputation, and Entry Deterrence."
132. "Ronald H. Coase — Prize Lecture."
133. Coase, "The Nature of the Firm."
134. "Ronald Coase, 1910–2013: A tribute." http://www.law.uchicago.edu/ alumni/magazine/spring14/coase
135. Milgrom and Roberts, 29.
136. Williamson, *Markets and Hierarchies*, 4, 9, 25; Ghoshal, "Bad for Practice," 18.
137. Williamson, *Markets and Hierarchies*, 7.
138. A manufacturer's perspective is usually taken, but the example of a franchisor is used here because it may be more familiar to many readers.
139. Williamson, *Markets and Hierarchies*, 26.
140. Cowling and Dugden, "Control, Markets and Firms," 73.
141. The term *supply chain management* was coined in 1982. See Tim and Oliver, "When Will Supply Chain Management Grow Up?."
142. Helms and Inman, "Supply Chain Management."
143. Kumar, "The Power of Trust."
144. Frankel, *Trust and Honesty*, 126.
145. Frankel, *Fiduciary Law*; Rodwin, *Conflicts of Interests and the Future of Medicine*; Gibson and Singh, *The Treatment Trap*; Toffler and Reingold, *Final Accounting*.
146. I use the term *professional* loosely in this sentence to describe those who do what they do for money rather than fun. This group is in contrast to the

learned professions, such as law and medicine, where practitioners are licensed, expected to serve the public, and possess a high level of technical skill.

147. Smith, *An Inquiry into the Nature and Causes of the Wealth of Nations*, 746.
148. Marshall, "Introduction."
149. Jensen and Meckling, "Theory of the Firm."
150. "SSRN Top 10,000" Papers, Social Science Research Network, last updated February 1, 2015, hq.ssrn.com
151. Jensen, *A Theory of the Firm*, 57.
152. Jensen and Meckling, "Theory of the Firm," 312.
153. The paper is saying that the proof rests on the assumption that the *efficient market hypothesis* is true because the *theory of rational expectations* is true.
154. See "The Power of Self-Belief," *The Economist*, December 6, 2014, 86.
155. Jensen and Meckling, "Theory of the Firm," 310.
156. Ibid., 312.
157. Dobbin and Jung, "The Misapplication of Mr. Michael Jensen," 331–66.
158. Jensen *et al.*, "Organizations and Markets."
159. Jensen and Meckling, "The Nature of Man," 4.
160. A sixth model was added later. See Jensen *et al.*, "Organizations and Markets," 10.
161. Jensen and Meckling, "The Nature of Man," 5.
162. Ibid., 5.
163. Jensen, "Self-Interest, Altruism, Incentives, & Agency," 3.
164. Jensen and Meckling, "The Nature of Man," 10. The authors also write on page 5: "The usefulness of any model of human nature depends on its ability to explain a wide range of social phenomena; the test of such a model is the degree to which it is consistent with observed human behavior. ... Greater detail limits the explanatory ability of a model because individual people differ so greatly." If this is so, then saying all economic behavior is intentional is more inclusive than saying that all economic behavior is selfish.
165. Jensen *et al.*, "Organizations and Markets," 28.
166. Jensen and Meckling, "The Nature of Man," 9.
167. Milgrom and Roberts, *Economics, Organization and Management*, 35.
168. Ghoshal and Moran, "Bad for Practice"; Dobbin and Jung, "The Misapplication of Mr. Michael Jensen," 331–66.
169. Stigler, *Memoirs of an Unregulated Economist*, 53.
170. Jensen, *A Theory of the Firm*, 57.
171. Jensen and Meckling, "Theory of the Firm," 310. Italics in the original.

172. Swedberg, "The Structure of Confidence and the Collapse of Lehman Brothers."

173. Jensen, *A Theory of the Firm*, 57.

174. Shearer, "Piece Rates, Fixed Wages and Incentives."

175. Baye, *Managerial Economics and Business Strategy*; Kreps, *Microeconomics for Managers*; Milgrom and John, *Economics, Organization & Management*; Thomas and Charles, *Managerial Economics*; Webster, *Managerial Economics*; Wilkinson, *Managerial Economics*.

176. "Milton Friedman on self-interest and the morality of corporations pursuing profits," From Friedman, "Speaks, Lecture 3."

177. Easterbrook and Fischel, "Antitrust Suits". Stable URL: http://www.jstor.org/stable/1288576, the bold type has been added.

178. Burns, "Qwest Chief's Appeal Hinges on Chicago's Daniel Fischer."

179. Heath, *Morality, Competition, and the Firm*, 19.

180. "Which Heads Rolled at GM Over Ignition Switch Scandal? Mostly Executives."

181. Knight, *The Ethics of Competition*, 85.

182. Ibid., 97.

183. Ibid., 29.

184. Ibid., 30.

185. Ibid., 42.

186. Ibid., 94

187. Ibid., 63.

188. Coase, "The Problem of Social Cost."

189. Posner, *Economic Analysis of Law*, 11–12, 265.

190. Margolis, "Hidden Curriculum."

191. Pierce and Paulman, "The Preceptor as Ethics Educator"; Hafferty and Hafler, "The Hidden Curriculum."

192. Khurana *et al.*, "Management as a Profession."

193. Gordon and Howell, *Higher Education for Business*, 3.

194. Bach, "Some Observations on the Business School of Tomorrow," 354–58.

195. Datar *et al.*, *Rethinking the MBA*.

196. Smith, *Fifty Years of Education*, 71.

197. AACSB International, "Business School Data Trends 2013," 32.

198. Dawkins, *The Selfish Gene*. Incidentally, it is the genes rather than the individuals they inhabit that cause them to act so uncivilly.

199. Kronman, *Education's End*; Neiman, *Evil in Modern Thought*.

200. Mearsheimer, "The Aims of Education."

201. Boesky, *Merger Mania*.
202. Berkeley Haas, "Commencement Speakers."
203. http://www.nytimes.com/1987/12/19/business/boesky-sentenced-to-3-years-in-jail-in-insider-scandal.html?pagewanted=all&src=pm
204. Protess and Ahmen, "Michael Douglas Tackles Greed for F.B.I."
205. Smith, *Ayn Rand's Normative Ethics*, 23.
206. Heath, *Morality, Competition, and the Firm*, 114.
207. Gentile, *Giving Voice to Values*, xi, 26.
208. Turner, *Cambridge Dictionary of Sociology*, 503.
209. Gould, *The Mismeasure of Man*.
210. Colby *et al.*, *Rethinking Undergraduate Business Education*.
211. Ibid., 87.
212. Hume, *A Treatise of Human Nature*.
213. Kahneman *et al.*, "Fairness and the Assumptions of Economics," S286.
214. Shover and Hochsteller, *Choosing White-Collar Crime*, 12–13.
215. Banaji *et al.*, "How (Un)Ethical Are You?"; Prentice, "Ethical Decision Making."
216. Bazerman and Tenbrunsel, *Blind Spots*.
217. Wright, *The Moral Animal*, 280.
218. Zimbardo, *The Lucifer Effect*.
219. Ibid., 438.
220. Belfort, *The Wolf of Wall Street*.
221. Armstrong, "Social Irresponsibility in Management."
222. Liberman and Ross, "The Name of the Game."
223. Ghoshal and Moran, "Bad for Practice"; Ferraro *et al.*, "Economics Language and Assumptions"; Mastilak *et al.*, "Self-Fulfilling Prophecy?."
224. Merton, "The Self-Fulfilling Prophecy,"195.
225. Brehm, *Theory of Psychological Reactance*, 4.
226. The expectations are not false in all instances of reactance.
227. Packard, *The HP Way*, 135–36.
228. Rogers, *Diffusion of Innovations*, 11.
229. Khurana, *From Higher Aims to Hired Hands*, 318.
230. Jensen, "Eclipse of the Public Corporation," 61–74.
231. Dobbin and Jung, "The Misapplication of Mr. Michael Jensen," 335–38.
232. Stigler, *Memoirs of an Unregulated Economist*, 211.
233. Khurana, *From Higher Aims to Hired Hands*, 320–21.
234. Business Roundtable, "2012 Principles of Corporate Governance."
235. Burkhard, "Proposed Model Bylaws." Boldface added here and in next two quotes for emphasis.

236. Business Roundtable, "Statement on Corporate Governance," 3.

237. Business Roundtable, "2012 Principles of Corporate Governance," 2–3.

238. "When Did It Happen? The Colonies Commit Treason, Revolutionary America 1763–1783," April 20–November 3, 2002, http://www.hoover. archives.gov/exhibits/RevAmerica/3-When/56Men.html

239. Peace Corps, "Fast Facts."

240. Charities Aid Foundation, "World Giving Index 2014."

241. Business Roundtable, "2012 Principles of Corporate Governance."

242. Fudenberg *et al.*, "Slow to Anger and Fast to Forgive."

243. Guth *et al.*, "An Experimental Analysis of Ultimatum Bargaining."

244. Frank, *Luxury Fever*; *What Price the Moral High Ground?.*

245. Brosnan, "Fairness and Other-Regarding Preferences in Nonhuman Primates," 92.

246. Fehr and Gachter, "Fairness and Retaliation."

247. Marwell and Ames, "Economists Free Ride, Does Anyone Else?," 307.

248. Ledyard, "Public Goods."

249. Hoffman, *Empathy and Moral Development.*

250. Bloom, "The Moral Life of Babies."

251. Gazzaniga, *The Ethical Brain.*

252. de Waal, "How Selfish an Animal."

253. de Waal, *The Age of Empathy.*

254. de Waal, "How Selfish an Animal," 67–72.

255. See Falk and Fischbacher, "A Theory of Reciprocity"; Dohmen *et al.*, "Homo Reciprocans."

256. Bowles and Gintis, "Behavioral Science," 128.

257. Hauser, *Moral Minds.*

258. See Major, "Public Choice Theory," http://go.galegroup.com.ezproxy.lib. utexas.edu/ps/i.do?id=GALE%7CCCX3045302118&v=2.1&u=txshracd259 8&it=r&p=GVRL&sw=w&asid=64eb5017cfca28c0395d1a509d7d0da1

259. Marwell and Ames, "Economists Free Ride, Does Anyone Else?," 299.

260. Ibid., 309.

261. Kahneman *et al.*, "Fairness and the Assumptions of Economics."

262. Frank *et al.*, "Does Studying Economics Inhibit Cooperation?."

263. Yezer *et al.*, "Does Studying Economics Discourage Cooperation?."

264. Frank *et al.*, "Do Economists Make Bad Citizens?"

265. McCabe *et al.*, "Academic Dishonesty in Graduate Business Programs," 295.

266. McCabe *et al.*, "Values and Moral Dilemmas."

267. Williams *et al.*, "Managers' Business School Education and Military Service."

268. Elegido, "Business Education and Erosion of Character."
269. CDA, "Healthcare-Associated Infections (HAIs)."
270. Fisman and Miguel, "Cultures of Corruption."
271. Transparency International. July 17, 2007, http://www.transparency.org/about/
272. World Bank, "GDP per Capita (Current US$)."
273. Encyclopædia Britannica Online, s.v. "civic virtue." December 21, 2015, http://www.britannica.com/topic/civic-virtue
274. *Oxford English Dictionary.*
275. Ghoshal and Moran, "Bad for Practice," 13–47; Dobbin and Jung, "The Misapplication of Mr. Michael Jensen"; Gintis and Khurana, "Corporate Honesty and Business Education."
276. Macey, *The Death of Corporate Reputation.*
277. Pascu-Nierth, "Enron Sails into New Markets."
278. Sachs, "Enron Corp. (ENE) Gas & Power Convergence."
279. http://online.wsj.com/article/SB11485750421063162.html?mod=+2_1040_3, 2/24/2009
280. Bogle, *The Battle for the Soul of Capitalism*, 92.
281. Ibid., 28, 10–11.
282. Congressional Budget Office, "The Budget and Economic Outlook."
283. Stengle, "Elder Stanford Dismayed by Son's Legal Travails."
284. See http://www.obitsforlife.com/obituary/523017/Goswick-O.php
285. July 25, 2012: http://www.forbes.com/sites/walterpavlo/2012/06/14/allen-stanford-sentenced-to-110-years-in-prison/
286. Bogle, *The Battle for the Soul of Capitalism*, 13. Boldface added for emphasis.
287. Bebchuk and Fried, *Pay without Performance*, 198.
288. Cuomo, "No Rhyme or Reason."
289. Lucian and Fried, *Pay without Performance*, 212.
290. Moore, "John Thain's $35,000 'Commode on Legs' Outrage."
291. Chandler, *The Visible Hand.*
292. Coase, "The Nature of the Firm," 386–405.
293. Chandler, *The Visible Hand*, 10.
294. Cohen and Prusak, *In Good Company.*
295. Fukuyama, *The Great Disruption,* 16.
296. "The 10 Biggest Frauds in Recent US History," 2015, forbes.com
297. Department of Financial Institutions, State of Washington, "Securities Division in the matter of determining whether there has been a violation of the Securities Act of Washington by: Bernard L. Madoff; Bernard L. Madoff

Investment Securities, LLC. Order Number S-08-429-09-FO01." March 5, 2009.

298. Information in this section is taken from McLean and Elkind, *The Smartest Guys in the Room*. Quotations from this source and citations of other sources are cited. Generous speculation has been added.

299. Risk-taking is a characteristic of a psychopath. See Babiak and Hare, *Snakes in Suits*, 47.

300. Alex (writer/director), *Enron*; Dawkins, *The God Delusion*. 215.

301. McLean, and Elkind, *The Smartest Guys in the Room,* 55.

302. Ibid., 267.

303. "Ex-Enron CEO Skilling Resentenced to 14 Years," *Austin American-Statesman*, June 22, 2013, B5.

304. John Bogle deserves credit for this literary allusion to Pogo. See, Bogle, *Battle for the Soul of Capitalism*, 93.

305. Chu, "Changing Credit Card Terms Squeeze Consumers," 2A.

306. Macey, *The Death of Corporate Reputation*.

307. Ritholtz, "A Memo Found in the Street."

308. Phillips, "Would You Pay $103,000 For This Arizona Fixer-Upper?," A1, A6.

309. http://www.fbi.gov/phoenix/press-releases/2012/loan-originator-sentenced-to-10-years-in-federal-prison-for-leading-a-multi-million-dollar-mortgage-fraud-scheme

310. Braga *et al.*, "'Flip that House' Fraud Cost Billions."

311. Braga *et al.*, "King of the Sarasota Flip," 1A, 8A, 9A.

312. Braga, "Craig Adams Sentenced to 3 Years in Flipping Fraud."

313. Panchuk, "Ocwen Finalizes Acquisition of Homeward Residential."

314. Smith, *The Theory of Moral Sentiments*, 86.

315. For a narrow but fascinating view of the cold war see Macintyre, *A Spy Among Friends*.

316. Jones, *Masters of the Universe*; Fourcade, *Economists and Societies*, Chap. 2; Mirowski and Piehwe, *The Road from Mont Pelerin*.

317. Friedman, *Capitalism and Freedom*, 17. For a discussion of the important role of Harold Luhnow, president of the Volker Fund, who acted as a venture capitalist in establishing the Chicago School and the Mont Pelerin Society. See Van Horn, Rob and Philip Mirowski. "The Rise of the Chicago School of Economics and the Birth of Neoliberalism" in Mirowski and Piehwe, eds., *The Road from Mont Pelerin*.

318. http://www.usgovernmentspending.com/spending_chart_1900_2019USp_XXs1li111mcn_F0t_US_Total_Government_Spending#tabbed

319. Hayek, *The Road to Serfdom*, 17.
320. Hayek, "The Intellectuals and Socialism," 417.
321. Ibid., 418.
322. Ibid., 417.
323. Ibid., 422.
324. Hartwell, *A History of the Mont Pelerin Society*, 26–27.
325. Ibid., 220.
326. The last paragraph of the society's "Statement of Aims" written on April 8, 1947, reads "The group does not aspire to conduct propaganda. It seeks to establish no meticulous and hampering orthodoxy. It aligns itself with no particular party. Its object is solely, by facilitating the exchange of views among minds inspired by certain ideals and broad conceptions held in common, to contribute to the preservation and improvement of the free society." It is not clear how welcoming the group became to those whose views were not libertarian. https://www.montpelerin.org/montpelerin/mpsGoals.html
327. Hartwell, *A History of the Mont Pelerin Society*, 11.
328. Only a few issues of *The Mont Pelerin Society Quarterly* were printed, but the organization's *Newsletter* has been in existence since 1971. See Hartwell, *A History of the Mont Pelerin Society*, 66.
329. Hartwell, *A History of the Mont Pelerin Society*, 45.
330. Ibid., 65, 66, 90.
331. https://socialthought.uchicago.edu
332. Dzuback, *Robert M. Hutchins*, 215.
333. Hayek, *The Counter-Revolution of Science*, 24.
334. The Royal Swedish Academy of Sciences, "Press Release."
335. Silk, *The Economists*, 47.
336. Friedman, "The Invisible Hand."
337. Quotation taken from Friedman, "The Methodology of Positive Economics," 3. Bold added for emphasis.
338. Friedman, "The Methodology of Positive Economics," 5.
339. Fourcade, *Economies and Societies*, 93.
340. Friedman, "The Methodology of Positive Economics," 32.
341. Ibid., 7–9.
342. Ibid., 40.
343. Ibid., 38–39.
344. Darity, "Economics, Experimental."
345. Keynes, *The Scope and Method of Political Economy*, 67–69. It is tempting to use *libertarian* as a synonym for *laissez faire* here, but according to the

Oxford English Dictionary, the term with this usage did not appear in print until 1944.

346. Friedman, *Capitalism and Freedom*, xi.
347. Ibid., 200.
348. Ibid., 25.
349. Ibid., 12.
350. Ibid., 2.
351. Ibid., 25.
352. Ibid., 2.
353. Ibid., 2.
354. Ibid., 3.
355. Friedman, "The Social Responsibility of Business is to Increase Its Profits."
356. Smith, *An Inquiry into the Nature and Causes of the Wealth of Nations*, 26, 27.
357. Smith, *The Theory of Moral Sentiments*, 235–36.
358. Sisodia *et al.*, *Firms of Endearment*.
359. See Mackey and Sisodia, "Rethinking the Social Responsibility of Business"; Mackey and Sisodia, *Conscious Capitalism*.
360. Jensen, "Value Maximization, Stakeholder Theory, and the Corporate Objective Function."
361. Hoover Institution, Stanford University. http://www.hoover.org.
362. Friedman and Friedman, *Free to Choose*, 5.
363. Ibid., 36.
364. Smith, *An Inquiry into the Nature and Causes of the Wealth of Nations*, 342–43.
365. Spencer, *Social Statistics*, 323.
366. Spencer, *Social Statistics, Abridged and Revised*, 156.
367. Spencer, *Principles of Biology*, 444.
368. Ghent, *Our Benevolent Feudalism*, 29.
369. Darwin, *The Descent of Man*, 165–66.
370. Hartwell, *A History of the Mont Pelerin Society*, 151, 229–30.
371. Jones, *Masters of the Universe*.
372. Hartwell, *A History of the Mont Pelerin Society*, 186.
373. Hayek, "The Intellectuals and Socialism," 422.
374. Hartwell, *A History of the Mont Pelerin Society*, 220.
375. Overtveldt, *The Chicago School*, 91.
376. Silk, *The Economists*, 52.
377. Clarke, "An Interview with Paul Samuelson, Part One."

378. *The Official Report, House of Commons* (5th Series), November 11, 1947, V. 444, cc. 206–07.
379. Lars Peter Hansen‡, 2013; Eugene F. Fama*‡, 2013; Thomas J. Sargent, 2011; Leonid Hurwicz, 2007; Roger B. Myerson‡, 2007; Edward C. Prescott, 2004; Daniel L. McFadden, 2000; James J. Heckman‡, 2000; Robert A. Mundell, 1999; Myron S. Scholes*, 1997; Robert E. Lucas Jr.*‡, 1995; Robert W. Fogel, 1993; Gary S. Becker*‡, 1992; Ronald H. Coase, 1991; Harry M. Markowitz*, 1990; Merton H. Miller, 1990; Trygve Haavelmo, 1989; James M. Buchanan Jr.*, 1986; Gerard Debreu, 1983; George J. Stigler*, 1982; Lawrence R. Klein, 1980; Theodore W. Schultz, 1979; Herbert A. Simon*, 1978; Milton Friedman*, 1976; Tjalling C. Koopmans, 1975; Friedrich August von Hayek, 1974; Kenneth J. Arrow, 1972; and Paul A. Samuelson*, 1970. ‡ denotes current faculty and * designates alumni. See http://www.uchicago.edu/about/accolades/22/
380. See Hunt and Lautzenheiser, *History of Economic Thought*, 493. They write "Samuelson's *Economics* enshrined macroeconomic (Keynesian) and microeconomic (neoclassical) theories as the twin pillars of orthodoxy."
381. Kaufman, "Chicago and the Development of Twentieth-Century Labor Economics."
382. Stigler, *Memoirs of an Unregulated Economist*, 162.
383. Shiller, *Irrational Exuberance*, 193.
384. Jensen and Meckling, "The Nature of Man," 9.
385. Fama, "The Twin Pillars of Asset Pricing."
386. Clement, "Interview with Eugene Fama." National Bureau of Economic Research, "US Business Cycle Expansions and Contractions."
387. Lewis, *The Big Short*; Zuckerman, *The Greatest Trade Ever*.
388. Olkin, "A Conversation with W. Allen Wallis."
389. Nik-Khah, "George Stigler," 124.
390. Augier and March, *The Roots, Rituals, and Rhetorics of Change*, 168.
391. "Merton H. Miller — Biographical."
392. Memo to Miriam Chamberlin, a Ford Foundation project director, quoted in Augier and March, *The Roots, Rituals, and Rhetorics of Change*, 168.
393. Schultz and Aliber, *Guidelines, Informal Controls, and the Marketplace*.
394. Quotation taken from Nik-Khah, "George Stigler," 127.
395. Ibid., 135.
396. Landau, *Regulating New Drugs*, 2.
397. Stigler, "Regulation," 9–19.
398. "George Stigler," http://research.chicagobooth.edu/stigler/about-the-center/george-stigler and http://www.chicagobooth.edu/about/nobel

399. Nik-Khah, "George Stigler," 136; "Stigler Center Annual Report," 2013–2014, https://research.chicagobooth.edu/~/media/94A00099AE464DC8B3 02F324ADEFBC8C.pdf., 30.

400. Stigler, *Memoirs of an Unregulated Economist*, 146–47.

401. Buchanan, "Socialism Is Dead."

402. Samuelson, "Credo of a Lucky Textbook Author," 158–59.

403. Fourcade, *Economists and Societies*, 89.

404. Stigler, *Memoirs of an Unregulated Economist*, 214.

405. Smith, *An Inquiry into the Nature and Causes of the Wealth of Nations*, 243.

406. Ibid., 47, 393, 525, 527, 709.

407. Ibid., 393.

408. Ibid., 760.

409. Scholars aware of Smith's religious views argue his language in *Moral Sentiments* was designed to appeal to his students, most of whom were entering the clergy, and to protect him from religious conservatives who might harm his career. He surely had learned the lesson of David Hume, who never obtained an academic appointment because of his controversial views. The counterargument to the position of these scholars is that Smith's deistic views were sincere and Smith exposed himself to great risk in declaring them because they were incompatible with the Westminster Confession of Faith that both he and those emerging clergymen were required by the University of Glasgow to embrace. His deistic views were not added to the five revisions of *Moral Sentiments* published after he quit teaching. The last appeared in the year of his death, when he had few earthly concerns beyond his intellectual legacy. Scholars also argue Smith's naturalistic social theory does not require the providence of God to support humankind and that vital aspects of his philosophical system — the emotion of sympathy and the virtues resulting from it — can easily be explained without requiring the existence of God. Smith would have responded that his religious (teleological) views were neither superfluous nor insincere. The *a priori* assumption supporting his system was that God created the universe and did not need to intervene thereafter because all of creation, including commercial institutions, was an adaptive system designed to promote the happiness of humankind. He referred to God as masculine and used a number of synonyms, including "the Deity," "the Author of nature," and "the divine Being." He also used "Providence," a term commonly used in eighteenth-century Scotland to refer to "the foreknowing and beneficent care and government of God." "Nature," as Smith used it, was feminine and referred to the universe and everything in it that had been created according to God's great

design. Thus, Smith's philosophical system was comprised of a designer, a design, and the operations of a great social machine. All that remains today of these three parts for economists is the price mechanism and the poetic but now empty metaphor of the invisible hand.

410. Leonidas Montes makes a persuasive case that neither Newton nor Smith was Newtonian in their methods of inquiry. See Montes, *Adam Smith in Context.*

411. Newton, *The Principia,* 940.

412. Neiman, *Evil in Modern Thought,* 31.

413. Smith, *The Theory of Moral Sentiments,* 236.

414. Ibid., 166.

415. Ibid., 87.

416. Ibid., 237.

417. Ibid., 183–85. In this same lengthy paragraph, he writes "It is this deception [that wealth brings happiness] which rouses and keeps in continual motion the industry of mankind. It is this which first prompted them to cultivate the ground, to build houses, to found cities and commonwealths, and to invent and improve all the sciences and arts, which ennoble and embellish human life; which have entirely changed the whole face of the globe, have turned the rude forests of nature into agreeable and fertile plains, and made the trackless and barren ocean a new fund of subsistence, and the great high road of communication to the different nations of the earth." Nowhere in this discussion does Smith indicate that ambition and the desire for wealth causes harm to others — that the motivating force is malicious greed.

418. Raphael and Macfie, "Introduction"; Smith, *The Theory of Moral Sentiments,* 8.

419. Smith, *An Inquiry into the Nature and Causes of the Wealth of Nations,* 422.

420. Ibid., 786–88.

421. Ibid., 493.

422. Ibid., 316.

423. Ibid., 26–27.

424. Smith, The Theory of *Moral Sentiments,* 309.

425. Smith, *An Inquiry into the Nature and Causes of the Wealth of Nations,* 760.

426. Alexander, *An Essay on Man,* 126, xiii. Also see Spacks, "Acts of Love and Knowledge," 176–91.

427. Mizuta, *Adam Smith's Library,* 202.

428. Smith, *An Inquiry into the Nature and Causes of the Wealth of Nations,* 454.

429. Ibid., 295.

430. Smith, *The Theory of Moral Sentiments,* 50.

431. Ibid., 149.
432. Ibid., 150.
433. Ibid., 25.
434. Ibid., 341.
435. Ibid., 99.
436. Griswold, *Adam Smith and the Virtues*, 102–03.
437. Smith, *The Theory of Moral Sentiments*, 163.
438. Ibid., 309.
439. Ibid., 313.
440. Smith, *An Inquiry into the Nature and Causes of the Wealth of Nations*, 342–43.
441. Smith, *The Theory of Moral Sentiments*, 163.
442. Ibid., 79.
443. Ibid., 82, 83.
444. Ibid., 86.
445. Ibid., 88.
446. Ibid., 235, 236.
447. Ibid., 85, 86.
448. Ibid., 116.
449. Ibid., 86.
450. Greenwald, *The McGraw-Hill Encyclopedia of Economics*, 632.
451. von Mises, *Liberalism*, 17, 18, 145.
452. Smith, *An Inquiry into the Nature and Causes of the Wealth of Nations*, 324.
453. Ibid., 687.
454. Meek *et al.*, *Lectures on Jurisprudence*, 16.
455. Smith, *An Inquiry into the Nature and Causes of the Wealth of Nations*, 724.
456. Ibid., 724.
457. Ibid., 719.
458. Ibid., 726.
459. Ibid., 728.
460. Ibid., 394.
461. https://www.gov.uk/right-of-way-open-access-land/public-rights-of-way; http://www.hampsteadramblers.org.uk/history/14-history-highways.html
462. Smith, *An Inquiry into the Nature and Causes of the Wealth of Nations*, 758.
463. Ibid., 781.
464. Ibid., 788.
465. Ibid., 793.
466. Ibid., 796.
467. Meek *et al.*, *Lectures on Jurisprudence*, 299.

468. Smith, *An Inquiry into the Nature and Causes of the Wealth of Nations*, 814.
469. Ibid., 297n25, 322–23.
470. Ibid., 258, 508.
471. Ibid., 842.
472. Ibid., 825.
473. Ibid., 521.
474. Ibid., 61.
475. Ibid., 61.
476. Meek *et al.*, *Lectures on Jurisprudence*, 295.
477. Ibid., 537–38.
478. Smith, *An Inquiry into the Nature and Causes of the Wealth of Nations*, 356–58.
479. Ibid., 831.
480. Ibid., 463. The navigation acts were inspired by England's hostile relationship with Holland in their struggle for naval supremacy. The first Navigation acts, imposed before the creation of Great Britain in 1707, were prejudicial to Scotland and led later to the first American tea party. This situation was all personal to Smith. He gave a copy of *Wealth of Nations* to Charles Townshend, who was so impressed with the work he wanted his stepson (Henry Campbell Scott, 3rd Duke of Buccleuch) to study with Smith in Europe. Townshend, British chancellor of the exchequer, proposed what became known as the Townshend Acts, imposing duties on products imported by American colonists, encouraging some Bostonians to host a tea party in his honor. Smith sent a letter of condolences in September to Townshend concerning his younger brother, Colonel Roger Townshend, who had been killed the previous summer by cannon fire from Fort Ticonderoga in the French and Indian Wars. Townshend surely thought that if he paid taxes and sacrificed his brother to protect the colonists from the French, then they should support Britain's efforts to defend them.
481. Smith, *An Inquiry into the Nature and Causes of the Wealth of Nations*, 582.
482. Ibid., 577–78.
483. Ibid., 739.
484. Frank, *Passions within Reason*.
485. Evensky, *Adam Smith's Moral Philosophy*.
486. Sen, *On Ethics and Economics*.
487. Sen, *The Idea of Justice*, 184, 32.
488. Sen, "Adam Smith's Prudence," 43; Sen, *The Idea of Justice*, 184.
489. Sen, *The Idea of Justice*, 186.
490. Frank, *Passion within Reason*, xi.

491. Smith, *The Theory of Moral Sentiments*, 83.
492. Friedman, *Capitalism and Freedom*, 27.
493. Hang, "Golf's Honor Code Limits."
494. Associated Press, "Furyk tops David in Hilton Head playoff."
495. Friedman and Friedman, *Free to Choose*, 36, 201.
496. Posner, *A Failure of Capitalism*, xiii.
497. Meek *et al.*, *Lectures on Jurisprudence*, 7.
498. Milton and Friedman, *Free to Choose*, 201.
499. Smith, *The Theory of Moral Sentiments*, 187.
500. Fukuyama, *Trust*, 11.
501. Ibid., 7.
502. Barker, *America's Crisis of Values*, 96.
503. "The Worst Country on Earth."
504. Heritage Foundation, "2015 Index of Economic Freedom."
505. Elsewhere, Fukuyama argues that the tradeoff between authoritarianism and trust also differentiates the traditional hierarchical organization that characterized automobile manufacturing from the time of Henry Ford with its strict chain of command and the modern flat organization producing automobiles employing lean manufacturing. See Fukuyama, *The Great Disruption*, 222–24.
506. Smith, *The Theory of Moral Sentiments*, 86.
507. Hobbes, *Leviathan*, 84.
508. Fukuyama, *The Great Disruption*, 244.
509. Ibid., 63–64.
510. Ibid., 62.
511. Ibid., 155.
512. Palank, "Madoff Investors to Get Over $1 Billion in Added Recoveries."
513. Federal Bureau of Investigation, "Uniform Crime Report: Crime in the United States, 2009," September 2010.
514. Shiller, *Finance and the Good Society*.
515. Dawkins, *The Selfish Gene*, 2.
516. Ostrom, "Collective Action," 138.
517. February 5, 2010, http://nobelprize.org/nobel_prizes/economics/laureates/2009/Ostrom-lecture-slides.pdf
518. Smith, *An Inquiry into the Nature and Causes of the Wealth of Nations*, 760.
519. de Tocqueville, *Democracy in America*, 122.
520. Heclo, "Varieties of American Exceptionalism," 30–32.
521. Hylton and Stein, "U.S. Fire Department Profile."
522. "Firefighters Let Home Burn Over $75 Fee — Again."

523. Smith, *An Inquiry into the Nature and Causes of the Wealth of Nations*, 23.
524. Ibid., 14–15.
525. Smith, "'Early Draft' of Part of *the Wealth of Nations*"; Meek and Stein, *Lectures on Jurisprudence*, 338–39, 489.
526. Smith, *An Inquiry into the Nature and Causes of the Wealth of Nations*, 22. "The shepherd, the sorter of the wool, the wool comber or carder [untangled the shorn wool], the dyer, scribbler [produced thin, continuous 'ropes' of wool to be spun into yarn], the spinner, the weaver, the fuller [cleaned and thickened the cloth], the dresser [removed the nap, or irregularities, from the cloth's surface]...."
527. Ibid., 687.
528. Smith, *The Theory of Moral Sentiments*, 86.
529. von Mises, *Liberalism: The Classical Tradition*, 1.
530. Ibid., 14.
531. Ibid., 16.
532. Ibid., 18, 85.
533. Stigler, *The Theory of Price*; Chamberlin, *The Theory of Monopolistic Competition*; Schumpeter, *Capitalism, Socialism, and Democracy*.
534. Robinson, *The Economics of Imperfect Competition*.
535. A major response to the challenge of monopolistic competition to neoclassical economics, especially by those of the Chicago School, was to assert the applicability of price theory under conditions of imperfect competition. See Stigler, *Memoirs of an Unregulated Economist*, 161–66.
536. Economists refer to this as the opportunity costs of capital for firms that do not need to borrow money.
537. Stigler, *The Theory of Price,* rev. ed.
538. Stigler attributes profits to differences among firms or because a market is not in equilibrium. Ibid., 180–81.
539. The nearest approximation is oligopoly with some differentiated products, but without administered prices. See Samuelson and Nordhaus, *Economics,* 165–66.
540. Chamberlin, *The Theory of Monopolistic Competition*, 56.
541. Schumpeter, *Capitalism, Socialism, and Democracy.*
542. See "The First Automobile — Cugnot's Steam Vehicle," http://patentpending.blogs.com/patent_pending_blog/2004/10/the_first_autom.html; Also Bellis, "Automobile History."
543. "History's 10 Best Selling Cars of all Time," February 9, 2015, http://www.autoblog.com/photos/historys-10-bestselling-cars-of-all-time/#image-10

544. Samuelson and Nordhaus, *Economics*, 182–83.

545. See Posner, *A Failure of Capitalism*; Posner, *The Crisis of Capitalistic Democracy*.

546. Thier, "Microsoft Stores are Very Sad Places."

547. Drucker, *The Practice of Management*, 30, 31.

548. Alderson, *Marketing Behavior and Executive Action*, 444.

549. See "Staples Marks Retail Milestone with Opening of 1,000th Store in Atlanta."

550. Drogin, "To Assess Romney, Look Beyond the Bottom Line."

551. Gavin and Pfeiffer, "Reaping Profit in Study, Sweat." The *Los Angeles Times* article cited in note 550 estimates the total to be $102 million.

552. It is common for powerful drugs to take lives of some of those who take it, but what is important is that no lives would have been lost if the Upjohn board had shared the information in their possession with potential users.

553. Thurow, "Ethics Doesn't Start in Business Schools."

554. Federal Bureau of Investigation, "Uniform Crime Report: Crime in the United States, 2009," September 2010.

555. See Bogle, *Battle for the Soul of Capitalism*, 10–11; and Morris, *The Two Trillion Dollar Meltdown*, xix. The authors do not employ the same measures.

556. Jackall, *Moral Mazes*. As quoted in Shover and Hochstetler. *Choosing White-Collar Crime*.

557. Shover and Hochstetler, *Choosing White-Collar Crime*, 70.

Bibliography

AACSB International. "Business School Data Trends 2013," Tampa, Florida.

Alderson, Wroe. *Marketing Behavior and Executive Action.* Homewood, IL: Richard D. Irwin, 1957.

American Association of Collegiate Schools of Business. "Faculty requirements and standards in collegiate schools of business." Proceedings of a Conference on Professional Education for Business, Harriman Campus of Columbia University, Arden House, October 27–29, 1955.

Applbaum, Michael. *Ethics for Adversaries.* Princeton, NJ: Princeton University Press, 1999.

Ariely, Dan. *Predictably Irrational: The Hidden Forces That Shape Our Decisions.* New York: Harper Perennial, 2010.

Armstrong, J. Scott. "Social Irresponsibility in Management." *Journal of Business Research* 5, no. 3 (1997): 185–213.

Arrow, Kenneth J. "Discrimination in the Labour Market." In *Readings in Labour Economics: Readings with Commentaries,* edited by J. E. King, 17–136. Oxford: Oxford University Press, 1980.

Arrow, Kenneth J., and F. H. Hahn. *General Competitive Analysis.* San Francisco: Holden-Day, 1971.

Associated Press. *Furyk Tops Davis in Hilton Head Playoff.* April 18, 2010. http://www.thegolfchannell.com/tour-insider/furyk-tops-davis-hilton-head-playoff-36109/.

Augier, Mie, and James G. March. *The Roots, Rituals, and Rhetorics of Change: North American Business Schools After the Second World War.* Stanford, CA: Stanford University Business Books, 2011.

Babiak, Paul, and Robert D. Hare. *Snakes in Suits: When Psychopaths Go to Work.* New York: HarperCollins, 2006.

Bach, George Leland. *Economics: An Introduction to Analysis and Policy,* 8th ed. Englewood Cliffs, NJ: Prentice-Hall, 1974.

———. "Managerial Decision Making as an Organizing Concept." In *The Education of American Businessmen: A Study of University-College Programs in Business Administration,* edited by Frank C. Pierson *et al.,* New York: McGraw-Hill, 1959, 319–54.

———. "Some Observations on the Business School of Tomorrow." *Management Science* 4, no. 4 (July 1958): 351–54. http://www.jstor.org/stable/2627458.

Bach, George Leland, Melvin G. de Chazeau, Donald W. O'Connell, Arthur M. Weimer, and Ewald T. Grether. "Economics in the Curricula of Schools of Business: Discussion." *American Economic Review* (Papers and Proceedings of the Sixty-Eighth Annual Meeting of the American Economic Association) 46, no. 2, (1956): 563–77. http://www.jstor.org/stable/1910710.

Baker, Wayne. *America's Crisis of Values.* Princeton, NJ: Princeton University Press, 2005.

Banaji, Mahzarin R., Max H. Bazerman, and Dolly Chugh. "How (Un)Ethical Are You?" *Harvard Business Review* 81, no. 12 (December 2003): 56–64.

Barth, James R., Tong Li, Wenling Lu, Triphon Phumiwasana, and Glen Yago. *The Rise and Fall of the U.S. Mortgage and Credit Markets.* Hoboken, NJ: John Wiley & Sons, 2009.

Baumol, William J. "Smith Versus Marx on Business Morality and the Social Interest." In *Adam Smith and the Wealth of Nations: 1776–1976 Bicentennial Essays,* edited by Fred R. Glahe, Boulder, CO: Colorado Associated University Press, 1978, 111–22.

Baye, Michael R. *Managerial Economics and Business Strategy,* 7th ed. New York: McGraw-Hill Irwin, 2010.

Bazerman, Max H., and Ann E. Tenbrunsel. *Blind Spots: Why We Fail to Do What's Right and What to Do About It.* Princeton, NJ: Princeton University Press, 2011.

Bebchuk, Lucian, and Jesse Fried. *Pay Without Performance: The Unfulfilled Promise of Executive Compensation.* Cambridge: Harvard University Press, 2004.

Becker, Gary S. "Crime and Punishment: An Economic Approach." *Journal of Political Economy* 76, no. 2 (March–April 1968): 169–216. http://www.jstor.org/stable/1830481.

Belfort, Leonardo. *The Wolf of Wall Street.* New York: Bantam Books, 2013.

Bellis, Mary. *Automobile History: The History of Cars and Engines.* http:// inventors.about.com/od/cstartinventions/a/Car_History.htm.

Berkeley Haas. *Commencement Speakers.* http://www.hass.berkeley.edu/hass/ about/commencementspeakers.html.

Black, John. *A Dictionary of Economics,* 2nd ed. Oxford: Oxford University Press, 2002.

Black, William K. *The Best Way to Rob a Bank Is to Own One: How Corporate Executives and Politicians Looted the S&L Industry.* Austin, TX: University of Texas Press, 2005.

Bloom, Paul. "The Moral Life of Babies." *New York Times,* May 5, 2010. http:// www.nytimes.com/2010/05/09/magazinebabies-t.html.

Boesky, Ivan F. *Merger Mania: Arbitrage, Wall Streets Best Kept Money Making Secret.* New York: Holt, Rinehart and Winston, 1985.

Bogle, John C. *The Battle for the Soul of Capitalism.* Yale University Press: New Haven, 2005.

Boudon, Raymond. "Rational Choice Theory." In *The New Blackwell Companion to Social Theory,* edited by Bryan Turner, Chitchester: Wiley-Blackwell, 2009, 179–95.

Bourke, Helen. "Mayo, George Elton (1880–1949)." *Australian Dictionary of Biography* 10 (1968). http://adb.anu.edu.au/biography/mayo-george-elton-7541.

Bowles, Samuel, and Herbert Gintis. "Behavioral Science: Homo recpirocans." *Nature* 415 (January 10, 2002): 125–28.

Boyer, Ernest L. *Scholarship Reconsidered: Priorities of the Professoriate.* Princeton, NJ: The Carnegie Foundation for the Advancement of Teaching, 1990.

Brehm, Jack W. A. *Theory of Psychological Reactance.* New York: Academic Press, 1966.

Broadie, Alexander, ed. *The Cambridge Companion to the Scottish Enlightenment.* Cambridge: Cambridge University Press, 2003.

Brosnan, Sarah F. "Fairness and Other-Regarding Preferences in Nonhuman Primates." In *Moral Markets: The Role of Values in the Economy,* edited by Paul J. Zak, Princeton, NJ: Princeton University Press, 2008, 77–106.

Brossard, James H. S., and J. Frederick Dewhurst. *University Education for Business: A Study of Existing Needs and Practices.* Philadelphia: University of Pennsylvania Press, 1931.

Bryce, Robert. *Pipe Dreams: Greed, Ego, and the Death of Enron.* New York: Public Affairs, 2002.

Buchanan, James M. *The Collected Works of James M. Buchanan. 5, The Demand and Supply of Public Goods.* Foreword by Geoffrey Brennan. Parts 5.5.25–5.5.26. Indianapolis: Liberty Fund, 1999. http://oll.libertyfund.org/title/1067.

———. "Socialism is dead, but Leviathan lives on." The Seventh John Bonython Lecture, Center for Independent Studies, Sydney, Australia, 1990.

Burkhard, James R. "Proposed Model Bylaws to be Used with The Revised Model Business Corporation Act (1984)." *The Business Lawyer* 46 (November 1990): 244.

Burns, Greg. *Qwest Chief's Appeal Hinges on Chicago's Daniel Fischer.* February 27, 2009. http://articles.chicagotribune.com/2009-02-27/news/0902260442_1_joseph-nacchio-stock-sales-edward-nottingham.

Business Roundtable. *2012 Principles of Corporate Governance.* March 27, 2012. http://businessroundtable.org/resources/business-roundtable-principles-of-corporate-governance-2012.

———. *Statement on Corporate Governance.* September 1997.

Byrne, John A. *The Whiz Kids: Ten Founding Fathers of American Business — and the Legacy They Left Us.* New York: Doubleday, 1993.

Callahan, David. *The Cheating Culture: Why More People Are Doing Wrong to Get Ahead.* Orlando, FL: Harcourt, 2004.

Campbell, R. H., and Skiller, A. S. *Adam Smith.* New York: St. Martin's Press, 1985.

Cassin, Richard L. "Oscar Wyatt, Founder of Coastal Corporation, Pleads Guilty to Iraq Bribes." Monday, October 1, 2007. http://www.fcpablog.com/blog/2007/10/1/oscar-wyatt-founder-of-coastal-corporation-pleads-guilty-to.html#sthash.XcYqzvbV.dpuf.

CBS News. *Ebbers Sentenced to 25 Years.* http://www.cbsnews.com/news/ebbers-sentenced-to-25-years/

CDA. *Healthcare-associated Infections (HAIs).* Accessed January 12, 2015. http://www.cdc.gov/HAI /surveillance/.

Chamberlin, Edward Hastings. *The Theory of Monopolistic Competition.* Cambridge: Harvard University Press, 1933.

Chandler, Alfred D., Jr. *The Visible Hand: The Managerial Revolution in American Business.* Cambridge: Belknap Press, 1977.

Charities Aid Foundation. *World Giving Index 2014: A Global View of Giving Trends.* November 4, 19, 2014. www.cafon.org/pdf/CAF_WG12014_Report_1555AWEBFinal.pdf.

Clarke, Conor. An Interview with Paul Samuelson, Part One. *The Atlantic,* June 19, 2009. http://www.theatlantic.com/politics/archive/2009/06/an-interview-with-paul-samuelson-part-one/19572/.

Clement, Douglas. Interview with Eugene Fama. *The Region.* Minneapolis: The Federal Reserve Bank of Minneapolis. December 1, 2007. http://www. minneapolisfed.org/publications_papers/pub_display.cfm?id=1134&&.

Coase, Ronald H. Prize Lecture. *Nobelprize.org.* February 25, 2011. http://www. nobelprize.org/nobel_prizes/economic-sciences/laureates/1991/press.html.

———. "The Nature of the Firm." *Economica* 4, no. 16 (November 1937): 386–405.

———. "The Problem of Social Cost." *Journal of Law and Economics* 3 (October 1960): 43, 44.

Cohen, Don, and Laurence Prusak. In *Good Company: How Social Capital Makes Organizations Work.* Boston: Harvard Business School Press, 2001.

Colby, Anne, Thomas Ehrlich, William M Sullivan, and Jonathan R. Dolle. *Rethinking Undergraduate Business Education: Liberal Learning for the Profession.* San Francisco: Jossey-Bass, 2011.

Columbia Business School. *The Power of Possibility: The Columbia MBA Program.* https://www.gsb.columbia.edu/ipimages/mba/CBS-MBA-Program-Viewbook.pdf.

Congressional Budget Office. *The Budget and Economic Outlook: 2015 to 2025.* January 1, 2015. https://www.cbo.gov/publication/49892.

Cournot, Augustin. *Recherches sur les Principes Mathematiques de la Theorie des Richesses.* New York: A. M. Kelly, 1971.

Cowling, Keith, and Roger Dugden. "Control, Markets and Firms." In *Transaction Costs, Markets, and Hierarchies,* edited by Christos Pitelis. Oxford, UK: Blackwell, 1993: 66–76.

Curtin, Kevin M. "Operations Research." In *Encyclopedia of Social Measurement,* edited by Kimberly Kempf-Leonard, vol. 2, Amsterdam: Elsevier, 2005, 925–31.

Darby, Alex (writer/director). *Enron: The Smartest Guys in the Room.* Los Angeles: Magnolia Home Entertainment, 2005.

Darity, A. William. "Economics, Experimental." In *International Encyclopedia of the Social Sciences,* 2nd ed., vol. 2, edited by William A. Darity, Jr. Detroit: Macmillan Reference USA, 2008. 505–06. *Gale Virtual Reference Library,* (accessed October 7, 2015).

Darwin, Charles. *The Descent of Man, and Selection in Relation to Sex.* Princeton, NJ: Princeton University Press, 1871/1981.

Dash, Eric. Former Chief Will Forfeit $418 Million. *New York Times,* December 7, 2007 (July 7, 2009). http://www.nytimes.com/2007/12/07/business/07options.html.

Datar, Srikant, David Gavin, and Patrick Cullen. *Rethinking the MBA: Business Education at a Crossroads.* Boston: Harvard Business Press, 2010.

Dawkins, Richard. *The Selfish Gene.* Oxford: Oxford University Press, 2006.

————. *The God Delusion.* Boston: Houghton Mifflin, 2006.

de Tocqueville, Alexis. *Democracy in America,* vol. 2. New York: Alfred A. Knopf, 1976.

de Waal, Frans. B. M. *The Age of Empathy: Nature's Lessons for a Kinder Society.* New York: Three Rivers Press, 2009.

————. "How Selfish an Animal." In *Moral Markets: The Role of Values in the Economy,* edited by Paul J. Zak, Princeton, NJ: Princeton University Press, 2008, 63–65.

Dobbin, Frank, and Jiwook Jung. "The Misapplication of Mr. Michael Jensen: How Agency Theory Brought Down the Economy and Why it Might Again." In *Markets on Trial: The Economic Sociology of the US Financial Crisis,* edited by Michael Lounsbury and Paul M. Hirsch, Bringley, UK: Emerald, 2010, 331–66.

Dohmen, Thomas, Armin Falk, David Huffman, and Uwe Sunde. "Homo Reciprocans: Survey Evidence on Behavioral Outcomes." *Economic Journal* (Conference Papers) 119, no. 536 (March 2009): 592–612.

Donham, Wallace B. "Foreword." In *The Social Problems of an Industrial Civilization,* 4th printing, by Elton Mayo. Andover, MA: Andover Press, 1945.

Dougherty, Peter L. *Who's Afraid of Adam Smith: How the Market Got Its Soul.* Hoboken, NJ: John Wiley & Sons, 2002.

Drogin, Bob. To Assess Romney, Look Beyond the Bottom Line. *Los Angeles Times,* December 16, 2007. http://articles.latimes.com/2007/dec/16/nation/na-mittbain16.

Drucker, Peter. *The Practice of Management.* Hoboken, NJ: Taylor & Francis, 2012.

Dzuback, Mary Ann. *Robert M. Hutchins: Portrait of an Educator.* Chicago: The University of Chicago Press, 1991.

Easterbrook, Frank H., and Daniel R. Fischel. *The Economic Structure of Corporate Law.* Cambridge: Harvard University Press, 1991.

————. "Antitrust Suits by Targets of Tender Offers." *Michigan Law Review* 80, no. 6 (May 1982): 1177, n57. http://www.jstor.org/stable/1288576.

Egan, Matt. 2008: Worse than the Great Depression?, *CNN* http://money.cnn.com/2014/08/27/news/economy/ben-bernanke-great-depression/.

Eichenwald, Kurt. *Conspiracy of Fools: A True Story.* New York: Broadway Books, 2005.

Elegido, Juan. "Business Education and the Erosion of Character." *African Journal of Business Ethics* 4, no. 4 (November 2009): 16–24.

Evensky, Jerry. *Adam Smith's Moral Philosophy: A Historical and Contemporary Perspective on Markets, Law, Ethics, and Culture.* New York: Cambridge University Press, 2005.

Falk, Armin, and Urs Fischbacher. "A theory of reciprocity." *Games and Economic Behavior* 54, no. 2 (February 2006): 293–315.

Fama, Eugene F. *The Twin Pillars of Asset Pricing.* Accessed December 8, 2013. http://www.nobelprize.org/nobel_prizes/economic-sciences/laureates/2013/ fama-lecture.html.

Fan, Jiayang. "Can China Stop Organ Trafficking?" *The New Yorker*, January 10, 2014. http://www.newyorker.com/news/news-desk/can-china-stop-organ-trafficking.

Farrer, J. A. *Adam Smith.* Altrincham, UK: J. Martin Stafford, 1988.

Fay, C. R. *Adam Smith and the Scotland of His Day.* Cambridge, UK: Cambridge University Press, 1966.

Feddersen, Timothy J. "Rational Choice Theory and the Paradox of Not Voting." *Journal of Economic Perspectives* 18, no. 1 (Winter 2004): 99–112.

Fehr, Ernst, and Simon Gachter. "Fairness and Retaliation: The Economics of Reciprocity." *Journal of Economic Perspectives* 14 (2000): 159–81.

Felton, Edwin, ed. *Carnegie Mellon 1900–2000: A Centennial History.* Pittsburgh: Carnegie Mellon University Press, 2000.

Ferguson, Niall. *The Ascent of Money: A Financial History of the World.* New York: Penguin Press, 2008.

Ferraro, F., J. Peffer, and R. I. Sutton. "Economics Language and Assumptions: How Theories Can Become Self-Fulfilling." *Academy of Management Review* 30, no. 1 (2005): 8–24.

Finn, Daniel K. *The Moral Ecology of Markets: Assessing Claims about Markets and Justice.* New York: Cambridge University Press, 2006.

"Firefighters Let Home Burn Over $75 Fee — Again." *NBC News.* December 7, 2011. http://usnews.nbcnews.com/_news/2011/12/07/9272989-firefighters-let-home-burn-over-75-fee-again.

Fisman, Raymond, and Edward Miguel. *Cultures of Corruption: Evidence from Diplomatic Parking Tickets* (Working Paper 12313). Cambridge, MA: National Bureau of Economic Research, June 2006.

Fleischacker, Samuel. *On Adam Smith's Wealth of Nations: A Philosophical Companion.* Princeton, NJ: Princeton University Press, 2004.

Flexner, Abraham. *Medical Education in the United States and Canada: A Report to the Carnegie Foundation for the Advancement of Teaching.* Bulletin no. 4. New York: Carnegie Foundation, 1910.

Fourcade, Marion, and Rakesh Khurana. "From Social Control to Financial Economics: The Linked Ecologies of Economics and Business in Twentieth Century America." *Theory and Society* 42, no. 2 (March 2013): 121–59.

———.*Economists and Societies: Discipline and Profession in the United States, Britain, and France, 1980s to 1990s.* Princeton, NJ: Princeton University Press, 2012.

Frank, Robert H. *Passions within Reason: The Strategic Role of the Emotions.* New York: W. W. Norton, 1988.

———.*Luxury Fever: Money and Happiness in an Era of Excess.* Princeton, NJ: Princeton University Press, 1999.

———.*What Price the Moral High Ground? Ethical Dilemmas in Competitive Environments.* Princeton, NJ: Princeton University Press, 2004.

Frank, Robert H., Thomas Gilovich, and Dennis T. Regan. "Does Studying Economics Inhibit Cooperation?" *Journal of Economic Perspectives* 7, no. 2 (Spring 1993): 159–71.

———."Do Economists Make Bad Citizens?" *The Journal of Economic Perspectives* 10, no. 1 (Winter 1966): 187–92.

Frankel, Tamar. *Trust and Honesty: America's Business Culture at a Crossroad.* New York: Oxford University Press, 2006.

———.*Fiduciary Law.* Oxford: Oxford University Press, 2011.

Frederick Taylor University. *Frederick Winslow Taylor, M.E., Sc.D.* http://www.ftu.edu/Frederick%20Taylor%20Bio.htm.

Friedman, Milton. The Social Responsibility of Business Is to Increase Its Profits. *Times Magazine.* New York: *The New York Times*, September 13, 1970. http://www.colorado.edu/studentgroups/libertarians/issues/friedman-soc-resp-business.html.

———."The Methodology of Positive Economics." In *Essays in Positive Economics.* Chicago: University of Chicago Press, 1953: 3–16, 30–43.

———."The Invisible Hand." In *The Business System: A Bicentennial View,* edited by Frederick E. Webster. Jr. University Press of New England, 1977.

———.*Speaks, Lecture 3: Is Capitalism Humane? Q & A Period.* Ithaca, New York: Cornell University, 1978. www.freetochoose.com.

———.*Capitalism and Freedom.* Chicago: University of Chicago Press, 2002.

———.*Why Government is the Problem.* Stanford, CA: Hoover Institution Press, 1993.

Friedman, Milton, and Rose Friedman. *Free to Choose: A Personal Statement.* San Diego, CA: Harcourt, 1980.

Friedman, Milton, John Mackey, and T.J. Rodgers. "Rethinking the social responsibility of business." *Reason* 37, no. 5 (2005): 28–37.

Fudenberg, Drew, David G. Rand, and Anna Dreber. "Slow to Anger and Fast to Forgive: Cooperation in an Uncertain World." *American Economic Review* 10 (2012): 720–49.

Fukuyama, Francis. *Trust: The Social Virtues & the Creation of Prosperity.* New York: Free Press, 1995.

———. *The Great Disruption: Human Nature and the Reconstruction of Social Order.* New York: Touchstone, 1999.

Galbraith, John K. "The Founding Faith: Adam Smith's Wealth of Nations." In *Annals of an Abiding Liberal.* Boston: Houghton Mifflin, 1979, 86–102.

———. "The Founding Faith: Adam Smith's *Wealth of Nations.*" In *The Essential Galbraith.* Boston: Houghton Mifflin, 2001, 152–68.

Gavin, Robert, and Sacha Pfeiffer. Reaping Profit in Study, Sweat. *Boston Globe,* June 26, 2007. http://www.boston.com/news/politics/2008/specials/romney/articles/part3_main/ and http://www.boston.com/news/daily/26/ampad.pdf.

Gazzaniga, Michael S. *The Ethical Brain: The Science of Our Moral Dilemmas.* New York: Harper Perennial, 2006.

Gentile, Mary C. *Giving Voice to Values: How to Speak Your Mind When You Know What's Right.* New Haven, CT: Yale University Press, 2010.

Ghent, William J. *Our Benevolent Feudalism.* New York: McMillan, 1902.

Ghoshal, Sumantra, and Peter Moran. "Bad For Practice: A Critique of the Transaction Cost Theory." *Academy of Management Review* 21 no. 1 (1996): 13–43.

Gibson, Rosemary, and Prasad Singh Janardan. *The Treatment Trap: How the Overuse of Medical Care Is Wrecking Your Health and What You Can Do to Prevent It.* Chicago: Ivan R. Dee, 2010.

Gintis, Herbert, and Rakesh Khurana. "Corporate Honesty and Business Education: A Behavioral Model." In *Moral Markets: The Critical Role of Values in the Economy*, edited by Paul J. Zak, 300–27. Princeton, NJ: Princeton University Press, 2008.

Gleeson, Robert E., and Steven Schlossman. "George Leland Bach and the Rebirth of Graduate Management Education in the United States, 1945–1975." *Selections* 11, no. 3 (Spring 1995): 8–46.

Goldman Sachs. "Enron Corp. (ENE) Gas & Power Convergence." Recommend List, October 9, 2001, 1.

Gordon, Robert Aaron, and James Edwin Howell. *Higher Education for Business*. New York: Columbia University Press, 1959.

Gould, Stephen J. *The Mismeasure of Man*. New York, Norton, 1981.

Greenwald, Douglas, ed. *The McGraw-Hill Encyclopedia of Economics*, 2nd ed. New York: McGraw-Hill.

Griswold, Charles L., Jr. *Adam Smith and the Virtues of the Enlightenment*. New York: Oxford University Press, 1999.

Guth, Werner, Rolf Schmittberger, and Bernd Schwarze. "An Experimental Analysis of Ultimatum Bargaining." *Journal of Economic Behavior and Organization* 3 (1982): 367–88.

Haakonseen, Knud. "Natural Jurisprudence and the Theory of Justice." In *The Cambridge Companion to The Scottish Enlightenment,* edited by Alexander Broadie. Cambridge: Cambridge University Press, 2003, 205–21.

———. ed. *The Cambridge Companion to Adam Smith*. New York: Cambridge University Press, 2006.

Hafferty, Frederic W., and Janet P. Hafler. "The Hidden Curriculum, Structural Disconnects, and the Socialization of New Professionals." In *Extraordinary Learning in the Workplace,* edited by Janet P. Hafler, Dordrecht, the Netherlands: Springer, 2011, 17–35.

Hallowell, John H. *The Moral Foundation of Democracy*. Indianapolis, IN: 2007.

Hang, Bob. Golf's Honor Code Limits 'Cheating' Incidents. *ESPN.com,* August 9, 2007.

Hartwell, R. M. *A History of the Mont Pelerin Society*. Indianapolis, IN: Liberty Fund: 1995.

Hauser, Marc D. *Moral Minds: How Nature Designed our Universal Sense of Right and Wrong*. New York: Harper Collins, 2006.

Hayek, F. A. *The Road to Serfdom*. Chicago: University of Chicago Press, 1944.

———. "The Intellectuals and Socialism." *University of Chicago Law Review* 16, no. 3 (Spring 1949).

———. *The Counter-Revolution of Science: Studies in the Abuse of Reason*. Indianapolis, IN: Liberty Funds, 1979.

Heath, Joseph. "Methodological Individualism." In *Stanford Encyclopedia of Philosophy,* edited by Edward N. Zalta. January 21, 2015. http://plato.stanford.edu/entries/methodological-individualism/.

———. *Morality, Competition, and the Firm: The Market Failures Approach to Business Ethics*, New York: Oxford University Press, 2014.

Heclo, Hugo. "Varieties of American Exceptionalism." In *American Exceptionalism: The Origins, History, and Future of the Nation's Greatest*

Strength, edited by Charles W. Dunn, Linham, MD: Rowland & Littlefield, 2013, 27–40.

Helms, Marilyn M., and R. Anthony Inman. "Supply Chain Management." In *Encyclopedia of Management,* 5th ed., edited by Marilyn M. Helms, 870–73. Detroit: Gale, 2006. *Gale Virtual Reference Library,* go.galegroup.com/ps/i. do?p=GVRL&sw=w&u=txshracd2598&v=2.1&id=GALE%7CCX3446300 279&it=r&asid=349a8cff5ba04f687db597f6f49dcd4d. Accessed 10 Jan. 2017.

Heritage Foundation. *2015 Index of Economic Freedom.* http://www.heritage.org/index/.

Heyne, Paul. *"Are Economists Basically Immoral?" and Other Essays on Economics, Ethics, and Religion.* Indianapolis, IN: Liberty Fund, 2008.

Hirst, Francis W. *Adam Smith.* Honolulu, HI: University of the Pacific, 2003.

Hobbes, Thomas. *Leviathan.* Oxford: Oxford University Press, 1996.

Hoffman, Martin. *Empathy and Moral Development: Implications for Caring and Justice.* New York: Cambridge University Press, 2000.

Hofstadter, Richard. *Social Darwinism in American Thought.* Boston: Beacon Press, 1983.

Hofstadter, Richard, and C. DeWitt Hardy. *The Development and Scope of Higher Education in the United States.* New York: Columbia University Press, 1952.

Hopper, Kenneth, and William Hopper. *The Puritan Gift: Reclaiming the American Dream Amidst Global Financial Chaos.* London: I. B. Tauris, 2009.

Hume, David. *A Treatise of Human Nature.* In reprint from original ed. (3 vols. with analytical index), edited by L. A. Selby-Bigge, Oxford: Clarendon Press, 1896, 319. http://oll.libertyfund.org/title/342.

Hunt, E. K., and Mark Lautzenheiser. *History of Economic Thought: A Critical Perspective,* 3rd ed. London: Routledge, 2011.

Hurdle, John, and Sabrina Tavernise. Former Judge Is on Trial in 'Cash for Kids' Scheme. *New York Times,* February 8, 2011. http://www.nytimes.com/2011/02/09/us/09judge.html?ref=markaciavarella.

Hutcheson, Francis. *An Inquiry into the Original of Our Ideas of Beauty and Virtue in Two Treatises,* edited by Wolfgang Leidhold. Indianapolis, IN: Liberty Fund, 2004. http://oll.libertyfund.org/titles/2462.

Hylton, J. G., and Gary P. Stein. *U.S. Fire Department Profile.* Accessed November, 2014. http://www.nfpa.org/research/reports-and-statistics/the-fire-service/administration/us-fire-department-profile.

Ingram, John K. *A History of Political Economy.* New York: J. J. Little, 1887.

Jackall, Robert. *Moral Mazes: The World of Corporate Managers.* New York: Oxford University Press, 1988.

————. "Value Maximization, Stakeholder Theory, and the Corporate Objective Function." *Journal of Applied Corporate Finance* 14, no. 3 (Fall 2001): 8–21.

————. *A Theory of the Firm: Governance, Residual Claims, and Organizational Forms.* Cambridge, MA: Harvard University Press, 2000.

————. "Self-Interest, Altruism, Incentives, & Agency." *Journal of Applied Corporate Finance* 7, no. 2 (Summer 1994): 2–16.

Jensen, Michael C., and William H. Meckling. "Theory of the Firm: Managerial Behavior, Agency Costs and Ownership Structure." *Journal of Financial Economics* 3, no. 4 (1976): 305–60.

————. "The Nature of Man." *Journal of Applied Corporate Finance* 7, no. 2 (Summer 1994): 4–19.

Jensen, Michael C., George P. Baker, Karen H. Wruck, and Carliss Y. Baldwin. "Organizations and Markets: History and Development of the Course and the Field." (December 10, 1997): 28. Available in electronic form from Social Science Research Network Electronic Library at http://papers.ssrn.com/.

Jensen, Michael C. "Eclipse of the Public Corporation." *Harvard Business Review* 67 (September–October 1987): 61–74.

Jevons, W. Stanley. *The Theory of Political Economy,* 4th ed. London: Macmillan and Company, 1931.

Jones, Daniel Stedman. *Masters of the Universe: Hayek, Friedman, and the Birth of Neoliberal Politics.* Princeton, NJ: Princeton University Press, 2012.

Jovanovic, Franck. "The Construction of the Canonical History of Financial Economics." *History of Political Economy* 40, no. 2 (2008): 213–42.

Kahneman, Daniel, Jack L. Knetsch, and Richard H. Thaler. "Fairness and the Assumptions of Economics." *Journal of Business* 59, no. 4 (1986): part 2, S285–S300.

Kaufman, Bruce B. "Chicago and the Development of Twentieth-Century Labor Economics." In *Elgar Companion to the Chicago School of Economics,* edited by Ross B. Emmett, Cheltenham, England: Edward Elgar, 2010, 128–51.

Kelly, Tom. "Learning from the 'Shadow Curriculum.'" *The Declaration* 1, no. 2 (May–August 1966).

Keynes, John Neville. *The Scope and Method of Political Economy.* London: Macmillan, 1891.

Khurana, Rakesh. *From Higher Aims to Hired Hands: The Social Transformation of American Business Schools and the Unfulfilled Promise of Management as a Profession.* Princeton, NJ: Princeton University Press, 2007.

Khurana, Rakesh, Nitin Nohria, and Daniel Prentice. "Management as a Profession." In *Restoring Trust in American Business*. Edited by. Jay W. Lorsch, Leslie Berlowitz, and Andy Zelleke, Cambridge, MA: The MIT Press, 2005, 43–60.

Khurana, Rakesh, and J. C. Spendler. "Herbert A. Simon on What Ails Business Schools: More than 'A Problem of Organizational Design.'" *Journal of Management Studies* 49, no. 3 (May 2002): 619–39.

Kingsbury, Kevin. "Apple Is Now More than Double the Size of Exxon — And Everyone Else." *Wall Street Journal*, Monday, March 23, 2015. http://blogs. wsj.com/moneybeat/2015/02/23/apple-is-now-more-than-double-the-size-of-exxon-and-everyone-else/.

Kiss, Elizabeth, and J. Peter Euben, eds. *Debating Moral Education: Rethinking the Role of the Modern University*. Durham, NC: Duke University Press, 2010.

Knight, Frank H. *The Ethics of Competition*. New Brunswick, NJ: Transaction Publishers, 2004.

Kreps, David M. *Microeconomics for Managers*. New York: W. W. Norton, 2004.

Krogh, Egil "Bud." *Integrity: Good People, Bad Choices and Life Lessons from the White House*. New York: Public Affairs, 2007.

Kronman, Anthony T. *Education's End: Why Our Colleges and Universities Have Given Up on the Meaning of Life*. New Haven, CT: Yale University Press, 2007.

Kumar, Nirmalya. "The Power of Trust in Manufacturer-Retailer Relationships." *Harvard Business Review* 74, no. 6 (November 1966): 92–106.

Laseter, Tim, and Keith Oliver. "When Will Supply Chain Management Grow Up?" *Strategy + Business*, Reprint No. 03304, 2003. http://www.strategy-business.com/article/03304?pg=all us.

Landau, Richard, ed. *Regulating New Drugs*. Chicago: University of Chicago Center for Policy Study, 1972.

Ledyard, John O. "Public Goods: A Survey of Experimental Research." In *The Handbook of Experimental Economics*, edited by John Kagel and Alvin Roth. Princeton, NJ: Princeton University Press, 1995.

Leslie, T. E. Cliffe. *Essays in Political Economy*, 2nd ed. New York: Augustus M. Kelley, 1969.

Levitt, Steven D., and Stephen J. Dubner. *Freakonomics: A Rogue Economist Explores the Hidden Side of Everything*. New York: Harper Perennial, 2009.

Lewis, Michael. *The Big Short: Inside the Doomsday Machine*. New York: W. W. Norton, 2010.

Liberman, Varda, Steven M. Samuels, and Lee Ross. "The Name of the Game: Predictive Power of Reputations Versus Situational Labels in Determining Prisoner's Dilemma Game Moves." *Personality and Social Psychology Bulletin* 30, no. 9: 1175–85.

Lorsch, Jay W., Leslie Berlowitz, and Andy Zelleke, eds. *Restoring Trust in American Business.* Cambridge, MA: MIT Press, 2005.

Lounsbury, Michael, and Paul M. Hirsch. *Markets on Trial: The Economic Sociology of the US Financial Crisis.* Bingley, UK: Emerald, 2010.

Lux, Kenneth. *Adam Smith's Mistake: How a Moral Philosopher Invented Economics and Ended Morality.* Boston: Shambhala, 1990.

Macey, Jonathan R. *The Death of Corporate Reputation: How Integrity Has Been Destroyed on Wall Street.* Upper Saddle River, NJ: FT Press, 2013.

Macintyre, Ben. *A Spy Among Friends: Kim Philby and the Great Betrayal.* New York: Crown Publishers, 2014.

Mackey, John, and Raj Sisodia. *Conscious Capitalism: Liberating the Heroic Spirit of Business.* Boston: Harvard Business Review Press, 2013.

Major, Solomon. "Public Choice Theory." In *International Encyclopedia of the Social Sciences*, 2nd ed., vol. 6, edited by William A. Darity, Jr., Detroit: Macmillan Reference USA, 2008. 606–07 *Gale Virtual Reference Library.* April 15, 2015.

Mandeville, Bernard. *The Fable of the Bees: Or, Private Vices, Public Benefits.* Indianapolis, IN: Liberty Fund, 1714, 1988.

Margolis, Eric. "Hidden Curriculum." In *Encyclopedia of Social Problems*, edited by Vincent N. Parrillo, Vol. 1, Thousand Oaks, CA: Sage, 2008. *Gale Virtual Reference Library*, March 9, 2015, 440–41.

Marshall, Alfred. *Principles of Economics*, vol. 1. London: Macmillan, 1980.

———. *Principles of Economics*, 8th ed. New York: Cosimo Classics, 2009.

Marshall, Ian. "Introduction," *Passage East.* Charlottesville, VA: Howell Press, 1997. www.nytimes.com/books/first/m/marshall-east.html.

Martin, John D., J. William Petty, and James S. Wallace. *Value-Based Management with Corporate Social Responsibility*, 2nd ed. New York: Oxford University Press, 2009.

Marwell, Gerald, and Ruth E. Ames. "Economists Free Ride, Does Anyone Else?" *Journal of Public Economics* 15, no. 3 (June 1981): 295–310.

Mastilak, Christian, Linda J. Matuszewski, Fabienne Miller, and Alex Woods. "Self-Fulfilling Prophecy? An Examination of Exposure to Economic Theory and Opportunistic Behavior." AAA 2014 Management Accounting Section (MAS) Meeting Paper, August 19, 2013. http://ssrn.com/abstract= 2312557.

Mayo, Elton. *The Social Problems of an Industrial Civilization*, 4th printing. Andover, MA: Andover Press, 1945.

McCabe, Donald, Kenneth Butterfield, and Linda Trevino. "Academic Dishonesty in Graduate Business Programs: Prevalence, Causes, and Proposed Action." *Academy of Management Learning & Education* 5, no. 3 (2006): 294–305.

McCabe, Donald, Janet M. Dukerich, and Jane E. Dutton. "Values and Moral Dilemmas: Comparing the Choices of Business and Law School Students." *Journal of Business Ethics* 10, no. 12 (December 1991): 951–60.

McLean, Bethany, and Peter Elkind. *The Smartest Guys in the Room*. New York: Portfolio, 2003.

Mearsheimer. John J. "The Aims of Education." *Philosophy and Literature* 22, no. 1 (1988): 137–55.

Meek, R. L., D. D. Rafael, and P. G. Stein, eds. *Lectures on Jurisprudence*. Indianapolis, IN: Liberty Fund, 1982.

Merton, Robert K. "The Self-Fulfilling Prophecy." *The Antioch Review* 8, no. 2 (Summer 1948): 193–210.

Middleton, Diana, and Joe Light. "Harvard Changes Course." *The Wall Street Journal*, February 3, 2011. http://www.wsj.com/articles/SB10001424052748 704124504576118674203902898.

Milgrom, Paul, and John Roberts. "Predation, Reputation, and Entry Deterrence." *Journal of Economic Theory* 27, no. 2 (August 1982): 280–312.

———. *Economics, Organization and Management*. Englewood Cliffs, NJ: Prentice-Hall, 1992.

Mill, John Stuart. *Utilitarianism*. London: Parker, Son, and Bourn, 1863.

Miller, Merton H. Biographical. *Nobelprize.org*. Nobel Media AB 2014. Accessed November 21, 2014. http://www.nobelprize.org/nobel_prizes/economic-sciences/laureates/1990/miller-bio.html.

Mintzberg, Henry. *Managers Not MBAs: A Hard Look at the Soft Practice of Managing and Management Development*. San Francisco: Berrett-Koehler, 2005.

Mirowski, Phillip, and Dieter Piehwe, eds. *The Road from Mont Pelerin: The Making of the Neoliberal Thought Collective* Cambridge, MA: Harvard University Press, 2015.

Mizuta, Hiroshi, ed. *Adam Smith's Library: A Catalogue*. Oxford: Clarendon Press, 2000.

Montes, Leonidas. *Adam Smith in Context: A Critical Reassessment of Some Central Components of His Thought*. Basingstoke, England: Palgrave Macmillan, 2004.

Moore, Heidi N. "John Thain's $35,000 'Commode on Legs' Outrage," *The Wall Street Journal*, 23 January 2009, http://blogs.wsj.com/deals/2009/01/23/ deal-journal-explainer-the-35000-commode-outrage/.

Morris, Charles R. *The Two Trillion Dollar Meltdown: Easy Money, High Rollers, and the Great Credit Crash, Revised and Updated.* New York: Public Affairs, 2008.

Mossner, E. C. *The Life of David Hume*, 2nd ed. Oxford, UK: Clarendon Press, 2001.

Muth, John F. "Rational Expectations and the Theory of Price Movements." *Econometrica* 29 (1961): 315–35.

National Bureau of Economic Research. *US Business Cycle Expansions and Contractions.* June 27, 2015. http://www.nber.org/cycles.html.

Neiman, Susan. *Evil in Modern Thought: An Alternative History of Philosophy.* Princeton, NJ: Princeton University Press, 2002.

———. *Moral Clarity: A Guide for Grown-Up Idealists,* rev. ed. Princeton, NJ: Princeton University Press, 2009.

Newton, Isaac. *The Principia: Mathematical Principles and Natural Philosophy.* Berkeley: University of California Press, 1999.

Nicholson, Colin. *Writing and the Rise of Finance: Capital Satires of the Early Eighteenth Century.* Cambridge: Cambridge University Press, 1994.

Nik-Khah, Edward. "George Stigler, the Graduate School of Business, and the Pillars of the Chicago School." In *Building Chicago Economics: New Perspectives on the History of America's Most Powerful Economics Program,* edited by Robert Van Horn, Philip Mirowski, and Thomas A. Stapleford. Cambridge, UK: Cambridge University Press, 2011, 116–47.

Noe, Thomas. "A Survey of the Economic Theory of Reputation: Its Logic and Limits." In *The Oxford Handbook of Corporate Reputation,* edited by Michael L. Barnett and Timothy G. Pollock, Oxford, UK: Oxford University Press, 2012, 114–39.

O'Day, Rosemary. *The Professions in Early Modern England, 1450–1800.* Harlow, England: Longman, 2000.

Olkin, Ingram. "A Conversation with W. Allen Wallis." *Statistical Science* 6, no. 2 (May 1991): 125. Accessed November 18, 2015. http://www.jstor.org/ stable/2245588.

Ostrom, Elinor. "Collective Action and the Evolution of Social Norms." *Journal of Economic Perspectives* 14, no. 3 (Summer 2000): 137–58.

Otteson, James R. *Adam Smith's Marketplace of Life.* Cambridge, UK: Cambridge University Press, 2002.

Overtveldt, Johan Van. *The Chicago School: How the University of Chicago Assembled the Thinkers Who Revolutionized Economics and Business.* Chicago: Agape, 2007.

Oxford English Dictionary. December 21, 2015. http://www.oed.com.ezproxy.lib.utexas.edu.

Packard, David. *The HP Way: How Bill Hewlett and I Built Our Company.* New York: Harper & Row, 1996.

Palank, Jacqueline. Madoff Investors to Get Over $1 Billion in Added Recoveries. *The Wall Street Journal,* November 18, 2015. December 21, 2015. http://www.wsj.com/articles/madoff-investors-to-get-over-1-billion-in-added-recoveries-1447868373.

Panchuk, Kerri Ann. Ocwen Finalizes Acquisition of Homeward Residential. Accessed December 31, 2012. http://www.housingwire.com/authors/8-kerri-panchuk/articles.

Pascu-Nierth, Vivian. "Enron Sails into New Markets." *Today's CPA* 27, no. 9 (November–December 2001): 27–28.

Persky, Joseph. "Retrospectives: The Ethology of Homo Economicus." *Journal of Economic Perspectives* 9, no. 2 (Spring 1995): 222–231.

Peace Corps. Fast Facts. July 6, 2015. http://www.peacecorps.gov/about/fast facts/.

Phillipson, Nicholas. *Adam Smith: An Enlightened Life.* New Haven, CT: Yale University Press, 2010.

Pierce, Jessica, and Audrey Paulman. "The Preceptor as Ethics Educator." *Family Medicine* 31, no. 10 (1999): 687–88.

Pierson, Frank C., *et al. The Education of American Businessmen: A Study of University-College Programs in Business Administration.* New York: McGraw-Hill, 1959.

Pitts, Leonard, Jr. Justice Falls Victim to Jail Privatization. *Austin American-Statesman,* February 27, 2011. http://www.eastbaytimes.com/2011/02/25/leonard-pitts-jr-justice-falls-victim-to-jail-privatization/.

Pope, Alexander. *An Essay on Man,* edited by Maynard Mack. London: Methuen, 1950.

Posner, Richard A. *Economic Analysis of the Law,* 6th ed. New York: Aspen, 2003.

———.*A Failure of Capitalism: The Crisis of '08 and the Descent into Depression.* Cambridge, MA: Harvard University Press, 2009.

———.*The Crisis of Capitalistic Democracy.* Cambridge, MA: Harvard University Press, 2010.

Prentice, Robert A. "The Case of the Irrational Auditor: A Behavioral Insight into Securities Fraud Litigation." *Northwestern University Law Review* 95, no. 1 (2000): 133–219.

———. "Ethical Decision Making: More Needed than Good Intentions." *Financial Analysts Journal* 63, no. 6 (November–December 2007): 17–30. http://www.jstor.org/stable/4480886.

Protess, Ben, and Azam Ahmen. Michael Douglas Tackles Greed for F.B.I. *The New York Times*, February 12, 2012. http://dealbook.nytimes.com/2012/02/27/michael-douglas-tackles-greed-for-the-f-b-i/?_r=0.

Quammen, David. *The Reluctant Mr. Darwin: An Intimate Portrait of Charles Darwin and the Making of His Theory of Evolution*. New York: Atlas Books, 2006.

Rae, John. *Life of Adam Smith*. Honolulu, HI: University Press of the Pacific, 2002.

Reiff, Phillip. *Freud: The Mind of the Moralist*, 3rd ed. Chicago: University of Chicago Press, 1979.

Robinson, Joan. *The Economics of Imperfect Competition*. London: Macmillan, 1933.

Rodwin, Marc A. *Conflicts of Interests and the Future of Medicine: The United States, France, and Japan*. Oxford: Oxford University Press, 2011.

Rose, David C. *The Moral Foundation of Economic Behavior*. New York: Oxford University Press, 2013.

Rogers, Everett. *Diffusion of Innovations*. New York: Free Press, 1962.

Ross, Don. "Game Theory." In *Stanford Encyclopedia of Philosophy*, 2006, part 7. http://plato.stanford.edu/entries/game-theory/.

Ross, Ian Simpson. *The Life of Adam Smith*. Oxford, England: Oxford University Press, 1995.

Sargent, Thomas J. "Rational Expectations." In *Concise Encyclopedia of Economics,* edited by David R. Henderson, Indianapolis, IN: Liberty Fund, 2008, 432–35.

Samuelson, Paul A. *Economics: An Introductory Analysis*. New York: McGraw-Hill, 1961.

———. *Economics,* 10th ed. New York: McGraw-Hill, 1976.

———. "Credo of a Lucky Textbook Author." *The Journal of Economic Perspectives* 11, no. 2 (Spring 1997): 153–60. Accessed November 1, 2015. http://www.jstor.org/stable/2138241.

Samuelson, Paul A., and William D. Nordhaus. *Economics,* 14th ed. New York: McGraw-Hill, 1992.

Schlefer, Jonathan. "Today's Most Mischievous Misquotation: Adam Smith Did Not Mean What He Is Often Made to Say." *Atlantic Monthly Magazine* 281, no. 3 (March 1998): 16–19.

Schultz, George, and Robert Aliber, eds. *Guidelines, Informal Controls, and the Marketplace.* Chicago: University of Chicago Press, 1966.

Schumpeter, Joseph A. *Capitalism, Socialism, and Democracy.* New York, London: Harper & Brothers, 1942.

Scott, William Robert. *Adam Smith as Student and Professor.* New York: Augustus M. Kelley, 1965.

Sen, Amartya. *On Ethics and Economics.* Malden, MA: Blackwell Publishing, 1988.

———. *The Idea of Justice.* Cambridge, MA: Belnap Press, 2009.

———. "Adam Smith's Prudence." In *Theory and Reality in Development: Essays in Honour of Paul Streeten,* edited by Sanjaya Lall and Frances Stewart. London: Macmillan, 1986.

Shapiro, Carl. "Premiums for High Quality Products as Returns to Reputations." *Quarterly Journal of Economics* 98, no. 4 (November 1983): 599–680.

Shearer, Bruce. "Piece Rates, Fixed Wages and Incentives: Evidence from a Field Experiment." *Review of Economic Studies* 71, no. 2 (2004): 513–34.

Shiller, Robert J. *Irrational Exuberance,* 2nd ed. New York: Broadway Books, 2005.

———. *Finance and the Good Society.* Princeton, NJ: Princeton University Press, 2012.

Shover, Neal, and Andy Hochsteller. *Choosing White-Collar Crime.* New York: Cambridge University Press, 2006.

Silk, Leonard. *The Economists.* New York: Basic Books, 1976.

Simon, Herbert. "Constructing a University." In *The Innovative University,* edited by Daniel P. Resnick and Dana S. Scott, Pittsburgh: Carnegie Mellon University Press, 2004, 1–13.

Simon, Herbert A. *Models of Man: Social and Rational: Mathematical Essays on Rational Human Behavior in a Social Setting.* New York: John Wiley, 1957.

Sisodia, Raj, Jag Sheth, and David B. Wolfe. *Firms of Endearment: How World-Class Companies Profit from Passion and Purpose,* 2nd ed. Upper Saddle, NJ: Pearson, 2014.

Skousen, Mark. "The Perseverance of Paul Samuelson's *Economics.*" *Journal of Economic Perspectives* 11, no. 2 (Spring 1997): 137–52.

Small-Jordan, Dianne. "Organ Harvesting, Human Trafficking, and the Black Market." *Decoded Science*, March 23, 2016. http://www.decodedscience. org/organ-harvesting-human-trafficking-black-market/56966.

Smith, Adam. *An Inquiry into the Nature and Causes of the Wealth of Nations.* Indianapolis, IN: Liberty Fund, 1981.

———. *Essays on Philosophical Subjects.* Indianapolis, IN: Liberty Fund, 1982.

———. *The Theory of Moral Sentiments.* Indianapolis, IN: Liberty Fund, 1976.

———. "'Early Draft' of Part of the Wealth of Nations." In *Lectures on Jurisprudence,* edited by R. L. Meek, D. D. Raphael, and P. G. Stein, 562–63. Oxford: Clarendon Press, 1978.

Smith, C. Aubrey. *Fifty Years of Education for Business at the University of Texas.* Austin, TX: College of Business Administration Foundation, 1962.

Smith, Tara. *Ayn Rand's Normative Ethics: The Virtuous Egoist.* New York: Cambridge University Press, 2006.

Spacks, Patricia Meyer. "Acts of Love and Knowledge: Pope's Narratives of Self." In *Augustan Subjects: Essays in Honor of Martin C. Battestin,* edited by Albert J. Rivero. Newark, NJ: University of Delaware Press, 1977.

Spencer, Herbert. *Social Statistics.* London: John Chapman, 1851.

———. *Social Statistics, abridged and rev together with The Man Versus the State.* New York: Appleton, 1896.

———. *Principles of Biology.* New York: Appleton, 1897.

Stengle, Jamie. Elder Stanford Dismayed by Son's Legal Travails. *Austin American-Statesman* (Sunday, February 22, 2009): D2.

Stewart, Dugald. "Account of the Life and Writings of Adam Smith, LL.D. from *Transactions of the Royal Society of Edinburgh,* read by Mr. Stewart on January 21 and March 18, 1793." Republished in *Essays on Philosophical Subjects,* edited by I. S. Ross, 268–69. Indianapolis, IN: Liberty Fund, 1980.

Stigler, George J. *The Theory of Price,* rev. ed. New York: Macmillan, 1965.

———. "Regulation: The Confusion of Means and Ends." In *Regulating New Drugs,* edited by Richard L. Landau, Chicago: University of Chicago Center for Policy Study, 1973, 9–19.

———. "Economics — The Imperial Science?" *Scandinavian Journal of Economics* 86, no. 3 (1984): 301–13.

———. "The Economist as Preacher." In *The Economist as Preacher and Other Essays.* Chicago: University of Chicago Press, 1982.

———. *Memoirs of an Unregulated Economist.* New York: Basic Books, 1988.

Stiglitz, Joseph E. *Making Globalization Work.* New York: W. W. Norton, 2006.

Swedberg, Richard. "The Structure of Confidence and the Collapse of Lehman Brothers." In *Markets on Trial: The Economic Sociology of the US Financial Crisis,* edited by Michael Lounsbury and Paul M. Hursh. Bingley, UK: Emerald Group Publishing, 2010, 69–112.

Taylor, Frederick Winslow. *The Principles of Scientific Management.* Norwood, MA: Plimpton Press, 1911.

"The First Automobile — Cugnot's Steam Vehicle." http://patentpending.blogs.com/patent pending_blog/2004/10/the_first_autom.html.

The Royal Swedish Academy of Sciences. "Press Release." Accessed October 14, 1976. http://www.nobelprize.org/nobel_prizes/economic-sciences/laureates/1976/press.html.

"The Worst Country on Earth." *The Economist.* November 12, 2009. http://www.economist.com/node/14742450/print.

Thier, Dave. Microsoft Stores are Very Sad Places. Forbes.com, Accessed February 13, 2012. http://www.forbes.com/sites/davidthier/2012/02/13/microsoft-stores-are-very-sad-places/.

Thomas, Christopher R., and S. Charles Maurice. *Managerial Economics,* 9th ed. New York: McGraw-Hill Irwin, 2008.

Tickle, Phyllis A. *Greed: The Seven Deadly Sins.* New York: Oxford University Press, 2004.

Toffler, Barbara Ley, and Jennifer Reingold. *Final Accounting: Ambition, Greed, and the Fall of Arthur Anderson.* New York: Random House, 2003.

"Top Gun for Hire." *The Economist,* December 3, 2005, 32.

Transparency International. Corruption Perceptions Index 2014. https://www.transparency.org/cpi2014/results.

Turner, Bryan S., ed. *Cambridge Dictionary of Sociology.* Cambridge: Cambridge University Press, 2006.

Twain, Mark, and Charles Dudley Warner. *The Gilded Age.* New York: Modern Library, 2006.

Ubel, Peter A. *Free Market Madness: Why Human Nature Is at Odds with Economics — and Why it Matters.* Boston: Harvard Business Press, 2009.

von Mises, Ludwig. *Liberalism: The Classical Tradition.* Indianapolis IN: Liberty Fund, 2005.

Webster, Thomas J. *Managerial Economics: Theory and Practice.* San Diego, CA: Academic Press, 2003.

"Which Heads Rolled at GM Over Ignition Switch Scandal? Mostly Executives." *Detroit Free Press.* May 16, 2015. freep.com.

Wilkinson, Nick. *Managerial Economics: A Problem Solving Approach.* Cambridge: Cambridge University Press, 2005.

Williamson, Oliver E. *Markets and Hierarchies: Analysis and Antitrust Implications.* New York: Free Press, 1975.

Williams, Robert J., J. Douglas Barrett, and Mary Brabston. "Managers' Business School Education and Military Service: Possible Links to Corporate Criminal Activity." *Human Relations* 53, no. 5: 691–712.

World Bank. *GDP Per Capita (Current US$).* Accessed May 4, 2015. http://data. worldbank.org/indicator/NY.GDP.PCAP.CD?page=1.

Wright, Robert. *The Moral Animal: Why We Are, the Way We Are: The New Science of Evolutionary Psychology.* New York: Vintage Books, 1994.

Yezer, Anthony M., Robert S. Goldfarb, and Paul J. Poppen. "Does Studying Economics Discourage Cooperation? Watch What We Do, Not What We Say or How We Play." *Journal of Economic Perspectives* 10, no. 1 (Winter 1996): 177–86.

Yip, George S., ed. *Disrupt or Be Disrupted: A Blueprint for Change in Management Education.* San Francisco: Jossey-Bass, 2013.

Yonay, Yuval P. *The Struggle over the Soul of Economics: Institutional and Neoclassical Economists in America Between the Wars.* Princeton, NJ: Princeton University Press, 1998.

Young, Lawrence A., ed. *Rational Choice Theory and Religion: Summary and Assessment.* New York: Routledge, 1997.

Zak, Paul J. *Moral Markets: The Critical Role of Values in the Economy.* Princeton, NJ: Princeton University Press, 2008.

Zimbardo, Philip. *The Lucifer Effect: Understanding How Good People Turn Evil.* New York: Random House, 2007.

Zuckerman, Gregory. *The Greatest Trade Ever: The Behind-The-Scenes Story of How John Paulson Defied Wall Street and Made Financial History.* New York: Broadway Books, 2009.

Index

AACSB, 17, 67
Adams, Craig, 117
A Dictionary of Economics, 35
agency theory, 50, 56, 58
Air Force, 18
Alderson, Wroe, 192
Ames, Ruth, 91
Ampad, 197
Applbaum, Michael, 231
Archimedes, 87
Armstrong, J. Scott, 80
Arrow, Kenneth, 32, 47, 127
Arthur Andersen, 45
Astor, John, 137
Atlas Shrugged, 70
attorneys, 13, 50
Augier, Mie, 28
automobiles, 189

Bach, Lee
  at Carnegie Tech, 23
  vision, 66
Bain Capital, 197
Banaji, Mahzarin, 77

Bank of America, 135
Barrett, Douglas, 97
Barton, Joe, 111
Battle for the Soul of Capitalism, 104
Baumol, William, 32
Bazerman, Max , 77
Bear Stearns, 115
Bebchuk, Lucian, 106
Becker, Gary, 35, 126, 139
Bernanke, Ben, 1
bioethics, 92
Blackberry, 190
black market, 14
Blind Spots, 78
Bloom, Paul, 92
Boesky, Ivan, 70
Bogle, John, 104
Boone, Daniel, 137
Boswell, James, 6
Bowles, Samuel, 93
Brabston, Mary, 97
brand recognition, etc., 188
Buchanan, James, 36, 43, 126, 139,
  148

Burke, Edmund, 6
business degrees, first
    doctoral, 21
    masters, 12
    undergratuate, 12
Business Roundtable, 88, 191
Butterfield, Kenneth, 96

Capitalism and Freedom, 119
Carnegie Foundation, 2, 18, 19, 75
Carnegie Institute of Technology, 19
Catholics, 151
Causey, Rick, 194
caveat emptor, 14
Chamberlin, Edward, 131, 185, 191
Chandler, Alfred, 107
Chicago School of Economics
    definition, 142
    merger with neoliberalism, 139
    Nobel Memorial Prizes, 39
    seat of Mont Pelerin Society, 126
Chugh, Dolly, 77
Churchill, Winston
    description of democracy, 141
Ciavarella, Mark, 9
Citigroup, 106
civic virtues, 15, 99, 108, 162
Clark, William, 137
Coase, Ronald, 139
    "The Problem of Social Cost",
        63, 215, 235
    "Nature of the Firm", 213, 235
    in Chicago law faculty, 47
    theory of the firm, 46
Coase, Ronaldo
    Nature of the Firm, 218
Cohen, Don, 108
Colby, Ann, 75
College of William and Mary, 13

Columbia University, 19, 39
competition, 187
conservativism, 163
consumer behavior, 191
Cooper, William, 26, 61
Corruption Perceptions Index, 178
Cournet, Augustin, 38
creative destruction, 189, 196
Crocket, Davy, 137
Cullen, Patrick, 68
Cunningham, Chuck, 9
Cuomo, Antonio, 106
curriculum
    formal, 65, 66
    formal overshadowed, 73
    hidden, 65
    old, 27
    recommendations, 22
    shadow, 65, 68, 79, 86, 97, 193
    standard, 20, 24

Dartmouth College, 12, 15
Datar, Srikant, 68
Davis, Brian, 174
Dawkins, Richard, 110, 181
Deloitte, 114
Democracy in America, 183
de Tocqueville, Alexis, 182
de Waal, Frans, 42, 92
diffusion of innovation, 83
Diffusion of Innovations, 83
Director, Aaron, 123, 126
Dobbin, Frank, 56, 84
Dolle, Jonathan, 75
dot.com bubble and bust, 104, 105,
    106
Dreber, Anna, 88
Drucker, Peter, 192
Dukerich, Janet, 96

Durkheim, Émile, 65
Dutton, Jane, 96

Easterbrook, Frank, 45, 61
Ebbers, Bernie, 9, 109
economic man, 36
   aggressive, 32
   criminal, 35
   deliberate, 41
   immoral, 32
   opportunisitc, 47
   rational, 35
   selfishness, 31
Economics
   aggregative economics, 22
   ethics, 64
   legislative art, 128
   mainstream/neoclassical, 29, 141
   marcroeconomics, 22
   microeconomics, 22
   neoclassical price theory, 142
   normative science, 128
   positive science, 128
Economists and Societies, 120
efficient market theory, 40, 53, 75, 84
Ehrlich, Thomas, 75
Elegido, Juan, 97
Empathy and Moral Development, 92
Enron, 45
Ernst & Young, 114
Ethics of Competition, 62
Evensky, Jerry, 171

Fama, Eugene, 26, 52
FBI, 199
Fehr, Ernst, 90
fiduciary duty, 13, 58, 72, 114, 134, 197

Financial Fraud Enforcement Task Force, 116
Fischel, David, 61
Fitch, 115
Ford, David, 83
Ford F150, 190
Ford Foundation, 2, 18, 20
Ford II, Henry, 18
Ford Motor Company, 18, 60, 190
Ford Pinto, 62
formal curriculm, 97
Foundations, 126
Fourcade, Marion, 120, 149
Francis Fukuyama
   The Great Disruption, 179
   Trust, 177
Frankel, Tamar, 13
Franklin, Benjamin, 6
Frank, Robert, 89, 92, 95, 172
Frederick Taylor, 16
free riders, 91, 95, 181, 183
Freud, Sigmund, 69
Fried, Jesse, 106
Friedman, Milton
   "The Methodology of Positive Economics", 213, 220, 238
   "The Social Responsibility of Business is to Increase Profit", 134
   Adam Smith, 127, 150, 185
   Capitalism and Freedom, 132, 150
   Chicago School of Economics, 142, 145
   Cornell University, 60
   Free to Choose, 136
   Mont Pelerin Society, 126, 139
   natural history of regulation, 176
   Paul Samuelson, 140

Phil Donahue Show, 36, 120, 140, 150
profit maximization, 35
research validity, 39
sports metaphor, 173
Friedman, Rose, 136
From Higher Aims to Hired Hands, 28
Fudenberg, Drew, 88
Fuld, Richard, 109, 176

Gachter, Simon, 90
Galbraith, John Kenneth, 35
games
  dictator, 90
  ultimatum, 59, 90, 94
game theory, 44
  experimental, 91
  mathematical modelling, 42
  Prisoner's Dilemma, 42, 43
Gavin, David, 68
Gazzaniga, Michael, 92
Gekko, Gordon, 70, 73
General Motors, 62
Gentile, Mary, 73
Ghoshal, Sumantra, 56
Gibbon, Edmund, 6
Gilovich, Thomas, 95
Gintis, Herbert, 93
Giving Voice to Values, 73
God, 7, 69, 76, 138, 153, 154, 156, 157, 159–161, 164
  diestic, 153
God-fearing, 109
Goldfarb, Robert, 95
Goldman Sachs, 103, 106, 114, 115, 218, 239
Gordon-Howell report, 20, 23
Gould, Jay, 137

Great Depression, 1, 82, 121, 122, 137, 148
greed defined, 9
Griswold, Charles, 159

Hahn, F. H., 32
Halterman, Marvene, 116
Hammurabi's Code, 13
Hardy, Charles, 126
Harvard Business School, 16, 18–21, 54, 110
Hauser, Mark, 93
Hayek, Frederich
  Road to Serfdom, 123
  The Road to Serfdom, 122, 126, 132
Hayek, Frederich
  Committee on Social Thought, 126
  scientism, 127
  vision, 125
Heath, Joseph, 14, 62, 73
Heclo, Hugo, 183
Heritage Foundation, 178
Hobbes, Thomas, 159, 178
Hochstetler, Andy, 77, 200
Hoffman, Martin, 92
Homo economicus, 87, 100
Homo reciprocans, 100, 182
Hoover, Herbert, 148
HSBC, 116
Hume, David, 6, 76, 163
Hutcheson, Francis, 41

Index of Economic Freedom, 178
indoctrination, 97
inefficient market theory, 143
In Good Company, 108, 191

institutional approach, 22, 67
invisible hand, 3, 7, 30, 31, 35, 107,
153, 154, 163, 181
irrational exuberance, 4, 116, 144

Jensen, Michael, 50
"Elipse of the Public
Corporation", 84, 216, 242
"The Nature of Man", 55, 214,
222, 242
agency theory, 52, 102
CCMO course, 54
diffusion of innovation, 85
production function, 136
Theory of the Firm, 84
Jevons, Stanley, 4
Johnson, Samuel, 6
J. P. Morgan Chase, 106, 118
Jung, Jiwook, 56, 84
justice
Adam Smith's definition, 161
distributive or social, 4, 137
Social or distributive, 4

Kahneman, Daniel, 76, 94
Keynesian-Marxist, 148
Keynes, John Maynard, 123
Keynes, John Neville, 128
Khurana, Rakesh, 28, 84
Kirkcaldy, Scotland, 6
Knetsch, Jack, 94
Knight, Frank, 62, 123, 126
Kozlowski, Dennis, 107
KPMG, 114

laissez faire
contradictory interpretations,
163
Lay, Ken, 104, 109, 194

Lehman Brothers, 59, 115, 176, 215,
251
Leviathan, 148, 178
Lewis, Meriwether, 137
liar's loans, 113
Liberalism
The Classical Tradition, 185
Liberman, Varda, 81
libertarianism, 163
London School of Economics, 46
lost-letter experiment, 95
Lucifer Effect, 79

Macey, Jonathan, 114
macroeconomics, 141, 148
Madoff, Bernie, 50, 108, 176, 180, 200
management science, 26
managerial approach, 22, 67
Mandeville, Bernard, 159
March, James, 28
market failures, 163
marketing mix, 187
market segmentation, 189
Markowitz, Harry, 39, 130
mark-to-market, 111
Marshall, Alfred, 41
Marwell, Gerald, 91
Masters of the Universe, 120
Maxwell, R. M., 139
Mayo, Elton, 15, 17, 22, 23, 25
human relations movement, 16
Social Problems, 16
McCabe, Donald, 96
McCarthy, Joseph, 149
McGuire, William, 9
McKinsey & Company, 110
McNamara, Robert, 18
Mearsheimer, John, 69
Meckling, William, 52, 54, 55, 84

Merger Mania, 70
Merrill Lynch, 106, 107, 115
Merton, Robert, 82
microeconomics, 48, 74
Microsoft, 144
Milgrom, Paul, 45
Miller, Merton, 26, 52
Millie, Grandma, 112
Mill, John Stewart, 41
MIT, 19, 39, 149
Modigliani, Franco, 26
monopolistic competition, 3, 131, 185
Mont Pelerin Society
    choice of name, 126
    domination by the Chicago
        School, 139
    formation of, 124
Moody's, 115, 116
Moral Minds, 93
Moral Sentiments
    in context, 7
Morality, Competition, and the Firm,
    208, 215, 216, 240
Moran, Moran, 56
Morgan Stanley, 106, 115
Mossner, Ernest, 8

NASDAQ, 115
National Bureau of Economic
    Research, 144
naturalistic fallacy, 76
natural theology, 7
Neiman, Susan, 153
neoclassical
    neoclassical economics defined,
        29
New Deal, 123
Newton, Sir Isaac, 153
New York CPAs, 17

New York Stock Exchange, 115
New York University, 17
New Zealand, 178
Nietzsche, 69
nineteenth-century liberalism, 163
Nobel Memorial Prize in Economics,
    39
Nohria, Hitin, 1
Nokia, 190
North Korea, 178

off balance sheet entities, 111
On Ethics and Economics, 171
Operation Stolen Dreams, 116
Ostrom, Elinor, 181
Oxford English Dictionary, 33
Oxford University, 6

package insert model, 60
Packer, David, 82
Panalba, 80
Passion within Reason, 172
Pay without Performance, 106
perfect competition defined, 2
Phillips, Michael, 116
physicians, 13
Pierson report, 20
Pogo, 113
Poppen, Paul, 95
Posner, Richard, 64, 176
Powers, William, 195
premises of professionalism, 13
Prentice, Robert, 78
price mechanism, 11, 46, 181
PriceWaterhouse, 114
Principia, 153
prisoner's dilemma, 81
Proctor & Gamble, 49
product differentiation, 188

profits, 186
propane explosions, 8, 61
Prusak, Laurence, 108
public goods game, 91
PWC, 114

radical individualism, 71, 86, 138,
    140, 151, 159
Rand, Ayn, 70, 140
Rand, David G., 88
rational, 42
rational choice theory, 40, 43, 77
rational expectations, 40
Reagan, Ronald, 139
Regan, Dennis, 95
reification, 75
reputation theory, 44, 101
*Research into the Principles
    of the Mathematics of the Theory
    of Wealth*, 38
Rethinking the MBA, 68
Reynolds, Joshua, 6
Ritholt, Barry, 115
robber barons, 137
Roberts, John, 45
Robinson, Joan, 186, 191
Rockefeller, John, 69, 138
Rogers, Everett, 83, 124
Ross, Lee, 81
Rousseau, 6

Samuelson, Paul
    Adam Smith, 8, 30
    Alan Greenspan, 140
    *Economics
        An Introductory Analysis*,
        30
    Milton Friedman, 140
    political pressure, 148

Samuels, Steven, 81
Sarbanes-Oxley Act, 104, 105
Scholes, Myron, 52
School of Economics, 124
Schumpeter, Joseph, 185, 189,
    191
SEC, 115
Securities and Exchange
    Commission, 115
self-fulfilling prophecy, 82
self-serving bias, 77
Sen, Amartya, 171
Shapiro, Carl, 44, 249
Shaw, George Bernard, 31
Shiller, Robert, 26, 143, 180
Shover, Neal, 77, 200
Simon, Herbert, 26
Skilling, Jeff, 109, 176
Smith, Adam
    acquaintences, 6
    benevolence, 161
    biography, 6
    conflicting views of, 2
    dramatic over-statement, 164
    East India Company, 51
    false quote, 31
    government's role, 164
    growth, 137
    invisible hand, 152, 153
    jurisprudence lectures, 7
    justice, 119, 161
    laborer's coat, 184
    laissez faire, 151, 162
    Lectures on Jurisprudence, 164,
        171
    misrepresentation of, 30
    moral philosophy course, 7
    political economy, 7
    prudence, 9, 157, 161

public goods, 163
rejects concept of economic man,
  159
self-command, 161, 162
self-love, 157
Smith, Adam, 161
socialism, 161
sports metaphor, 174
strait pin production, 184
unintended consequences,
  154
vanity, 10
Smith, Vernon, 131
social capital, 108, 179
Social Darwinism, 138
socialism defined, 149
socialization, 79
Southern Methodist University, 109
Spencer, Herbert, 138
Standard & Poor's, 115, 116
Stanford Encyclopedia of Philosophy,
  43
Stanford, R. Allen, 105
Stanford University, 19, 81
Staphylococcus aureus, 98
Staples, 196
Stedman Jones, Daniel, 120
Stigler, George, 152
  Coase, Ronald, 34
  diffusion of innovation, 85
  fairness and justice uncongenial,
    35
  law and economics, 33
  memoirs, 143
  Mont Pelerin Society, 126
  The Theory of Price, 185
Stiglitz, Joseph, 35, 39
street criminals, 200

subprime bubble and bust, 85, 113,
  118, 122
Sullivan, William, 75
supply chain, 49
syllogism, 77

Target, 135
Taylor, Frederick, 22, 23, 25
Tenburnsel, Ann, 78
Thain, John, 107
Thaler, Thaler, 94
Thatcher, Margaret, 139
The Age of Empathy, 92
The Chicago School, 140
The Death of Corporate Reputation,
  114
The Economist, 177
*The Elgar Companion to the Chicago
  School of Economics*, 142
The Epidemiology of Greed, 74
The Ethical Brain, 92
The Fountainhead, 70
The Idea of Justice, 171
*The Principles of Scientific
  Management*, 15
*The Problems of an Industrialized
  Civilization*, 16
The Road to Serfdom.
  The Road to Serfdom, 148
*The Roots, Rituals, and Rhetorics
  of Change*, 28
The Selfish Gene, 110
The Visible Hand, 107
The Wolf of Wall Street, 80
Theory of the Firm
  Coase article, 46
  Jensen and Meckling article, 52,
    84

Peter Drucker's view, 192
Wroe Alderson's view, 192
Thornton, Charles, 18
Thurow, Lester, 199
Tiffany & Co., 188
Today's CPA, 103
tragedy of the commons, 181
transaction cost theory, 47
Trevino, Linda, 96
Trojan horse, 2, 71
trust/control pyramid, 177
twin pillars
    mainstream economics, 38
twin pillars of free-market capitalism,
    30, 37, 55, 119
        mainstream economics,
        101
twin pillars of free-market capitalism
    defined, 2
Tyco, 107

UCLA, 19
UnitedHealth Group, 9
United Nations diplomats, 98
University of California Berkeley, 19,
    22, 129
University of Chicago, 19–21, 39
University of Colorado, 32
University of Glasgow, 7, 41
University of Pennsylvania, 12, 15
University of Rochester, 54
University of Texas, 20, 61, 68

Upjohn Company, 80
utilitarianism, 41

Vanderbilt, Cornelius, 137
van Overtveldt, Johan, 140
Viner, Jacob, 152
Voltaire, 6
von Mises, Ludwig, 3, 163, 185
vulture capitalism, 195

Wallis, Allen, 145
Walmart, 49
warning labels, 56
Watkins, Sharron, 195
Watt, James, 6
Wealth of Nations
    in context, 7
Wells Fargo, 116
Westfall, Gabriella, 117
Wharton, Joseph, 13
white-collar criminals, 200
Whiz Kids, 19
Whole Foods, 135
Will, George, 10
Williamson, Oliver, 48
Williams, Robert, 97
WorldCom, 9, 109
Wyatt, Oscar, 9

Yale University, 19
Yezer, Anthony, 95

Zimbardo, Philip, 79

Printed in the United States
By Bookmasters